It's a London thing

MANCHESTER
1824

Manchester University Press

Music and Society

Series editors   Peter J. Martin and Tia DeNora

Music and Society aims to bridge the gap between music scholarship and the human sciences. A deliberately eclectic series, its authors are nevertheless united by the contention that music is a social product, social resource, and social practice. As such it is not autonomous but is created and performed by real people in particular times and places; in doing so they reveal much about themselves and their societies.

In contrast to the established academic discourse, *Music and Society* is concerned with all forms of music, and seeks to encourage the scholarly analysis of both 'popular' styles and those which have for too long been marginalised by that discourse – folk and ethnic traditions, music by and for women, jazz, rock, rap, reggae, muzak and so on. These sounds are vital ingredients in the contemporary cultural mix, and their neglect by serious scholars itself tells us much about the social and cultural stratification of our society.

The time is right to take a fresh look at music and its effects, as today's music resonates with the consequences of cultural globalisation and the transformations wrought by new electronic media, and as past styles are reinvented in the light of present concerns. There is, too, a tremendous upsurge of interest in cultural analysis. *Music and Society* does not promote a particular school of thought, but aims to provide a forum for debate; in doing so, the titles in the series bring music back into the heart of socio-cultural analysis.

The land without music: music, culture and society in twentieth-century Britain
  Andrew Blake

Networks of sound, style and subversion: The punk and post-punk worlds of Manchester, London, Liverpool and Sheffield, 1975–80
  Nick Crossley

Music and the sociological gaze: art worlds and cultural production
  Peter J. Martin

Sounds and society: themes in the sociology of music
  Peter J. Martin

Popular music on screen: from the Hollywood musical to music video
  John Mundy

Popular music in England 1840–1914: a social history (2nd edition)
  Dave Russell

The English musical renaissance, 1840–1940: constructing a national music (2nd edition)
  Robert Stradling and Meirion Hughes

Time and memory in reggae music: the politics of hope
  Sarah Daynes

Essays on The Smiths: Why Pamper Life's Complexities?
  Sean Campbell and Colin Coulter (eds)

It's a London thing

How rare groove, acid house and jungle remapped the city

Caspar Melville

Manchester University Press

Published by Manchester University Press
Altrincham Street, Manchester M1 7JA

www.manchesteruniversitypress.co.uk

British Library Cataloguing-in-Publication Data
A catalogue record for this book is available from the British Library

ISBN 978 1 5261 3123 2   hardback

ISBN 978 1 5261 3125 6   paperback

First published 2020

Typeset in Minion and Frutiger
by R. J. Footring Ltd, Derby, UK

Contents

The plates section begins opposite page 80

v

Figures

List of figures

Plates

Preface

More than thirty years ago I stood on a London rooftop looking out over St Paul's Cathedral and the City of London as the sun came up into a pale blue summer sky. I was not alone: there were dozens of us on the roof, smiling and smoking, dazzled by the new morning. We had come up a dusty staircase from two floors below, where for the past eight hours we, and thousands of others, had been dancing to the music – soul, funk, disco, boogie, reggae and hip hop – supplied by DJ Norman Jay and his bass-heavy Good Times sound system. While it was musicians and producers – from Chicago, New York, New Orleans and Kingston, Jamaica – who originally made the music and Norman Jay who had put it in potent juxtaposition, what happened that night was an act of collective creation, a co-production by musician, producer, DJ, technology and us, the dancing crowd. Together we had brought the dead space of an abandoned and seemingly unloved warehouse to life and made it a space of collaboration and joy.

I felt an exhausted euphoria. Some of this was, no doubt, the result of the subconscious chemical processes of the body releasing endorphins after long hours of dancing, and the pretty sunrise. I was young then, and optimistic. But still I felt and still feel that I had been a part of something important: a group of disparate individuals synchronised by rhythm, orchestrated difference. This seemed especially important because the city we were in, the London in which I was born and grew up, was divided, especially by race. The forces that conspired to keep us apart, assigned to different spaces, had tenuously and temporarily perhaps been defeated that night. This was not the result of an organised political campaign or programme but a night-long moment in which racial division was overcome. For me, it had the force of epiphany.

The intake at my London state schools had been diverse in terms of class and race, reflecting the economic and ethnic diversity of Lambeth. At primary school in Kennington we played happily side by side, though at the school gates we went our separate ways. By the time I got to secondary school in the late 1970s – a large comprehensive of 2,000 kids from Pimlico, Stockwell, Vauxhall, Brixton and Fulham – friendships across class and race lines were commonplace, forged by everyday proximity and shared rituals of sport, classroom disruption and viciously funny schoolyard cussing. But these bonds were vulnerable and loosened as we moved from the classroom and playground back into the streets and the private sphere of home. School was policed by the deputy head, who enforced no-running-in-the-corridor rules, which we could all equally ignore, but the space outside was subject to more complex and divisive kinds of regulation, which was anything but equal.

Outside school we shared streets, buses, shops, tube carriages and hospital waiting rooms. But something I was not then able to name kept us separate. Class distinctions played out in space – my white middle-class family had a garden, and close by were the park and my friends' houses; the children from Dorset Road Estate, the large social housing block at the end of my road, 'played out' (though not all were not allowed to); friends 'knocked for them' and they slipped away from parental surveillance. I'd have liked to do this too, but I never did. My parents might have let me, but equally it might have contravened some of their basic middle-class values to allow their child to 'run wild' in the streets. A spatial taxonomy was maintained, policed by mutual misunderstanding. As the anthropologist of class difference Pierre Bourdieu remarked, you get the city that goes with your social and cultural capital. In this sense, though we lived in shared space, we lived in different cities.

Race was an even more conspicuous divider. The political and social conflicts over race which defined the British city in the 1970s and '80s intruded into my school in the form of racist graffiti, overtly National Front-supporting skinheads and a mini race riot (which was really a battle between racists and anti-racist pupils, black and white). This led to the school having the dubious honour of being the first in London to employ security guards to keep the peace. A racially mixed social world survived, in class, in sport and at school discos and parties, but it was precarious.

Meanwhile, in the smoke-plumed basement of my best friend's house, I was introduced to punk and roots reggae simultaneously – the Sex Pistols' *Never Mind the Bollocks* and the Clash's 'White Riot', Max Romero's *War Ina Babylon*, Bob Marley's *Catch a Fire* – the rebel edge of both genres synchronised with our teenage sense of injustice, and the cadence of the streets. Records by Bob Andy and by Burning Spear were played in the intervals of the punk shows I went to at the Greyhound pub in Fulham. The two genres came together again in Victoria Park, at the Rock Against Racism shows that featured punk, the Pop Group and the Slits, alongside reggae, Misty in Roots and Aswad, under the slogan 'Black and White Unite and Fight'. But despite these optimistic intentions, closer to home such unity seemed out of reach.

Therefore, I knew about how social divisions of race and class were reproduced spatially in the city long before reading social geography. But there was also a lot about how city space was policed, how the 'right to the city' was differentially granted, that my black friends knew about, but that I did not (they didn't talk much to me about it). If looked at from a certain distance, we were part of a lived multiculture in one of the most diverse cities in the world. But proximity did not necessarily build solidarity.

This is why that rooftop of an abandoned warehouse next to the Thames, on a summer night in 1986, seemed to me to matter. The party attracted a crowd of a couple of thousand from across London. Though I have no way of confirming this beyond the testimony of people who were there, it appeared to be a cross-class and multiracial mix and instantiated a solidarity that actually did exist and could be built on. It suggested that social difference (re)produced through spatial division

Figure 0.1 Flyer for the first Bear Wharf riverside party, 5 July 1986. Courtesy Dan Benedict

could be overcome and that music might be key to how this could happen. Music had turned one kind of space, the carcass of imperial trade, into another, a space of multicultural collaboration. Black music from America and the Caribbean channelled new information, relayed from vinyl disc via diamond-tipped needle down copper wires to paper cones, that we took in through our ears and organs and embodied in collective dance. In the space that music creates, the social structures imposed on us were reworked, imperial space remade as post-colonial space, the past reconfigured in the present, divided city space made over as a space of multiculture.

If this book seems unduly preoccupied with the relations between city space, social divisions and music in the last decades of the twentieth century, this is because these relations have formed me just as they have formed London. But there are no guarantees of permanence: political gains and progressive changes are always subject to reversal. I want to recover the history of these spaces in order to strengthen commitments to a common culture that faces a new set of challenges in the twenty-first century. These are my 'reasons of the heart' (Hall 1990: 222–3).

Acknowledgements

Writing a book can be lonely but that has not been my experience, because of the many people who generously gave their time to talk to me about music, London and life. In no particular order my deep thanks go to Norman Jay, Jazzie B, Trevor Nelson, Colin Dale, Gilles Peterson, Roni Size, Rob Playford, MJ Cole, DJ Spoony, Mikee P, Joy White, Dan Benedict, Rachael Bee, Paul Gilroy, Jamie D'Cruz, Stan Shock, Simon Payne, DJ Dodge, Marie Loney, 'Dubplate' Pearl Boatswain, Dennis Bovell, Gordon Mac, Sam Kelly, Rodney P, Linton Kwesi Johnson, H Patten, Asher Senator and June and Ade from Nzinga Soundz.

I'd also like to thank Mykaell Riley, Chris Christodoulou, Jacqueline Springer, Kate Theophilus, Aisha Forde and Les Back (my colleagues on the Bass Culture research project, from which I've learned so much). I am indebted to both David Hesmondhalgh and Angela McRobbie for their support and guidance, and Laurie Taylor, Morgan Jackson, Anamik Saha, Ilana Webster-Kogen, Sam Harman, Patrick Turner and Malcolm James for their friendship and music insight. Massive respect to Les Back, Kenny Monrose and my anonymous reviewer for reading the manuscript and their kind and acute comments and suggestions. Thanks also to Steve Swindells (the Lift), Paul Stone (RIP) and Dan Benedict (Family Funktion) for permission to reproduce their club flyers, Mochles Simawi for permission to use his lovely photograph of Kokoroko, and Dave Swindells, whose brilliant photographs culled from his extensive four-decade archive of club culture form the plates section of the book.

Acknowledgements

Bringing a book to life is a team effort and I'd like to thank the MUP gang, my editor Tom Dark, Jen Mellor in production and Rebecca Mortimer in marketing, Ralph Footring for his meticulous copy-editing, and Paula Clarke Bain for indexing.

This book is dedicated to all the DJs, promoters, sound system operators, pirate radio stations, record stores and dancers who made London club culture what it is, and to the memory of jazzi-funk promoter and DJ George Power and DJ-dancer extraordinaire Paul 'Trouble' Anderson, who both died far too young, as I was finishing this book.

For my mum, Sarah and Saul, and in fond memory of Richard Melville (1938–2019), a man who loved to dance

Introduction: London's sonic space

London provides a vast space – bigger in some senses than the nation – in which cultures can be differently imagined and conceived. (Kevin Robins)

This book is about three black music multicultures in London in the 1980s and 1990s: rare groove, acid house and jungle. It is a critical exploration of the role they have played in the production of what Stuart Hall once identified as London's 'workable, lived multiculture' (Hall 2004). These are not the only important black music scenes in London: that list would include soca, jazz and Afrojazz, Afrobeat, dancehall, hip hop, UK garage, R&B and grime, and to include them all would have called for a much bigger book. So, this is not a comprehensive study of all black music produced and consumed in the city. I focus on rare groove, acid house and jungle because they are three moments that involved inter-racial collaboration, in terms of both production and consumption, around black music. They were music scenes which put the racial divisions of the city into question and worked against the logic of spatial separation. They explored new ways in which culture could be inhabited collectively. In ways both deliberate and contingent, these musical scenes involved collaboration between young people from different sides of what the great black American sociologist W. E. B. Du Bois (1903) identified as 'the color line', and hosted lived multiculture on the dancefloor. Around each scene, discourses developed to address this cultural intermixture, and within them were forged new ways of dancing, listening and making

1

culture together. This was a complex. contested process, where gains were often temporary, but it was also one within which new forms of interculture emerged that transformed the city.

We can conceive of these musical scenes as moral economies (Gilroy 2010; Davies 2018). They are economies because they are organised around economic objectives: promoters, DJs and the music markets which sustained them all had the underlying motivation of making money, of getting paid. Dancers paid to enter the dance. Though they were largely informal economies, they were driven by the ambition to build a viable future in the midst of de-industrialisation and brutal urban neoliberalisation. They are moral because they are bounded by particular social and ethical norms and amount to networks of affiliation and creation which are not reducible to financial exchange – many dancers did not have to pay but could get on the guest-list (known in the parlance of the time as a 'squeeze'), which built strong bonds of obligation and mutual care. Something of the moral underpinnings of the club scenes this book focuses on can be heard in the lexicon of the time. Among the most common words used in these scenes – for greeting, assent and parting – were the words 'safe' and 'respect', keywords taken, as was so much of the basic form of these scenes, from reggae sound system culture, a pointer to the core values of security and mutual recognition which underpinned these informal social movements against a backdrop of a city and a society which were, for many, unsafe and often unable to accord citizens recognition of their worth.

The solidarity made available here was easily won, pliable, as is true of all the black music cultures of the city, because it was essentially open. Anyone who was down with the music, and especially anyone who was willing to dance, was welcome. This amounted to a flat rejection of the racist injunction to 'stick with your own kind' which held sway outside the dance. This can help us understand the apparent paradox that London's black music ecosystem took its particular form both *despite* and *because of* the enduring power of urban racism. The legacy of these scenes became a resource for the creation of new ones – like the garage and grime of the 1990s and the Afro-rap and jazz resurgence of 2018, all of which were or still are in some ways continuous with black music scenes of the 1980s and 1990s – and they can also be used as a resource by which to write an alternative history of London's culture. These scenes created and were created by multicultural constituencies which reconstituted, remixed, the moral and political geographies of everyday life in the city. But they have been largely overlooked in histories of the city and accounts of British culture or the creative economy.

As the cultural theorist Paul Gilroy, who is particularly sensitive to the political and cultural impact of the forms of cultural mixture made possible by music, has frequently argued, such informal music scenes and their 'mechanisms of cultural transmission' (Gilroy 2000: 271) are 'poorly understood and only partially mapped' (Gilroy 2003: 387–8). Such a mapping, to which this book seeks to contribute, forms part of a larger project of coming to terms with the legacy of empire and the post-colonial constitution of the British nation, a necessary rediscovery of a hidden history (Hall 1990: 224) which contributes to 'the unfinished history of the black British diaspora and its intricate interweaving with British life' (Hall 2002).

Mapping space, music and multiculture

Part of the project of this book, then, is to map the emergence of musical multiculture in London – where it happened, who participated, the conditions of emergence and decline, and the music, from Jamaica, America, Brazil, the Latin Caribbean and from London itself, which was always at the centre. The notion of mapping is a spatial metaphor. I think a fruitful way to understand the shape of these music scenes – which perhaps has implications for how we understand all popular music – is by thinking about them in terms of space. We can understand how they were formed and what they felt like inside by thinking about what was happening in the space around them, in what sociologists call 'the constitutive outside'.

As the feminist social geographer Doreen Massey has convincingly argued, space and the social are mutually constitutive and space is always 'an expression of and a medium of power' (Massey 1994: 104). Black music scenes in London, because they were black, were subject to extreme forms of spatialised power, and they responded by making new spaces, where new ideas about how social space could be organised were front and centre – imaginary spaces with real social consequences, the kind that music can take you to. Race, gender and class, as well as other forms of social inequality, are produced, and reproduced, spatially. Massey coins the useful term 'power geometry' to describe the process by which distinctions of class, race and gender are enacted spatially and spaces become coded in particular ways that reveal underlying power relations (for example 'a woman's place is in the home', 'no-go areas', 'sink estates').

In recent times, at the interface between geography and critical race studies sometimes called 'black geography', particular attention has been paid to the way race is produced, and racial division maintained, spatially (McKitterick 2006; Woods and McKitterick 2007; Neely and Samura 2011; Brand 2018). This work continues the project of anti-racist sociologists who analysed how race is reproduced spatially under 'racial rule', such as David Theo Goldberg's comparative analysis of the forms of spatial segregation that produced race in apartheid South Africa and the segregated American city (2004). In each case, Goldberg argues, racial ideology is produced and reinforced through a variety of spatial policies both judicial, like the passbook laws under apartheid, or extra-judicial, like urban zoning policies and spatialised policing, which often draws its power from the 'discretionary' power of police officers, security guards or club bouncers. In each case the effect of racial power geometry is to contain racialised populations 'in their own' areas, to circumscribe their access to private space (lunch counters, cinemas) and curtail their free movement in public space. Thus spatial power upholds 'the fundamental principle of racial rule': segregation (Goldberg 2004).

Britain has never had state-mandated racial separation like South Africa or the degrees of segregation characteristic of the American city – which, as the geographer Ceri Peach shows (1996), in some cities can reach 100 per cent – yet it has enacted its own forms of racialised power geometry. Between 1969 and 1975, for example, as a response to the perceived threat of the 'ghettoisation' of migrant populations from the former colonies, Birmingham and a number of other British cities instituted a 'set ratio dispersal policy' for social housing which mandated that no more than one property in six could be allocated to black tenants (see James and Harris 1993; Huttman et al. 1991). The policy led to the 'shunting out' of black families from their homes in familiar areas to 'the white hinterland' in the interests of integration (James 1993: 262). This is just one example of the way race and space have been articulated together in British urban policy.

Writing about New Orleans, the music historian George Lipsitz (2007) has shown how struggles over space are often the way race is most directly experienced in the city, and music often plays a central part in these conflicts. He notes that these conflicts involve both actual geographical spaces and a clash of opposed 'spatial imaginaries'. Exploring the conflicts between the New Orleans black community and police over the ritualised marching of the Mardi Gras Indians – 'social clubs of black men who masquerade as Plains Indians and parade through their neighborhoods in flamboyant costumes twice a year' (2007: 10) – Lipsitz shows how spatial struggles, which are also often sonic struggles over the right to play music, are processes of racialisation, part of the way that race is made in the city (Banton 1977; Brand 2018).

The reason why music is so strongly implicated in these processes is that it, too, is a spatialising technology, as geographers concerned with music and music scholars alert to space have argued (see Eisenberg 2015). Music, according to musicologist Steven Connor, 'procures' space for its own sonic purposes and makes particular 'spacings' available to the listener – the studio, the concert, New Orleans or Havana, the space of technology, outer space… music can take you entirely out of the place you are occupying geographically and take you elsewhere.

> The kind of sound we feel minded to call music is sound as space rather than sound in place. What matters in music is not the space that the music is in, but the space and *the spacings that the music puts its listener in*. (Connor 2010: 6, emphasis added)

In his canonical book *The Production of Space* (1971), the Marxist social geographer Henri Lefebvre brings these two ideas – that space and the social are mutually constitutive and that music has the potential to disrupt spatial power – together in an exploration of the social and political technologies which 'produce' space. For Lefebvre, space is a product of the relations between physical form (the *perceived*), instrumental knowledge (the *conceived*) and symbolic practice (the *lived*) (Eisenberg 2015). He characterises the social formation as a spatial struggle between the forces of rationality, the 'established order', who dominate the right to define (he consequently calls this power 'Logos', the power of the word), attempting to fix, dominate and control space in the interests of power, and those – the 'Anti-Logos' – like the founders of the Paris commune of 1871 – who attempt to 'divert' or 'appropriate' space, to 'restore it to ambiguity' and 'dramatise' it in the interests of freedom (Lefebvre 1994: 392). In this 'unequal struggle between Logos and Anti-Logos' over space, Lefebvre reserves a special role for music. Despite the scale of the forces attempting to dominate, spatial practice is not finally 'determined by an existing system', he claims, because of the potential energy of those who can divert space for their own purposes: 'Space is liable to be eroticized and restored to ambiguity, to the common birthplace of needs and desires, by means of music' (Lefebvre 1994: 390). Lefebvre did not have in mind the music of James Brown, Joe Smooth or Roni Size when he wrote this, but his arguments are applicable to the way in which rare groove, acid house and jungle in London, as continuations of the long lineage of Afro-diasporic dance musics, deployed music to divert space, recode the libidinal energies of the post-industrial city and create the space for new forms of culture.

Lefebvre, as the music writer Greil Marcus demonstrates in *Lipstick Traces* (1989), developed a line of thinking influenced by Dada of the 1920s and the Situationists of the 1950s (he was friends with both Tristan Tzara and Guy Debord, though he fell out with both) which Marcus calls a 'theory of moments', within which the everyday and temporary zones of the festival, occupations (like those of Parisian factories in 1968 or of Wall Street in 2011) or indeed the nightclub can be imagined as opening up new spatial possibilities and political alternatives in the face of attempts to dominate and fix space in the service of the status quo. This might sound fanciful – it *is* fanciful – but it takes imagination to think beyond the world as it is and, having been French Marxism's leading theoretician in the 1940s, Lefebvre had become convinced that instead of focusing on the structures of economic production and social control that are the usual grist to the Marxist mill, it was the tiny epiphanies of *la vie quotidienne* (everyday life) which mattered. They were temporary: 'they passed out of consciousness as if they had never been, yet in their instants they contained the whole of life' (Marcus 1989: 134).

Could it be that those fleeting moments of common feeling forged on the dancefloor on a Saturday (or a Sunday, a Wednesday or any other) night were more than merely a way to let off steam, more than mere distraction from the important arenas where real political change is forged?

This book was written to try to convince you that they were. Combining these ideas about space and music – that social distinctions are produced and maintained spatially, that music lays hold of space and can 'divert' space and put into play new spatial ideas and practices – it approaches these three musical scenes from the perspective of the racialised power geometry in which they emerged. It asks you to consider the ways in which they challenged the racialisation of city space, 'diverted' space in the interests of alternative ideas about how to build a good society and unleash new spatial imaginaries which materialise both a diasporic spatiality – a 'history of other spaces' in the words of Barnor Hesse (1993) – and the imaginative resources for forging new worlds.

Time keeps on ticking

I began the research on which this book is based in 1997 as a study of jungle, then a relatively new music scene. Jungle, although it is a globally successful branch of club culture, is now well into middle age; V Recordings, the London-based jungle and drum and bass label run by Nigel 'Jumping Jack Frost' Thompson and Bryan 'Gee' Guerrero,[1]

7

for example, celebrated its twenty-fifth anniversary in 2018. Much has changed since the end of the twentieth century. Entirely unanticipated circumstances – from the development of the internet, social media and mobile phones as ubiquitous technologies, to 9/11, the war on terror and the 7/7 terror attacks in London, to the financialisation of the London housing market (Minton 2017) and the privatisation of public space – have transformed the space of London, and the possibilities for new kinds of culture it appeared to promise back then. But it is too early to let the music multicultures of the 1980s and 1990s pass unnoticed into history. One aim of writing a book about these historical cultural forms now is to render musical cultures that are in danger of being forgotten into text, to get them in the archive and make them part of the debate around British urban culture, where their example might better inform our understanding of both the relation between music, race and space and the history of the post-colonial city.

There is plenty of academic discussion of popular music cultures of the 1970s through to the 1990s, punk and post-punk (Savage 1991; Reynolds 2006; Cabut and Gallix 2017), Brit pop (Gilbert 1997; Stratton 2010) and hip hop (Turner 2017), but very little on the London club cultures of rare groove or jungle, and what there is about acid house is in my view partial (as I argue in chapter 3). One of the reasons Paul Gilroy's work (1987, 1993, 2000, 2003, 2010) is so important to this discussion is that he remains one of the only theorists who has taken seriously the role black music and dance cultures in the city have played in consolidating an 'alternative public sphere', bonded through social dance rituals and what he calls the 'ethics of antiphony', offering 'a different rhythm for living' (1993: 200–2).

Gilroy's work has foregrounded the expressive cultures of reggae and soul and their role in creating the grounds of 'black particularity' and an emergent black British subjectivity, in the light of histories of racialised terror and contemporary forms of urban racism. I apply these precious insights to a new set of objects: the post-soul and reggae dance cultures of rare groove, acid house and jungle, and focus on the constitution of forms of multicultural alliance and subjectivity made available through them. Gilroy's depiction of the importance of black music cultures and their real-time performance traditions in the city in his first book, *Ain't No Black in the Union Jack* (1987), are largely affirmative, but by the time Gilroy writes *The Black Atlantic* in 1993 he is already taking a more pessimistic tone, noting that 'the power of music and sound are receding' relative to the 'relentless powers of visual culture'. This sense of loss becomes the dominant tone in his later work, where he mourns the loss of analogue recording in the light of now ubiquitous 'deskilling' digital production technologies (1999) and sees the life-enhancing potential and oppositional spirit of black music subordinated to the process of neoliberal marketisation and commodification (Gilroy 2000; see also Hesmondhalgh 2013: 169). But I think he moves rather too quickly in this direction. In this book I offer evidence that while black Atlantic musical culture may have receded as the central force in articulating a black subjectivity in the late twentieth century, in the spaces of the warehouse party, the rave and the jungle club, even when produced using digital technology, this music and its cultures served as a vital resource to build and sustain multicultural forms of sociality and, to use Gilroy's own term, politically significant multicultural 'conviviality'.

Multiculturalism versus multiculture

Multiculturalism is a horrible word; it's too long and there is an unfortunate sense of the doctrinaire with that 'ism'. It's a word that is 'stubbornly imprecise' (Gilroy 2000: 244); and even those, like Stuart Hall, who are assumed to be its strongest advocates have baulked at using it: 'I don't like the word multiculturalism,' he told Bill Schwarz, 'but I am interested in the multicultural question' (Schwarz 2007: 150). Part of the problem has been that the term has been employed to describe at least two different processes: on the one hand 'descriptive multiculturalism', the manifest and everyday fact of diversity, especially in post-colonial cities like London; and on the other hand, 'prescriptive multiculturalism', which attempts to manage the problems that are presumed to be attendant with this diversity, through forms of regulation and state policy.

In his 2014 book *Multiculturalism and Its Discontents* the journalist and author Kenan Malik argues for a clear delineation between the two: while the fact of lived diversity in the city is to be welcomed, for the cosmopolitan benefits it brings and the way it acts as a solvent on racism and ethno-nationalism, prescriptive multiculturalism amounts to an 'authoritarian and anti-human outlook' (2002), which, through its promotion of an ideology of absolute cultural difference and the empowerment of dubious 'civic leaders' assumed to speak for whole communities, merely reinforces cultural difference and attempts to 'manage and institutionalize diversity by putting people into ethnic and cultural boxes' (Malik 2014: xi). This works against genuine social cohesion, Malik argues, partly by disallowing the idea of universal values, which are taken to breach the requirement to respect cultural difference.

The events of 11 September 2001 in New York ('9/11') and the threat of fundamentalist Islamic terror it announced to the world lent a hysterical tone to debates over multiculturalism, pivoting around the fears over the incompatibility of Islam and the West, over unchecked immigration (of which the Brexit vote of 2016 was only the most obvious articulation) and a concomitant sense that multicultural policies had been responsible for enabling the rise of domestic terror. In February 2011, for example, the Prime Minister, David Cameron, announced that 'state multiculturalism' had failed and that what was required to address the threat of terror and enable social cohesion was a renewed sense of national identity.[2]

Such views found support from journalists like David Goodhart, who had long been arguing that social cohesion and national unity were being undermined by a population which was, in the words of a notorious 2004 article for *Prospect* magazine, 'Too Diverse' (to be fair, the headline had a question mark at the end, but the thrust of the argument was that too much diversity was a bad thing because it meant that 'the idea of fostering a common culture, in any strong sense, may no longer be possible'). As sociologists Alana Lentin and Gavan Titley show (2011), since the turn of the millennium, there has been a 'crisis in multiculturalism' in which 'a grab bag of societal problems, from terrorism, "radicalization" and "ghettoisation" to youth unemployment, sexism and homophobia are pinned squarely on multiculturalism'. They note the way in which the debate over multiculturalism provides 'a shorthand for all that was wrong with the guilt-ridden, relativist, overly permissive West'. This perspective, they argue, has licensed a return to the idea that mixture is a threat.

This book is not about the official regulation of diversity, or multicultural policy, but about the everyday politics of diversity and the role that music cultures have played in creating spaces for living with and through difference. It is not about multicultural*ism* as policy but about multiculture, those everyday forms of what Gilroy specifies as 'convivial post-colonial interaction … that enrich our cities and drive our cultural industries' (Gilroy 2004).

It explores club cultures where the idea that mixture is threat and that 'people prefer their own kind' (Goodhart 2004), and the racialised power geometry which mandates separation, are questioned and overcome through what sociologist Ash Amin defines as 'everyday mixity' (2010). It argues that we still do not know enough about these conduits of crossover, and that examining how they emerge, constitute themselves and decline will aid our understanding of how multiculture is made. This is an analysis of the role that music cultures have played in fostering the forms of everyday mixity and cross-race collaboration which 'descriptive multiculturalism' describes.

Methods, disciplines, sounds

As a latecomer to academia, trained in the anti-discipline of cultural studies (Turner 2012), I have always bridled against the tendency to subdivide critical enquiry into camps, disciples and subdisciplines that, despite the lip service paid to interdisciplinarity, remain separate and often antagonistic, and do little to challenge hierarchies of knowledge. The black-studies scholar Christina Sharpe argues that we should strive to crash these disciplinary borders, to become 'undisciplined' (2016: 13). In this book I follow Sharpe's lead by making use of ideas from across disciplines – cultural history, cultural studies, critical race theory, musicology and popular music studies, radical geography and creative industries – ranging as wide as I can to find ideas I can use.

Academic accounts of culture can too often proceed without the voices and experiences of those who participate. I want to put the voices of the people who made and participated in these cultures into the centre of these debates. The first decades of my working life were spent as a music journalist, mainly writing for small London-based music publications *Touch* magazine and *Blues & Soul* and the jazz magazine *On the One* in San Francisco in the 1990s.[3] Many of the musicians, rappers and producers I spoke to as a journalist talked eloquently about their lives and work and its wider connection to history and politics, but the limitations of music journalism, attuned to the priorities of record-company release schedules and personal brand management, restricted the space for wider discussion of the political and social significance of popular music (which is not to say that many music journalists do not write brilliantly about these issues[4]). In this book I put these voices into conversation with the cultural theory to which my life as an academic now gives me access. I'm not suggesting that the producers of art and culture should necessarily monopolise their interpretation. But I am arguing that those involved in the production of a form of culture which the Jamaican scholar Sylvia Wynter has described as an 'underground reservoir of cultural heresy'[5] need to be brought into the ongoing debate about these cultures, how they were made and what they mean.

This book draws on a large collection of interviews I've recorded since 1997, as well as some unpublished interviews by other people (a full list of interviewees and interviews is given in the Appendix). In radio stations and record stores, pubs, clubs, coffee shops and the back seats of cars I spoke to a wide range of cultural producers – DJs, promoters, MCs, dancers, white and black, male and female – and attended a wide range of events, concerts, club nights and other places where music and dancing happened in the city. This book includes the voices, and draws on the experience of, musicians, DJs and club promoters across a range of genres, from reggae and jazz funk to techno and jungle, and the non-professional dancers – the ravers – who were (and are) a vital, and too often overlooked, part of the production of music cultures. I supplement my own interviews by drawing on insider accounts and oral histories like Lloyd Bradley's *Sounds Like London* (2013), Mark 'Snowboy' Cotgrove's *From Jazz Funk and Fusion to Acid Jazz: The History of the UK Jazz Dance Scene* (2009), Luke Bainbridge's *Acid House: The True Story* (2013) and Brian Belle-Fortune's oral history of jungle *All Crews: Journeys Through Jungle/Drum and Bass Culture* (2004).

This research started well before Web 2.0. Since then, a growing archive of oral history – of a rich but variable and sometimes factually dubious kind – has become available on the internet. This book has made use of blogs, podcasts and discussion forums, much of it produced by club culture insiders like the DJ/writers Greg Wilson, Terry Farley, Bill Brewster, Frank Broughton, Seymour Nurse and Gilles Peterson.[6]

Researching club culture history is especially challenging because so much of it was not recorded or written down. Cultural activity around music and dance often takes place in performative spaces that are temporary or hidden by design, spaces that 'hosted a complex process of intercultural and transcultural syncretism' (Gilroy 2003: 387–8), which, though they largely depended on recorded music, took place in real-time relations between music, DJs and crowd. As historian Lara Putnam argues, reflecting on writing histories of the African diaspora within which technologies of remembrance were more frequently oral-sonic than written, 'it is far easier to trace the history of the print-centered public ... but the international consciousness generated by the black performative realm may have mattered more, and mattered to many more' (2013: 149). The forms of consciousness made available in London by the 'black performative realm', which both nurtured the emergence of a distinctly black British identity and became moral and economic resources available to all, are at the heart of this book. The place to seek an understanding of the development of multiculture in the city is in these black performative realms – the clubs, dances, sound systems, blues parties and raves which constituted the everynight life of late twentieth-century century London. Here we find 'the narratives and poetics of cultural intermixture' and can trace a history of the aspiration to build 'collective or shared space as a commons in which majorities and minorities participate as equals' (Amin 2010: 14).

It's a London ting[7]

Though rare groove, acid house and jungle drew on musical influences from across the African diaspora – New Orleans, New York, Chicago, Detroit, Kingston, Havana, Lagos – my focus is on just one place: London. This is not because London is the only place in the UK where significant black music club cultures emerged. There are linked, but distinct, stories to tell about the dance music cultures of Manchester (Haslam 1999), Bristol (Johnson 1996), Birmingham (Jones and Pinnock 2017), even the Yorkshire market town of Huddersfield (Huxtable 2014) and the Essex seaside town of Southend (whose musical history is yet to be written), both of which are surprisingly rich in black music culture.

Partly this London focus is pragmatic; a full accounting of black music cultures in the UK is beyond the scope of this, and perhaps any single, book. But equally there is much that is distinct about London, which fed the development of music in the city in particular ways. Trevor Beresford Romeo, aka Jazzie B, the DJ-entrepreneur behind the Soul II Soul clubs and recordings, may have been a little hyperbolic when he claimed in the foreword to Lloyd Bradley's *Sounds Like London* that London is 'probably the most important city in black music worldwide', but the reason he gives for his assertion – 'because it wasn't just one style that started here, it's been years of different movements' (Bradley 2013: 10) – bears further investigation. There are distinct characteristics of the city that have made it a cauldron of black musical innovation, pulled generations of black musicians and black music lovers from across the diaspora into its orbit, and produced forms of music and dance culture that have wielded a huge influence on the development of Afro-diasporic music and global club culture. Part of this is precisely because it has been the city where black music has stimulated the creation of racially mixed music cultures, and the legacy of this has been the flowering of new genres and new kinds of interculture which challenge the division of social life into discrete racially marked camps.

London is the historic capital city of the world's largest empire, with a large post-colonial population who are 'here because you were there' (Kushnick 1993). It is historically a city of migrants, defined by the traffic of wealth, goods and people to and through it; it 'is not, and has never been a city of native Londoners' (German and Rees 2012: 232). The key to understanding London, as historian Roy Porter insists in his social history of the city, is the British empire: 'As capital and port, finance and manufacturing centre all in one, London was the beneficiary-in-chief of Empire' (Porter 1994: 2). One axis of the argument in this book concerns precisely the traffic of people, ideas and commodities to and through London from the former colonies in America, Africa and the Caribbean that we might call, following Elam and Jackson (2005), black cultural traffic. Half of the migrants from the West Indies who arrived in Britain between 1948 and the late 1960s – 'the Windrush generation' (Phillips and Phillips 1998) – settled in London; of this group, more than 60 per cent were from Jamaica (James 1993). This settlement has had huge consequences for the cultural life of the city. This book considers these consequences with respect to the emergence of post-colonial music cultures within which the descendants of colonial migrants have played a leading role.

The migration and settlement patterns of imperial and post-imperial subjects is one factor powerfully affecting how the city was remade in the late twentieth century. Another axis concerns the unplanned 'patch-work' nature of the London to which they arrived, the consequence of centuries of messy speculator-driven construction and destruction, waves of local-authority planning, economic boom and bust, and the Blitz of 1940–1, which pockmarked London with bomb sites, reclaimed for public housing in the post-war period. London has never been subject to the kind of grand rationalisation like that of Baron Haussmann which transformed Paris in the 1860s; it remains a hodgepodge of medieval streets and alleyways, suburban sprawl, property speculation and distinctly un-joined-up local-authority planning – though London has had a degree of central planning under the Greater London Council (1965–86) and, since 1999, the Greater London Authority, overseen by a mayor (since 2000), it is still administered largely by thirty-three separate councils (thirty-two local authorities and the Corporation of the City of London). One consequence of this patchwork, as demonstrated in the famous 1885 map of London poverty based on the research of social reformer Charles Booth, is that the richest in London never live very far from the poorest – though, as Anna Minton shows in *Big Capital* (2017), this distance has been growing in the twenty-first century – and consequently London has escaped the kinds of absolute class and racial ghettoisation that is characteristic of many American cities (Moretti 1998; Goldberg 2006).

With late twentieth-century globalisation, London became defined as a 'global city' (Sassen 2001), linked through international flows of capital and financial services and information to other nodes – New York, Tokyo – of an emergent global information network, a challenge to the primacy of the nation-state. This book focuses on flows at another scale and considers how London operates as a node in a different supranational network which links it not to other global capitals of finance but to the cities of what has been called variously the 'West Atlantic' (Patterson 1994), the 'circum-Atlantic rim' (Roach 1996) and the 'black Atlantic' (Gilroy 1993).

Music and dance in black London

In *Black London: The Imperial Metropolis and Decolonization in the Twentieth Century* (2016), an account of how London came to serve as a hub for black activism and de-colonial politics in the early to mid-twentieth century, historian Marc Matera suggests that London in this period could be considered an 'Afro-metropolis'. Through a network of political clubs and ad hoc associations, and the intellectual labour of exiles and sojourners like Kwame Nkrumah, Amy Ashwood Garvey, George Padmore and C. L. R. James among many others, a transnational black political culture was nurtured in the city, with multiple connections to the Caribbean, Africa and the USA. Central to this political culture was the social culture around black music:

> London was a crossroads of musical cultures. African, Caribbean, and African American met regularly, collaborated, and shared the bandstand.... Their evolving sounds were artifacts and articulations of black internationalism, even when not explicitly political or oriented toward an immediate agenda. (Matera 2016: 149)

This internationalist black culture cohered in London as early as the 1920s, in places like the Urskine Club on Whitfield Street and the Black Man's Café on White Lion Street, among the first establishments catering to a black clientele. An informal black social and political culture grew in the bars and clubs of Soho, such as the legendary Florence Mills Social Parlour at 50 Carnaby Street, run by Amy Ashwood Garvey (who had been briefly, unhappily, married to Marcus Garvey) and founded in 1936, where 'music was an ever-present part of black sociability and anti-colonial activity' and, when live music was not being played, 'the 78 records of African American, Caribbean and African musicians spun late into the night' (Matera 2016: 145–7). This venue continued to be a significant black space in Soho until the 1980s, as the Blue Lagoon, the Sunset and the Roaring Twenties (later, Colombos), where sound system operator Count Suckle first brought Jamaican sound system culture to the West End in 1961.

The Florence Mills Social Parlour was one among many Soho venues of the 1930s and 1940s which hosted black music for a mixed crowd – 'blacks of all classes and jazz aficionados as well as homosexuals, socialists, and young white Britons drawn by the mix of exotic pleasures it offered' (Matera 2016: 162). Matera's list includes Frisco's on Frith Street, the Shim Sham on Wardour Street, the Big Apple and Cuba Club on Gerrard Street, the Nest and Bag O' Nails on Kingley Street, Jig's Club (raided and closed in 1942) as well as the Barbarian, Panama, Goose and Gander, Havana Club and the Café de Paris.[8] Black musicians from the Caribbean, Africa and the USA, often barred from the best-paying gigs, especially after the 1935 Musicians' Union ban on foreign musicians

(Williamson and Cloonan 2016), found space to play and mingle in cramped Soho basements, where new hybrid musical forms emerged – 'a black international in sound' – and alliances, personal and political, were forged:

> These spaces become models of a more egalitarian social order and for equality across ethnic, racial, regional and class differences, but like the utopian visions and oppositional subject positions they inspired and articulated, these spaces were fragile, susceptible to internal pressures, co-option and outside repression. (Matera 2016: 199)

This diasporic musical culture, which mixed American jazz, Caribbean calypso and West African highlife, was a music and dance culture that transformed the city's cultural landscape.

Parallel to the development of the black metropolis that Matera describes, dancing to black music was taking place, from around 1918, in the dance halls that were a significant form of entertainment for white mainly working-class Britons. In his cultural history of dance halls, *Going to the Palais* (2015), social historian James Nott argues that 'race and dancing were inextricably linked' in the dance hall because, though the crowd was predominantly white, the music and dance styles – from ragtime, jazz and swing to the jitterbug, black bottom and Charleston – were from black America. As the racial make-up of British cities changed over the twentieth century, the dance hall became one of the most significant sites of racial interaction in Britain (Nott 2015: 278). They were also, as Nott demonstrates, suffused with racial anxiety, particularly around the issue of black men dancing with white women, and spaces where stereotypes about the 'primitive', innately rhythmic and implicitly threatening nature of blackness circulated widely.

These concerns over 'cultural contamination' reached fever pitch during the Second World War, when 130,00 black US servicemen were stationed in the UK. Nott shows how the British government and the dance establishment responded with a variety of strategies designed to limit inter-racial mixing and institute 'proper' styles of dance – including banning 'primitive' jitterbugging, and promoting instead an 'English style' which mandated physical restraint.

One of Nott's examples is the Mecca Dance Hall at the Paramount on Tottenham Court Road in central London, which in the 1940s attracted an increasing number of black male dancers, who were often the preferred partners for white women, leading to growing tensions with local white men. After a series of fights, the Mecca introduced a number of measures designed to limit black attendance, including the requirement to bring a dance partner (difficult for the largely male black population of the time, who were going to dance halls specifically to find dance partners). In 1943, following a fight, black dancers were banned for forty-eight hours, 'for their own safety' (Nott 2015: 271). Although the Colonial Office objected to this colour bar, on the grounds that it was not government policy to support racialised exclusion, it remained in force. The Jamaican Enrico Stennett,[9] who had arrived in London in 1947, and was a regular and especially talented dancer at the Paramount, recalled that police would target black men who were leaving the venue with white women, deliberately provoking them (Stennett 2007).

Matera's and Nott's mappings of black London and the emergence of the intercultural dancefloor provide the context for what followed in the 1970s and 1980s, showing how music and dance became implicated both in racialised understandings of music and in creating the conditions of crossover and interculture. The forms of racial anxiety and spatial discipline that were written across the dance-hall period (which effectively ended in the 1960s, with the birth of pop music) reappear in club culture, as we shall see, in the exclusion of black youth from leisure spaces in the 1970s and in the founding of new spaces for interculture in the city, like the sound system, the warehouse party and the rave.

Journalist Lloyd Bradley's affirmative history *Sounds Like London: 100 Years of Black Music in the Capital* covers the period from 1919, when the Syncopated Southern Orchestra became 'the first black band to play in London' (2013: 14), to the twenty-first century, with rappers like Tinie Tempah and Dizzee Rascal. Bradley details the impact of West Indian musicians and bands from well before post-war migration, like the Trinidadian double-bass player Al Jennings, who arrived in the city in the 1920s, and the Guyanese clarinettist Rudolph Dunbar, who arrived in 1931 and became the first black conductor of the London Phil-harmonic, in 1941. Covering the emergence of calypso, steel drum, free jazz, Afro-rock, lovers rock and Brit funk and the rise of the DJ-led club culture of the 1980s, Bradley focuses on the emergence of new kinds of musical hybrids in the city, as Africans, West Indians and Americans met and collaborated with British musicians, producers and audiences, in many of the same Soho venues (though often with new names) that Matera writes about.

These books do an important job of showing how specific forms of black music arrived and were remixed in the city and the role music played both in founding and supporting internationalist and diasporic forms of black identity and in hosting encounters across the colour line that fed London's multiculture. Work emerging from British cultural studies of the 1970s, in particular that by John Clarke and Tony Jefferson (1973) as well as Dick Hebdige's work on subculture (1974, 1979), provides some of the theoretical coordinates that help understand how white youth subcultures of the 1960s and 1970s can be understood as ways in which white working-class youth were negoti-ating their identities, and their relation to blackness, through music. Hebdige's still pertinent assessment is that white youth subcultures like mod, skinhead and punk can be understood as a series of symbolic responses to the black presence on the streets in Britain; he reads punk, for example, as the invention of a 'white ethnicity' influenced by Rasta-farian style (1979).

Simon Jones's *Black Culture, White Youth: Reggae Tradition from Jamaica to UK* (1988), another book to emerge from Birmingham cultural studies, explores the role of reggae sound system cultures in Birmingham in creating the conditions for the emergence of shared forms of culture in the city. But it is in the work of Paul Gilroy, particu-larly *Ain't No Black in the Union Jack* and *The Black Atlantic*, that we start getting the sense of the emergence of *black subcultural space*, organised around sound (systems), and its intricate connections to the Caribbean, Afro-America and Africa. It is through music, he shows, that blacks who are born in Britain experience their relations to other parts of the diaspora, where those who are 'not Jamaican but connected to Jamaica, not African but connected to Africa, not American but connected to America' (Paul Gilroy interview, 21 September 2017), and not, because of racism, allowed to be fully British, negotiate their identities and subject positions and produce new possibilities not beholden to fixed biological ideologies of racial difference.

Yet despite these histories, black music in Britain continues to be underestimated. Residual, and not so residual, racism and conservative nationalist sentiment garnished with 'postcolonial melancholia' (Gilroy 2004) continue to support the view of black popular music 'as a kind of bastard tradition of minority interest made by people not really British' (Stratton and Zuberi 2014: 3) or as a threat to law and order, or even life itself (Thapar 2018a). This book, along with these vital antecedents,[10] suggests we need to think harder.

Structure of this book

This book is organised chronologically, taking the three moments of rare groove, acid house and jungle in the order in which they happened. But it starts with some historical framing. Chapter 1 examines the racialisation of London through processes of settlement and migration and authoritarian forms of spatial control that served to contain and exclude London's black populations and to militate against multiculture. Alongside discussions of specific judicial and extra-legal forms of spatial control, like the 'sus' law and the racialisation of leisure – pubs, football – it examines the emergence of specific kinds of semi-autonomous musical space in the city around reggae sound systems, which were, in part, a response to this racial containment, though they were also much more. The chapter also considers the emergence of multicultural space, in schools and the musical cultures of soul, which provided the resources for the development of 1980s club culture.

Chapter 2 focuses on the emergence of warehouse parties, and the interrelated cultural economy of record shops, pirate radio stations and informal clubs within which developed multicultural alliances around music. Against the background of London's racialised geography, the chapter maps the way the warehouse party scene diverted space, and it analyses the 'rare groove' genre, the rediscovered music of 1970s America, which provided its soundtrack.

Chapter 3 is about acid house and the rave culture it spawned. This much-mythologised musical culture is rarely included in the taxonomy of black music, something that, as I argue, fails to do justice to the race–space dynamics of house and techno, or the contribution of black London to the emergence and transformation of rave.

Chapter 4 is about jungle, arguably the first distinctly black British musical genre, which (re)combines house and techno with (other) diasporic genres like jazz, hip hop and reggae, and in its deployment of technology like sub bass and time stretching articulates a specifically Afro-diasporic approach to technology, put in the service of multiculture.

Throughout the discussion of these three musical scenes I draw attention to the way music became caught up in debates about race, and the way that the music diverted and procured space for the founding of important, though often temporary and vulnerable, forms of multicultural alliance. My aim is to contribute to an understanding both of how London has been produced as a particular kind of racialised space and of how self-generated musical cultures produced from the margins, often by those who had few other cultural or economic options, have opened up space for counter-narrative and the founding of multicultural alternatives.

The black arts

Black music is rarely considered a form of art but the music at the heart of these scenes and this book – from James Brown to Roni Size – is, in my view, undeniably beautiful as well as (and this is one of the reasons it is not considered proper art) socially useful: like in all black music traditions, dance is intrinsic. 'Throughout the history of black music', writes the musicologist Samuel Floyd, 'its black listeners have also been dancers' (1991: 269). It functions to carve out performative space for those whose access to other spaces – economic, public, moral – is severely limited and creates spaces which, in principle at least, are open to all.

It is art that creates the conditions for community (though it doesn't always achieve this) and that reflects but also moves beneath and beyond the social and political conditions in which it is born. It is an art defined, in Arthur Jafa's words, by its 'beauty, power and alienation' (cited in Brown 2018). While black music's more experimental manifestations – from the music of Sun Ra to jungle and grime – can sound alien, alienated, alienating (Eshun 1998), it can also work to 'unmake alienation' and allow the emergence of a repertoire of new cultural and political possibilities (Spillers 2006: 25). The stories and histories that this book tells matter, and not just as a contribution to black history, but to London history and the story of the nation. As the dub poet Linton Kwesi Johnson suggests, this story 'is a part of the fabric of British life, British culture' (Linton Kwesi Johnson interview, 20 February 2017). But this story of repeated, promiscuous border-crossing works against the idea that the national should be the primary frame of analysis. Black music has been one of the key resources for developing forms of affiliation and notions of belonging that exceed the narrow boundaries of the nation state. I would like to think that in the context of revivified ethno-nationalism, the backward-looking desire to put the 'great' back into Great Britain and the pervasive inhospitality to difference which seems to be currently defining Britain, placing these musical cultures at the heart of the history of the nation's capital might work in the opposite direction.

Notes

1 Throughout this book I use the names of DJs and producers that they use in their professional lives. If this is not their given name I will identify them, but it makes sense to cite them in their professional persona as these are the names by which they are known by the public; they are in effect their own personal brands and are not (always) identical with the private person, the

more so the more famous they are. See James (2015: 145) on the relationship between the person and the *corporate person.*

2 See 'State multiculturalism has failed, says David Cameron', BBC News website, 5 February 2011, accessed at https://www.bbc.co.uk/news/uk-politics-12371994 on 15 July 2019.

3 My music journalism career reached its nadir in 1999 with an awkward encounter with Jennifer Lopez in New York, when my desire to discuss popular music in the context of wider cultural politics came up against the immoveable force of brand JLo. See Melville (2001).

4 Of course, this is completely contradicted by the brilliant writing of music journalists like Nick Cohn, Jon Savage, Greil Marcus, Ellen Willis, Val Wilmer, Richard Williams, Penny Reel, Simon Reynolds, Dan Hancox, dream hampton and Greg Tate and others, who earned an autonomy in their writing which I never did.

5 This quote is taken from Sylvia Wynter's manuscript 'Black Metamorphosis', which at the time of writing remains unpublished; see Kamugisha (2016: 145).

6 See for example Greg Wilson's blog 'Being A DJ', at https://blog.gregwilson.co.uk; Gilles Peterson's podcast archive on Mixcloud, at https://www.mixcloud.com/gillespeterson/stream; and Seymour Nurse's 'The Bottom End', https://www.thebottomend.co.uk (all last accessed June 2019).

7 This heading is the title of a track by DJ Scott Garcia released in 1997, an example of the post-rave London-born genre UK garage. It was reused as the main sample for a grime reworking by Jammz in 2016. The nearly twenty-year distance between the two can be measured in the difference between the sunny but the inarticulate celebration of 1990s multiculture of the first versus the articulate anger of the second, which posits poverty, corporate gentrification and an act of street violence as the real 'London tings'.

8 On Saturday 8 March 1941, the twenty-six-year-old Guyanese bandleader Ken 'Snakehips' Johnson, leader of the West Indian Dance Orchestra, was killed, along with several other musicians and dancers, by a German bomb which fell on the Café de Paris (see Tackley 2014: 11).

9 Enrico Stennett, who was mixed race and spent his life battling racial discrimination in the UK, published an autobiography in 2011 that foregrounds his experience of living 'between race' in the title: *Bukra Massa Pickney (White Masters Child).*

10 Nabeel Zuberi does an excellent job of this in his discussions of Tricky, Massive Attack and Barry Adamson, in his book *Sounds English* (2001), as does the collection *Black Popular Music in Britain Since 1945* (2014) edited by Jon Stratton and Zuberi, which makes the case for the importance of, among other things, Brit funk and African jazz in Britain.

Chapter 1

Hostile environment: London's racial geography, 1960–80

This chapter charts the processes through which space became racialised in London between the 1950s and the 1980s and the emergence of specific forms of musical space, the reggae sound system[1] and the soul club, which flowed into and were reconfigured in the club cultures of London in the mid-1980s. It asks and tries to answer a series of questions. How was public space racialised in the post-war period? How was leisure patterned by race? How did it happen that those coded as non-white and considered thereby illegitimate presences in the city experienced public space differently to white Londoners? And, finally, how did this feed into the development of musical multicultures in the city? Answering these questions involves a brief examination of migration from the Caribbean, which peaked in the years between 1948 and 1962 (although it did continue thereafter), and the patterns of settlement that took West Indian migrants into particular parts of the inner city. Here, in areas like Notting Hill, Hackney and Brixton, we see the emergence of what Hall et al. call the 'self-defensive black colony' (Hall et al. 1978) as a response to specific strategies of spatial power, in particular the over-policing of black space and the racialised containment of black Londoners, underpinned by a 'law and order' discourse which perceived the changing racial composition of the city as a threat. Historian Bill Schwarz characterises this period the 're-racialisation of England' (Schwarz 1996).

Against this background I consider the emergence of multicultural space in the city, particularly in schools, where migrants and their British-born children forged a new inter-racial culture with their white friends, all of whom were, in Schwarz's words, 'learning how to be post-colonial'. The chapter ends with a discussion of leisure spaces that outlines both the racial exclusion from formal zones of working-class leisure like pubs and football, and the development of musical alternatives: the semi-autonomous zones of black sociability around music – sound systems and Notting Hill Carnival which emerged as symbolic sonic tactical ripostes to the racial coding of space and strategies of racial containment[2] – and the southern suburban circuits of white soul, which deployed black music in the context of white working-class leisure.

Reggae and soul, the linked but distinct black musics of Jamaica and the USA, are the most important musical precursors of the club cultures of the 1980s and 1990s. It is the fusing of these two musical traditions in the club cultures of the 1980s which gives London club culture its distinctive character. Though reggae and soul share a rhythmic core around the interplay of drum and bass, draw from the same historical resources ('African retentions', spirituals and gospel, jazz) and overlap continually (it's worth recalling that Bob Marley modelled himself on Curtis Mayfield), they were articulated in London before the 1980s in different ways and were sometimes mutually antagonistic.

Soul, especially after Motown, moved smoothly through the channels of the international music market and, relatively unmarked by strong versions of black particularity, found a ready market with white audiences, and especially within the mod subculture of the late 1960s. Reggae, once uptown ska gave way to 'sticker', more militant rocksteady and roots reggae in the early 1970s (Hebdige 1987), was largely ignored by the mainstream market and media, and it circulated instead through clandestine channels back and forth between Kingston and London, where it was put to use in the semi-autonomous zones of black London. Reggae and the rebellious independent Rastas who dominated it in the 1970s were exotic and mysterious to white youth – which is part of what made it such an influence on punk – but it was never something that white youth could claim as their own or constitute a subculture around, at least not in the racially mixed city, as they were able to with soul.

For black Londoners, reggae and soul were held in an unstable compound: Rastas derided soul for its triviality and Americanness, for its sappy celebrations of love, for being in thrall to, rather than stepping out of, Babylon; while for black soul boys and girls, reggae could be perceived as too heavy, too serious, too dread and too far removed from the reality of teenage life in the British city. The techno DJ Colin Dale, for example, growing up in the 1970s in Brixton, where reggae provided the dominant musical and social context, was drawn to soul and disco clubs in Soho precisely because of their difference from the heavily Jamaican-oriented reggae sound system culture around him. 'Although I liked reggae', he recalled in interview, 'I only reluctantly went to shebeens. I didn't feel comfortable there. It was a very rude-boy atmosphere and I wasn't a rude boy. [For me] It was definitely soul music, disco. Reggae was just out the window' (Colin Dale interview, 30 July 2017).

But in reality most fans of black music were happy to sup from both of the dominant black Atlantic musical streams of the day. As the DJ and filmmaker Don Letts argues, the cleavage between reggae and soul is too often exaggerated, and throughout this period 'Jamaicans', even the dreadest dread, 'loved American soul, James Brown, The Chi-lites; it was always there in the background' (Don Letts interview, 7 December 2017). Dancers like H Patten, for example, growing up in 1970s Birmingham, would comfortably alternate between reggae blues parties and the soul clubs of the city, though he was well aware of the need to adjust his clothing, dance styles and modes of interaction accordingly: the blues were black space, competitive and sexually charged but overlaid with a strong sense of common feeling and familial affinity, while the soul clubs in the city centre involved tense inter-racial mixing where H, a popular dance partner for white women, was always aware of the resentment of the white male patrons, who tended to cluster resentfully in the bar (H Patten interview, 8 July 2018). For Nigel Thompson (Jumping Jack Frost), a Brixton boy, soul – especially the funkier end of Sly Stone and

Bootsy Collins – was the soundtrack of home, what his parents listened to, while he would seek out the deepest roots reggae at Shepherd's Youth Club on the Brixton Frontline, played by sound systems like Dread Diamond, Frontline, Stereograph and especially Jah Shaka (Jumping Jack Frost interview, 27 March 2017). The jungle genre which Jumping Jack Frost helped create in the early 1990s braided deep dub and funky soul together, using the cut-and-mix techniques of hip hop and the pounding digital beats of house (see chapter 4).

The white soul scenes of Kent, Essex and south and east London, which emerged in the 1970s from the mod subculture of Soho, would feature music from across the jazz–soul–funk spectrum, but reggae was off the menu. Soul eschewed dread reggae in favour of a peppy feel-good emphasis on fun, sprinkled with a very English end-of-the-pier silliness. Though some moved back and forth between reggae and soul, the two were constructed around very different, mutually exclusive political and cultural discourses. Within these various moral economies, racial meanings circulated through the music, and within the discourses that structured them. But they were also formed against a specific backdrop; the constitutive outside of reggae and soul is provided by the way space was racialised in the city beyond the walls of the night club, church hall or blues party. This chapter examines these processes of racialisation.

A hostile environment: the racialisation of London space

London has always been a hotchpotch. It is one of the world's most ethnically diverse cities, and Europe's most diverse. In his biography of London Roy Porter (1994) details the long history of immigration to and settlement in the city, by Jews, Hugonauts, Germans, Greek-Cypriots, Maltese, Italians and Irish migrants, drawn to the city for work, and in some cases to escape poverty, famine and ethnic oppression. As a port city, one of the world's busiest until the 1980s, London has been made by the traffic of goods and people through it, and the temporary visits of sojourners, as well as those who decided to stay, has indelibly marked its character and culture.

There is a long history of black settlement in the city, as detailed in Peter Fryer's classic study *Staying Power: The History of Black People in Britain* (1984). Africans arrived in the UK with the Romans; black musicians worked in the court of Henry XIII; and black sailors from west and east Africa lived in the city in the sixteenth century. With the development of the Atlantic slave trade in the seventeenth century, in which Britain was the most rapacious slave-trading nation (Olusoga 2016), black slaves and servants became valued assets for fashionable London households. The black population of London swelled after 1784, when refugees who had fought with the British in the American War of Independence came to London pursuing the promise of freedom, which, as Fryer points out, was never kept: they found themselves exchanging 'the life of a slave for that of a starving beggar on the London streets' (Fryer 1984: 191).[3]

Workers from the Caribbean colonies arrived in the UK to labour in munitions factories during the First World War. During the Second World War around 16,000 West Indians volunteered to serve in the British army and around 130,000 black American troops were stationed in the UK (though the vast majority returned soon after it had ended). Post-war London also attracted migrants from West Africa, to study, perform and serve in the armed forces, the majority from Sierra Leone, Nigeria and Ghana (Bradley 2013: 131). But it was the post-war migration from the former colonies of the Caribbean that had the biggest impact on the development of a settled black population in London and that created the conditions for a profound change in the racial composition and cultural life of the city.

The British Nationality Act of 1948 gave citizens of British colonies the rights of citizenship and settlement in the UK. Following a series of campaigns aimed at recruiting Caribbean workers to aid post-war reconstruction and work for London Transport (founded 1933) and the National Health Service (founded in 1948) migrants began arriving in the UK from Jamaica, Barbados, Trinidad and Tobago, Antigua, Guyana, Saint Kitts and Nevis, the Grenadines and other islands of the British West Indies. The MV *Empire Windrush* docked in Tilbury in 1948, from which 492 Jamaican men disembarked, starting a flow of immigration that eventually brought around half a million black West Indians to Britain, until this was slowed after 1962 by increasingly stringent immigration laws, which reduced but never completely stopped the flows, which continued throughout the 1970s and 1980s.

West Indian settlement in the UK was, from the beginning, an urban phenomenon, one that transformed the political geography of Britain's cities. By 1971, 68 per cent of the West Indian population were concentrated in Britain's two biggest conurbations: 13 per cent in Birmingham and 55 per cent in London (Peach 1996). There were clear factors pushing Caribbean migration into British cities. The job market was one; another was the depopulation of those inner-city areas – London in 1981 had a population two million less than in 1938 (Porter 1994: 346) – a leakage concentrated in central boroughs like Hackney and Lambeth, which lost 18 per cent of their population between 1971 and 1981, and these were the areas where Caribbean settlement was highest. This population leakage was primarily a result of economic depression and the collapse of manufacturing and heavy industry, especially the decline of London's docks, which led to the contraction of the East End labour market. A high proportion of London's East End working-class population who had relied on the ports for employment relocated, from the late 1960s onwards, to parts of Kent and Essex and the New Towns of Basildon and Harlow, created following the New Towns Act of 1946 (Mandler 1999: 218). Once Caribbean migrants had started to settle in these emptying London boroughs, 'white flight', the abandonment of inner-city areas by whites as a consequence of the presence of the black population, led to increasing racial polarisation (Peach 1996).

The Blitz of late 1940 and 1941 had a devastating effect on London's housing stock, destroying 100,000 family dwellings and creating a 'gargantuan housing problem' (Porter 1994: 349–51). This further exacerbated the patchwork pattern of London identified by Charles Booth in 1885; by 1942 areas such as the Georgian squares in Islington and Clapham, which had been relatively homogeneous on Booth's map, were peppered with bomb craters. In post-war reconstruction, priority was given to housing, and by 1949 some 50,000 new homes had been built in London and 64,000 more were on the way (Porter 1994: 351). It was partly Winston Churchill's promise to build 300,000 homes a year that propelled him back into office as Prime Minister in 1951 (Pilkington 1988: 53). Much of this housing was built on bombsites and was low-income council housing, which sprang up cheek by jowl with Victorian middle-class housing, albeit much of it in fairly dilapidated condition by the late 1940s, but gentrified since, in increasing intensity towards the end of the century (see Mandler 1999).

The decision of many thousands of Commonwealth citizens from the Caribbean to make the long journey to Britain was the result both of the push factors – weak domestic labour markets and high unemployment, a fragility that was the legacy of plantation economics – and of the pull of the British labour market, which during reconstruction had more jobs than workers (Foner 1978: 120–51). Membership of the New Commonwealth meant that West Indians had British passports, and the right to live and work in the UK; moreover, they had been educated in a British system and conditioned to consider Britain the mother country, and themselves as fully British (Linton Kwesi Johnson interview, 20 February 2017).

But we should not overstate the lure of the mother country. The preferred work destination for many Jamaicans was the much closer United States and it was only with the passing of the Immigration and Naturalization Act of 1952 (known as the McCarran–Walter Act after its congressional sponsors), which severely limited Jamaican access to the American labour market, that Jamaican migration switched to the UK. And though some arrived in London with a song in their heart, like the calypsoan Lord Kitchener, who famously delivered his optimistic ode to 'this lovely city', 'London Is the Place for Me', to the Pathé News cameras from the deck of the *Windrush* at Tilbury, many took the journey reluctantly. Sam Kelly (who would become the drummer in the UK Afro-funk band Cymande), for example, born in Kingston in 1949 and brought to London in 1957 by his mother, was 'dragged kicking and screaming' to England: 'Yes, we had poverty in Kingston,' he says, 'but we were used to that and we loved our life there' (Sam Kelly interview, 12 June 2017). Lloyd Blackford, who arrived in October 1962 (who went on to found the Sir Coxsone sound system in south London and who is now more commonly known as Lloyd Coxsone) was similarly reluctant: 'In Jamaica I had [a] river to swim in, I have the sea to swim in, I have fruit, ripe banana, mangoes, sugarcane, everything. So, I didn't really want to come to England and leave all of that behind, you understand?' (Lloyd Coxsone interview, 25 July 2017).

Despite the promise of employment – a 'good life… among varied and interesting people', as one London Transport recruitment poster for bus conductors posted in Barbados promised – Caribbean workers were, from the outset, economically marginal, a 'labour surplus' required in times of shortage but prevented from full integration into Britain's skilled workforce (Pilkington 1988). Sam Kelly's father was a skilled baker but he found it impossible to get work in London. His mother managed to find a job in a Lyon's Tea House to support the family. Keen to find work to earn the airfare back home to Jamaica, Lloyd found his route into employment blocked. After repeated futile visits to the Labour Exchange in Balham, south London, he challenged the clerk: 'How come you have four boxes full of job tickets and you can't give me a job out of them?' he asked, finally unable to contain what he describes as 'mi Jamaican fire'.

> He pull out one of the cards and said 'I'm going to show you the reason why I can't send you……' and the card [was] marked NCP. He pulled out a couple more and said all of them are marked NCP. What [is] NCP? 'What does that stand for?', I said. 'No coloured people.' I was frightened. That's the first time I come up against racism in this country.' (Lloyd Coxsone interview)

Similar patterns of exclusion conditioned where Caribbean migrants could live. Initially, migrants settled around three of the main London transport termini: Paddington in the north-west of the city centre, Kings Cross in the east and Brixton in south London. Housing was an immediate problem, not just because of the chronic shortage but also because, at the beginning, 'the Caribbean population was effectively barred from the most significant source of working-class accommodation, council housing' (Peach 1998: 211), making migrants dependent on the 'racial tolerance' of landlords and especially vulnerable to the machinations of unscrupulous slumlords, like the infamous Peter Rachman (Pilkington 1988).[4]

In the first instance it was frequently the dilapidated Victorian and Edwardian houses of run-to-seed areas like Notting Hill which provided often overcrowded and unsanitary accommodation for newly arrived migrants. In the decades following the *Windrush*, London's black population grew steadily, 'clustering' in particular parts of the city like Notting Hill and Brixton. Racist logic suggested this clustering occurred because migrants 'chose' to stick together because they were unable or unwilling to adapt to 'the British way of life', and that they were the cause of the urban decay they had in fact inherited (Peach 1998). In this way the racial resentment unleashed by a British population who were, in Schwarz's words, 'discovering themselves as white' in the light of black settlement (Schwarz 1996: 68), could be explained as a reasonable reaction to strangers unwilling to integrate. Anti-immigration Conservative politician Norman Pannell, for example, argued in 1965 that 'the fact that coloured immigrants congregate in certain areas of the larger cities in deplorable conditions inevitably arouses resentment'. Such congregation, he claimed, amounted to an 'alien invasion' (Pannell and Brockway 1965: 18).

The clustering of Britain's black population in inner cities obeys both an economic and a social logic. When they arrived, migrants had to settle in those places that were prepared to accommodate them, often where pioneers had already established a foothold (Phillips and Phillips 1998: 92). Obviously, many newcomers to Britain, facing dislocation and unfamiliar weather and food, wanted to live close by family, friends and former neighbours. In Brixton, Sam Kelly's family lived among neighbours from the same yard in Kingston, providing familiarity and security in a hostile environment. New arrivals would stay in the houses of friends and family before finding accommodation for themselves, often nearby. The majority of those settling around Brixton in south London were Jamaicans, whereas those in north-west London were predominantly 'small islanders' from Trinidad, Antigua, Saint Kitts and Nevis, and the Grenadines. Pearl Boatswain's mother settled in Notting Hill, close to the community of settlers from her home island of Carriacou. Caribbean affiliations were reproduced in the city. But this 'chain' pattern of settlement, where familial, friendship and national ties dictated housing choices, was reinforced by the virulent and wholly unexpected everyday racism experienced by black migrants (Foner 1978).

Over the years the common experience of British racism pushed West Indians from different islands, who otherwise might have felt they had little in common, together. In this way those from the Caribbean who might have had little sense of the region's links to Africa or the plantation economics on which their local economies were based – such things were absent from the British school curriculum taught in colony schools, which was structured around Victorian texts like Thomas Nelson's 'Royal Reader' series, which made no mention of Caribbean history – came face to face with a new discourse of race. As Stuart Hall has written, in Britain, where the 'finely graded racial classificatory system of the colonial discourse of race' he had grown up with in Jamaica was replaced with the simple binary of white/not white (Hall 1985: 109), Caribbean migrants 'discovered themselves to be black' (Hall 1994: 231).[5]

Spatial discipline

In the 1960s and 1970s, economic marginalisation and everyday and institutional forms of racism formed the constitutive outside to the emergence of the self-defensive black areas of London. The violent racist attacks over four nights in 1958 in Notting Dale which became known as the Notting Hill Race Riots, where white crowds chanted 'Kill the niggers' and 'Keep Britain white' as black residents were openly assaulted in the streets and forced to barricade themselves in because police failed to provide adequate protection (Pilkington 1988), were a harbinger of a new toxic attitude to race in the city.

In 1966 a series of right-wing racist political groups, including the League of Empire Loyalists (the remnants of Oswald Mosley's British Union of Fascists) and the British National Party, joined forces to launch the National Front,[6] which duly fielded candidates in the 1969 local elections on an explicitly anti-immigration agenda. This overt racism was given a gloss of respectability two years later when, in April 1968, Enoch Powell, pretender to the leadership of the opposition Conservative Party, made his infamous 'rivers of blood' speech in Birmingham. Powell's racist rhetoric – offering the image of respectable English womanhood having dog faeces posted through her letterbox by 'picaninnies' running wild – polarised the debate around migration and race, gave support and inspiration to the gathering forces of populist racism and nationalism, and defined the terms of the 'race' debate until at least the 1980s (and arguably far beyond).[7] Though Powell was sacked by Edward Heath from the shadow cabinet for his 'racialist speech', his rhetoric licensed a new confidence among racists and he received overt backing from some London dockers and porters at London's Smithfield market, who marched in support of his views,[8] as well as from anti-immigration politicians both Conservative and Labour; he also received covert support from many other quarters.

Also in 1968, two significant pieces of legislation left their mark on the racial politics of the next decades. The rights of Commonwealth citizens to settle in Britain had already been rolled back by the 1962 Commonwealth Immigrants Act,[9] which introduced an 'employment voucher' system to limit migration. In that year, in the hysterical climate stoked by Powell's rhetoric and cranked to fever pitch by Idi Amin's expulsion of Uganda's Asian population, who mostly held British passports, triggering fears of a new 'flood' of non-white immigration, Harold Wilson's Labour government rushed through a new Commonwealth Immigrants Act, with what Barbara Castle, a minister in that government, subsequently admitted was 'indecent haste'.[10] This law introduced, among other restrictions and indignities, the infamous 'partial clause', which stipulated that migrants had to establish a link with a parent or grandparent already resident in the UK in order to be granted the right to settle. The implication was clear to those 'foreigners' residing at that time in Britain – non-whites were an unwanted threat (Joppke 1996: 471).

The other piece of legislation was the Race Relations Act 1968, which was framed as compensation for the strengthening of the immigration laws. This sought to toughen up the provision of the first such Act, of 1965, which had outlawed racial discrimination 'in places of public resort' (to little practical effect), by extending this to include housing and employment. The 1968 Act also established the Community Relations Council to adjudicate claims of direct discrimination. Home Secretary James Callaghan, under whose jurisdiction the legislation fell, who as an MP was sponsored by the Police Federation (effectively the police officers' trade union), exempted the police from the provisions of the Act. This effectively relieved the police force from any obligation to curb discriminatory practices and left them unaccountable for their policies in relation to race.[11] This exemption was a major contributory factor to the degree of discretionary power the police were able to use in the streets. The apparently arbitrary but actually systematic over-policing and harassment of black people (particularly, but not only, young men) and black areas in London in the 1970s from which no black Londoner was exempt relied on these discretionary powers for its effectiveness as a form of control (Carr-Hill and Davis 1988), one which manifested a particular spatial form (Keith 1993: 131).

Underpinning such over-policing was the 'common sense' that perceived the problem of 'race' in Britain not as a matter of white racism but of fundamental incompatibility and inherent black criminality, a stance that drew on long-standing discourses about the relation between blackness and vice. As far back as the sixteenth century, European adventurers were commenting on the African predisposition for vice and immorality in their diaries and memoirs. These kinds of 'factual' accounts, which were popular reading in Britain, helped structure the racial attitudes of the eighteenth and nineteenth centuries, which in turn 'influenced the emergence of more modern racialist thought' (Walvin 1982: 59).[12]

The apparently self-evident nature of the link between race and crime was reproduced in the racist rhetoric of ideologues from across the political spectrum. Accrington Labour MP John Hynd was an enthusiastic supporter of the lobby against black immigration, led by the Conservative Cyril Osborne, as was Labour MP George Rogers, whose Notting Hill constituency was the scene of the racist attacks in 1958. Rogers's proposed solution to the problems of racist violence was to curtail immigration (Pilkington 1988: 69, 84). Tory MP and former colonial officer in Nigeria Norman Pannell, another implacable opponent of immigration, argued that 'it can be stated on incontrovertible evidence that immigrants are far more prone to certain grave offences than are the rest of the community' (Pannell and Brockway 1965: 29). Such arguments served the ideological role of legitimising the political management of urban problems by deflecting attention away from racism and onto the moral character of black people themselves (see Smith 1993: 137).

In the period between the passing of the Commonwealth Immigrants Act of 1962 – which, though it had been drafted to curtail black immigration to Britain, had the opposite effect initially, as migrants rushed to 'beat the ban' – and the major racialised civil unrest of the early 1980s – the Brixton riots of 1981 and the riots in Tottenham and Brixton in 1985 – London's political geography became racialised, subdivided into white and black – 'no-go' – areas. Areas of black concentration became further subdivided into 'frontlines' and 'backyards', that is, the streets where black people were confronted by the forces of law and order and formed their own informal and self-protective infrastructures (see Monrose 2016) and the private 'semi-autonomous' sphere where black Londoners could escape racialised surveillance (Keith 1993; Hall 1997).

City space becomes understood by reference to race, just as race comes to be understood geographically – places where black people live are represented as 'trouble spots', with disproportionate rates of street crime, drug use, prostitution and associated social chaos. A similar metonymic slippage characterises the emergence, in the 1970s, of the figure of the 'innately criminal black youth', a folk devil known in the ideological parlance as the 'mugger' or 'dipper' (i.e. pickpocket) (Hall et al. 1978). The logic of racists like Pannell was to establish through statistics (compiled by the Home Office using questionable methodology, including a lack of consistency in racial categories: see Dumuth 1978) that a disproportionate amount of violent street crime was perpetrated by young black men. The term 'mugger' could then be indiscriminately attached to any male bearer of black skin (white criminals were far more likely to be called 'thief' or 'burglar') (Hall et al. 1978).

This discourse legitimised the racialisation of space in 1970s London, and the increasingly 'paramilitary' strategies enacted by the forces of law and order (Gilroy 1987; Carr-Hill and Davis 1988; Keith 1993; Smith 1993). These strategies included the deployment of a unit of the Metropolitan Police called the Special Patrol Group (SPG), active in London between 1961 and 1987. Centrally based rapid-response squads designed to quell public disorder, SPG units, comprising thirty officers, three sergeants and an inspector, would be deployed in vans equipped with riot gear at demonstrations and other public events where 'trouble was expected', charged to execute stop and search. SPG vans were an everyday sight during the 1970s and 1980s, partially concealed round corners and under railway arches, yet obvious to the whole local community, in areas such as Brixton, Tottenham and Hackney, black areas conceived to be trouble spots. During 1975 alone, 14,000 people were stopped by the SPGs (Phillips and Phillips 1998).[13] 'It's a time of almost internal colonization', Paul Gilroy told the authors of the 1999 book *Windrush*, 'the black settlement population at the middle of most cities are being policed like they're foreign territories' (Phillips and Phillips 1998: 296).

The use of tactical forces like SPG units turned the public space of certain areas of the city into a battleground where black Londoners were vulnerable to arbitrary 'stop and search'. At the same time, their access to other public spaces of the city was circumscribed by strategies of containment. Goldberg argues that spatial containment is the primary mode by which racial marginalisation has been (re)produced in the Western city. This does not require the absolute removal of undesired populations beyond the limits of the city but it is produced through 'their circumscription in terms of location, and their limitation in terms of access – to power, to (the realisation of) rights, and to goods and services' (Goldberg 1993: 47).

In the mid-1970s, the Metropolitan Police and other urban police forces began to employ another strategy of containment that came to be known by its colloquial appellation, 'sus'. Standing for 'suspected persons', the sus laws used section IV of the Vagrancy Act 1824, passed following the Napoleonic Wars to deal with the masses of returning soldiers thronging the cities or, to use the language of the ordinance, 'disorderly persons, rogues and vagabonds' (Jackson 2015: 162). Sus enabled police on the streets to stop and search anyone who they saw acting 'suspiciously' and committing or planning to commit a crime. The use of sus in Britain was concentrated in metropolitan regions, primarily Liverpool, Manchester and London. Even within these regions, however, it was not evenly applied but used only 'in certain very specific areas' (Dumuth 1978: 38). Claire Demuth, in a report for the Runnymede Trust, shows that sus systematically targeted black youth in an attempt both to confine them to 'their own' areas and to exclude them from other kinds of public space (Dumuth 1978).

Dumuth's detailed analysis reveals that sus laws disproportionately targeted young black men. This hinged on the unprecedented amount of discretionary power accorded to individual police officers,[14] with whom lay the decision of whom to stop and when. Even if it were not for the well documented high incidence of racist attitudes held by British police officers (see Smith and Gray 1983; Gilroy 1987), of the sort described by the 1999 Macpherson report into the murder of black teenager Stephen Lawrence as amounting to 'institutional racism', it would still be reasonable to assume that the 'common sense' notions of black criminality would have pre-structured these discretionary decisions.

Not only were blacks far more likely to be stopped – Carr-Hill and Davis (1988) report one estimate that blacks were fifteen times more likely to be stopped for sus than whites – but there was a large discrepancy between stopping and arrest rates. Although blacks stopped for sus were 30 per cent more likely to be arrested than whites, only a very small proportion of stops led to arrest, suggesting a lack of evidence of any crime. One study found that of 3,482 people stopped, only 179 were arrested (see Carr-Hill and Davis 1988).

On the question of who was likely to get stopped, Dumuth's research suggests that the social standing of the alleged perpetrator had little bearing. While 'good references', from, say, a school, college or employer, could help secure the dismissal of a criminal case that had arisen from a sus arrest, in terms of the 'dipping' cases, in which black people were disproportionately arrested, all kinds of black people (but mainly young, mainly male) – the employed and unemployed, school children, college students, musicians, drivers, teachers – who were in the places where sus arrests were concentrated were liable to be stopped and questioned.

Sus required the witnessing of two distinct acts of 'suspicious be-haviour' but it did not require independent witnesses: police testimony was sufficient. If the case did make it to court, the cards were stacked in favour of the arresting officers. As Dumuth puts it, in the politest of terms, because of the close relationship and professional contact between the police and magistrates, 'it is often difficult for the magis-trate to accept that police evidence may be open to question' (1978: 29). I will cite just a few examples of the many stories I was told.

In 1977 Colin Dale (a self-described 'good church boy') and his friend Fitzroy Heslop, both aged fourteen, were on Brixton High Street, looking at the rings in a jewellers' shop window. A woman was standing near them, and then moved away. Seconds later they were stopped by police, who claimed that the boys had attempted to steal the woman's bag, though they never asked her for corroboration. They were arrested and charged. 'It went all the way to court', Dale recalled, 'and I remember the judge looking at the case for about thirty seconds and then throwing it out. But they wasted all that time and absolutely scared us to death' (Colin Dale interview).

Sus was systematic: applied in 'trouble spots' as a method of con-tainment and in significant public space as a method of exclusion, to keep black youth away. In October 1977, for example, almost half the sus cases in London were heard at Marlborough Street Court, which covers the West End. Oxford Street is London's premier shopping street and statistically the place where most pickpocketing takes place, but this still does not account for the high rates of stop and search of black children, something that was routine, as activist and sound system operator Michael La Rose recalled: 'From twelve years old onward … when I used to walk up Oxford Street, I would be stopped four times by police, searched on the street and asked what I was doing and where I was going' (Michael La Rose interview in Harris and White 1999: 125). Pearl Boatswain (who works as a legal secretary but has a double-life as the reggae DJ Dubplate Pearl) lived in Notting Hill and liked to go shopping with her sister to the West End after school. She was stopped by police, who claimed that the girls fitted the description of two shoplifters. 'We didn't even have any bags with us, and we had plenty of money', she re-membered. Pearl, who is well spoken and articulate (her parents insisted that to succeed in England she needed to speak 'correctly'), wanted to know why they had been stopped and asked for the badge numbers of the officers. They retreated, saying it must have been a mistake. 'That's the kind of thing you're up against. At our functions, in the streets. Harassment from the police, we got that all the time' (Dubplate Pearl interview, 20 August 2017).

Femi Williams, the DJ and club promoter Femi Fem, from a middle-class West African home in west London, had a similar tale of being stopped in Oxford Street with school friends, when they went to visit girls they knew who worked on the make-up counter at Selfridges department store:

> All of a sudden we got stopped by plain-clothes police. We were happy to go to the station because we were innocent. Next thing we know we were fucking nicked, under sus or some kind of attempted this or that. That was really foolish – they concocted a story about some woman that we tried to mug but they couldn't even find her. Then because we didn't plead guilty we had to go to court. I had an uncle who was a judge who helped us out with lawyers. When the trial came up the police told a pack

of lies in court; it was so weak and cheap. It was thrown straight out. It was major stress; it's almost like I blocked that incident out of my mind. (Femi Fem interview, 8 July 1999)

The desire to keep black youth away from London's commercial and leisure centre was reflected in sentencing policy: one frequent condition for a non-custodial sentence was to stay away from central London (Dumuth 1978: 34).

The differential operation of sus laws meant that city space was experienced very differently depending on your race. I grew up in London and frequently visited Oxford Street and the West End. I have been stopped by police in London only once in my life, and this was when I was with black friends (they accused us of shoplifting and searched our bags). Of the people I spoke to for this book, all the black informants, male and female, had first-hand experience of sus. Being stopped and searched and even prosecuted on flimsy or no evidence became a common experience for black urban populations in this period, fuelling resentment and reinforcing the idea that they were being made unsafe on the streets by the very forces charged with protecting the public. Such incidents were commonplace for black Londoners but were little known or understood by white Britons – it was something black Londoners rarely discussed with their white peers. Femi says he tried to block the incident out because 'he didn't want to become bitter'. Colin Dale says his experience left a bitter taste but that it wasn't lasting. Such unwillingness to dwell on these incidents or even necessarily to attribute them to racism – Femi says 'When I deal with the police I still give them a chance; you'll get some who are alright and some who aren't' – can act as a form of self-preservation, a refusal to be a victim. Such refusals, argues Claire Alexander in *The Art of Being Black*, can transform 'a recognition of group powerlessness' into 'an assertion of individual control' (Alexander 1996: 121).

While all of my black interviewees acknowledged some experience of harassment by police on the streets of the city and a few made mention of 'run-ins' with the law where they acknowledged some fault ('I was a bit wild' Bryan Gee, DJ and label head, admitted in interview, 2 March 1999), few were willing to speculate on the psychological consequences of such encounters, or the racism they seem to demonstrate. That I am not black might well have presented a barrier to disclosing this kind of intimate detail with someone who had not experienced it themselves. But it is also evident that they didn't want to dwell on these often traumatic encounters, that to ascribe them too readily to racism could lead to psychologically damaging forms of resentment, and prevent them from pushing on with the everyday work of building a space for themselves in the multicultural city.

What is clear is that black music and its cultures launched a powerful critique of such structural racism. The message of 'sufferation' in the Kingston yard, and the iniquities of corrupt police, 'politricks', hypocrites, the CIA, crazy baldheads, informers and 'door peeps' – the serried ranks of the forces of the Babylonian 'shitstem' and what Bob Marley named as its 'evil philosophy' – which was made available in the 1970s through Rastafarian-informed reggae was adapted to the black British context through the sound systems. The black dance became a place where harassment and overpolicing were witnessed and placed in the larger context of imperialism, racism and inequality. It was also the place where alternatives were explored. Music became infused with a powerful political charge.

On 19 January 1981, after a political campaign organised by a cross-generational alliance within the black community, the sus law was scrapped (Phillips and Phillips 1998: 306–7). Although it was replaced by the Criminal Attempts Bill, which partially reinstated some elements of sus under the heading of a new offence, 'interfering with parked cars', which could be enacted in similarly arbitrary ways, the success of the 'Scrap Sus' campaign, an alliance of political activists, politicians, community leaders and ordinary people within which black women took a leadership role, not only strengthened the sense of the possibilities of black political gain but also 'drew young black people and older black people together' (Phillips and Phillips 1998: 307). External pressure created a strong internal sense of solidarity between old and young and between 'those who have chosen the respectable route and those who have chosen to hustle and survive' (Hall et al. 1978: 353).

Linton Kwesi Johnson argues that another response to this pressure was the establishment of independent institutions by the black community, like New Beacon Books, the first black bookshop and publishing house in London, founded in 1966 and the network of sound systems that became the primary cultural institutions of the 1970s by which Afro-diasporic music, ideas and politics were circulated. But before we get to the sound systems I want to consider the emergence of multicultural space during the same period.

Despite the forces of racial polarisation which blocked Caribbean migrants' full access to housing and employment, the rise of populist forms of racism on the streets of London, and the emergence of the self-defensive black colony, racial polarisation or ghettoisation in London was far from absolute. Geographer Ceri Peach shows that degrees of segregation in Britain are not only far below those of the United States but were falling through the 1970s and 1980s. There is nowhere in London where the Afro-Caribbean population has ever made up more than 31 per cent of the residents (Peach 1998: 208).

Several processes militated against the complete isolation of black communities. One was a change in policy in the 1960s that allowed local authorities to accommodate migrant families in council housing, where they shared space with the white working-class population and migrants from Greece, Italy, Ireland and Cyprus (Peach 1998: 211). Another was gentrification, which led to the large-scale renovation of Victorian and Georgian London by the urban middle class, who capitalised on the depressed housing market and mass suburbanisation of the 1960s and 1970s (Porter 1994) to 'reclaim' dilapidated single-family houses in many of the same areas of high migrant population: Notting Hill, Camberwell and Camden for example. Like many other urban middle-class couples, my parents bought their house in Stockwell, south London, cheaply in 1969, and converted it from small flats back into the family home it had been originally built as in the 1880s. Obviously, gentrification is a destructive process for marginal(ised) communities (Cohen 1972) and these movements provided much fuel for increased economic and racial conflict, resentment and 'border skirmishes'. However, through the unavoidable sharing of public space and services, an emergent multiculture was incubated alongside the emergence of 'colony culture'.

Learning multiculture

The seeds of multiculture where Caribbean and Asian migrants and their children shared space with other members of the urban working class were sown in everyday encounters in the contact zones of the city, on housing estates, in the streets and at school. In *London Crossings: A Biography of Black London*, journalist Mike Phillips, who came with his family from Guyana in 1956, describes how class solidarity could underpin cross-racial alliances:

> My experience of meeting London was never an encounter with a mono-lithic alien culture. For instance, the white boys and girls I met were as foreign as I to traditional ideas about Englishness, which was defined by a middle-class public-school elite, and which was part of the language of the politicians and the newspapers…. Our geography of London was the opposite of a clutch of institutions and landmarks which housed the engines of power. We met and struggled, instead, over a space which was physical and material and in which we could be ourselves, whatever we thought that was. What happened between us was a rite of passage which bound us together rather than drove us apart. (Phillips 2001: 28)

Some of the key sites for these spatial struggles and class alliances were London's schools. At state schools, secondary moderns and large comprehensives like the 2,000-pupil Tulse Hill school in south London, where both the dub poet Linton Kwesi Johnson and techno DJ Colin Dale went to school, Stockwell Manor comprehensive, where drummer Sam Kelly and Peter St Aubyn (reggae toaster Asher Senator) were pupils, Beaufoy School in Vauxhall and Pimlico School near Victoria (an audacious brutalist hulk designed by the Greater London Council's

Figure 1.1 Pimlico School, Lupus Street, London, 1970. Seier+Seier © CCBY

John Bancroft in 1967, where I went to school – see figure 1.1) black, white and brown children shared the classroom and playground, and, though these encounters were often far from convivial, new alliances could be forged.

Black children were ill-served by the school system (Runnymede Trust and Radical Statistics Group 1980; Solomos 1988), and not for the reasons of black intellectual inferiority, inability to assimilate or cultural difference that were often mooted by anti-immigration ideologues. To take just one example, Linton Kwesi Johnson was shocked – given what he had been led to believe about the superiority of English education – to discover that his Jamaican primary education meant he was much more academically advanced than his white classmates at Tulse Hill. Nevertheless, class stratification was reproduced in the school through streaming, which, although it was supposed to group children according to ability, reproduced class and race hierarchy: 'It was stratified. You had three streams, immigrant kids in the bottom stream, working class in the middle stream and the more middle-class kids in the top stream' (Linton Kwesi Johnson interview). Johnson was able to work his way up from the bottom to the middle stream but no further (he eventually went on to take a BA in sociology at Goldsmiths college and in 2017 was granted an honorary doctorate from Rhodes University in South Africa).

A decade later Colin Dale went to the same school. He grew up in Brixton Hill and was a bright child. He did well in the eleven-plus, the exams children took at the end of primary education, but he did not get a place at the Strand Grammar School close to his home, which he wanted to attend, and had to go to Tulse Hill instead. 'I definitely think I got let down. I was top of my class; people who were below me at school got in and I just couldn't figure out why that was. I didn't think about it as prejudice at the time, but looking back on it, I think now that it was' (Colin Dale interview).

Just because schools were racially mixed did not necessarily mean students mixed well. The tensions of heterogeneity were palpable, as class and race conflicts were played out among the children of the working and middle classes. For many it was the first time they had been in intimate space with children of other classes and races. When Sam Kelly arrived at the Stockwell Manor comprehensive in the early 1960s he was one of only about a dozen black children in a school of 1,500. He made friends with his white classmates, and race didn't seem to matter until it was pointed out: 'You didn't look at each other as colour; this person had a name and vice versa. It wasn't until the third party said 'Oh this' or called names or something and you both look up and 'Oh right'. You know, somebody would shout something' (Sam Kelly interview).

By the time Peter St Aubyn arrived at Stockwell Manor a decade later, the racial mix of the school had changed dramatically and was majority black, reflecting the changing demographics of the area (and the reluctance of white parents to send their children to school with a majority of black children). St Aubyn, who was born in Guyana, lived in a rented house in Clapham North, in a mainly white area: 'I thought they'd brought me to a town where there's no blacks. The people, like everyone I liked and all my friends were white. Then I went into Stockwell Manor and said "wow"'. For St Aubyn, school was the first time he had shared space with so many black children and his first exposure to Jamaican music and culture, to which he was inexorably drawn (he later grew dreadlocks and became a prominent reggae toaster).

For many white children, whose parents could not afford or whose liberal values precluded private education, the comprehensive school was the first time they were in social contact with black people. They carried with them assumptions about blackness inherited from racial ideology. One informant, who grew up in a working-class area of south London, described how the black boys he saw at school 'looked like they could handle themselves in a fight; they seemed cool and they seemed to be together' (Jaimie D'Cruz interview, 6 August 1998). From the outside, the forms of solidarity developed among black children as protection in a hostile environment could look intimidating, just as a group of friends, or even acquaintances, from the same area can look, through a racialised lens, like a gang. For some, especially middle-class children with no competence in the masculine codes of street culture, the encounter with difference could be traumatic, as can be seen in Jean Paul Flintoff's memoir about his time at Holland Park comprehensive, *Comp: A Survivor's Tale* (1998), in which he describes the black boys in his class as 'tougher, harder, stronger, cooler', and his own feelings of anxiety as a white middle-class boy thrown into contact with them, a situation he perceived only in terms of threat.

But at these schools music could take on a special role, in being able, under certain conditions, to provide a bridge across differences of race and class. Music plays an especially important part in adolescent life, serving as a badge of identity and helping young people establish group affinities (North and Hargreaves 1999). Subcultural affiliations, like all tastes, are a matter of distinction making (Bourdieu 1984; Thornton 1995). The period of the 1960s and 1970s in Britain has, especially in Birmingham cultural studies, been widely discussed as the era of 'subcultures' (Hebdige 1979; Hall and Jefferson 1991), when 'tribal' affinities to a succession of genres – starting with teds in the late 1950s, then mods and rockers, soul boys and up to the punks of the late 1970s – defined youth orientation towards popular music. This work has been critiqued for its concentration only on the cultural activity of boys and its celebration of 'spectacular' subcultures and for ignoring, and therefore tending to reproduce pejorative assumptions about, everyday 'mainstream' feminised pop consumption (McRobbie and Garber 1991) and romanticising working-class cultural practice (Thornton 1995; Branch 2014). Yet this tradition remains one of the most serious attempts to get to grips with the investments youth make in their musical choices and to understand how social and racial conflicts were being worked out through music.

However we view the legacy of subcultural theory, it is the case that London school populations of the 1970s subdivided themselves along the lines of musical affiliation. This is something the young Gilles Peterson was acutely aware of when his parents – one French, one Swiss – shifted him from the French lycée in South Kensington to John Fisher, a majority white Catholic 'rugby-playing school' in Purley, in suburban south-west London:

> The people I was meeting in this school were very different from those in the French school. It was very tribal. I remember thinking you had to belong to a scene or a gang or a movement. In France everyone could wear what they wanted … [at John Fisher] you had to make a decision; it was very different to the French way. You could have been a punk, heavy metal, or a soul boy. (Gilles Peterson interview, 3 August 2017)

Through a friend's sister he was introduced to soul – Maze, Bobby Caldwell – and to the uniform of the suburban soul boy. Soul became his 'tribe'.

As the subcultural theorists argue, these subcultures were often constituted around black music, but they were not necessarily zones of integration, and often the white youth taste for black music did not translate into racial tolerance of black people. As Dick Hebdige argues, the subcultures of ted, mod, skinhead and punk can be read as ways in which white working-class urban youth were responding to the changing racial composition of the city, but often they were a substitute for, not a prelude to, genuine intercultural sociality: the image of the black man in the white subcultural imagination was a constant, Hebdige argues, but it was a frozen, static image (Hebdige 1979: 40–1). The very ideology that romanticised black cultural expression was 'underpinned by racist commonsense' (Gilroy and Lawrence 1988: 127–30). The racial homogeneity (almost exclusively white) of these largely working-class subcultures ensured that black typification was relatively unchallenged by experience.

But mixed schooling did sometimes provide the means by which black Londoners could establish some (sub)cultural authority and everyday multiculture could emerge around music. Norman Jay (see plate 2), who was born in 1957 and grew up in west London, was steeped in the black musical culture (jazz, soul, ska) of his family and had been buying records from Webster's stall in Shepherd's Bush market to play at family get-togethers since he was eight. At school he used his musical knowledge and record collection as a form of currency with which to build affiliations outside the autonomous circuits of black expressive culture. His school had a music classroom with one old turntable in it. He began bringing in his records to play at lunchtime. An exchange economy emerged:

> All the kids who used to bunk off music to play football started coming in at lunchtime. The white kids would bring in their Simon and Garfunkel records, and I'd bring in my Marvin Gaye and reggae records. Soon it turned in to a disco session. We made the music teacher redundant. (Norman Jay interview, 22 November 1999)

Trevor Nelson, who later became a prominent club and BBC radio DJ, growing up a decade later in north-east London, got a scholarship to a local Hackney grammar school, Central Foundation, where he was among a small group of black pupils: three out of a class of thirty. He prospered in the school environment, becoming used to being 'a minority person in a white situation'. An early career as a record trader relied upon this ability to translate between the black Hackney culture in which he grew up, where black musical knowledge circulated through families (his uncle's record collection was a treasure trove of American soul and funk) and the sound systems, and the white culture beyond:

> School was a perfect ground for me. I would spend my dinner money on records and then sell them at school, make a bit of profit. I hustled. At school the kids would give me their Police albums, Stranglers, Stiff Little Fingers, and I would give them Bob Marley, Linton Kwesi Johnson and Earth, Wind & Fire. (Trevor Nelson interview, 7 August 1998)

Through these forms of exchange, black and white children acquired multicultural capital and networks developed which inverted the racial hierarchies of the wider culture of the city: here, sonic blackness ruled supreme.

Class distinctions cut sharply across the affiliations of school. Even the most mixed schools became distinctly more middle class, and white, with the transition to sixth form, after the majority of working-class kids, white and black, had left at the age of sixteen, which was as soon as the law allowed. Those working-class children who stayed on often faced estrangement from their friends and family as the price for academic achievement. Nonetheless, friendships across the colour line forged at school could be resilient and carried over into the cultural activity of generations of Londoners coming of age in the 1970s and early 1980s.

Segregated leisure: never in a pub

Pubs which were the centres of working-class London social life were, with very few exceptions, off-limits to black Londoners. There were a very few black-owned pubs in London (Bradley 2013) and others which were prepared to accommodate black drinkers, but only under certain conditions. The Apollo pub on All Saints Road in Notting Hill, for example, served black customers but initially only in the public bar and not the saloon, and these privileges could always be withdrawn.

Following the Notting Hill riots and a rise of racial violence, implied or actual, the Apollo decided to exclude black drinkers 'for their own safety' (Pilkington 1988: 61).

Black children like Norman Jay were socialised to avoid the inappropriately named 'public' house:

> You just knew you didn't go into pubs, no-one told you, you just knew that if you were black it could be 'oi nigger' and a glass in the face. So if we wanted a party we didn't hire the backroom of a pub: it was in someone's house or the church hall. (Norman Jay interview)

Generally, if Afro-Caribbeans wanted to drink they did so at home, or in drinking establishments of their own devising, many of which were unlicensed. Dillip Hiro estimates that by the mid-1960s there were at least fifty such unlicensed black clubs, known as shebeens or shubeens[15] (see Monrose 2016), in south London alone (Hiro 1991).

In his memoir of growing up in London in the 1960s and 1970s, Jamaican-born Ferdinand Dennis suggests the scale and the impact of this social exclusion. His father, an early migrant from the Caribbean, liked to sip rum of an evening, but for him and his generation it was 'never in a pub' (Dennis 1999: 318). Just as fathers were excluded from the zone of grown-up male working-class leisure, so their sons and daughters were excluded from youth clubs and from the other rituals of British working-class culture, like those of sport:

> As the [...] white boys reached their teens, the football culture seized them.[...] We, the boys from the Caribbean or with Caribbean parents, had fewer outlets for our adolescent energy [...] the football stadium, perhaps the most important arena for celebrating and affirming working-class belonging, was a no-go area for us. At a football ground, we knew, they likened us to monkeys and drew on an astonishingly rich vocabulary of offensive racial terms. The passion for football was also a passion for whiteness. (Dennis 1999: 315)

Some back youth refused to accept this exclusion. Norman Jay, although he lived in west London, decided to support the north London club

Tottenham, because he liked the smart, mod-ish, white strip and the extravagantly gifted striker Jimmy Greaves. But he, and his black friends who joined him, had to fight for space on the terraces, and established themselves as legitimate supporters through the masculine rituals of football violence.

While some played in mixed pick-up games, school teams and local leagues, for most black Londoners organised football and the other semi-formal zones of white working-class leisure remained off limits. They therefore created their own network of independent cultural institutions, where they could drink, play and socialise, and, just like in the Black Man's Café and Amy Garvey's Florence Mills Social Parlour of the 1930s, there was always music.

Stringing up: London sound systems

West Indian migrants to Britain used music as a source of connection with the culture of home (Hinds 1980; Dennis 1999). In the 1940s and 1950s this music was primarily Afro-American – swing, jump blues, jazz – played live in Jamaica's tourist hotels by musicians like guitarist Ernest Ranglin, and played on record by the early sound systems of Clement 'Coxsone' Dodd (who loved bebop), Duke Reid and Prince Buster (Bradley 2000).

In Britain this music was hardly played on the radio – the BBC had a long history of banning or severely limiting the playing of black American music, wary of its supposed sexual licentiousness – so migrants had to find their own ways of hearing the music they craved. The Blaupunkt 'Blue Spot' radiogram, one of the earliest models of domestic record player, was 'a standard piece of furniture' in West Indian homes (Monrose 2016: 78), which meant that Sundays, holidays and family gatherings would be accompanied by the platters spun by what Donald Hinds calls the 'Saturday night disc jockeys' (Hinds 1980: 51).[16] On the Blue Spot, West Indian families would listen to gospel, mento and American popular music, not only black music but the equally popular country music of Hank Williams and Jim Reeves (radio broadcasts of powerful AM stations from the southern United States, like Tennessee's WLAC, could be picked up in Jamaica, facilitating Reeves's huge popularity on the island).

The central place that the record player took in the domestic space of the West Indian household was matched by the increasingly central place of local sound systems in black London social life. The pioneers were friends Wilbert Campbell (Count Suckle) and Vincent Forbes (Duke Vin), who arrived from Jamaica in 1952 as stowaways on a banana boat, and who set about adapting the model of Kingston sound systems like Tom the Great Sebastian, for whom they had both worked in Kingston, to a London context. After settling in Ladbroke Grove, Duke Vin set up the UK's first sound system, 'Duke Vin the Ticklers', in 1955, which was swiftly followed by the second, run by his friend Count Suckle.

For black Londoners, sound systems, which proliferated over the following decades, shubeens and the informal businesses concentrated in the 'frontline' areas of black communities like Brixton, Notting Hill and Newham provided alternative forms of leisure and employment, cultural interaction and security. As criminologist Kenny Monrose argues, though frontlines like the north stretch of Upton Lane in Forest Gate and Railton Road in Brixton acquired a reputation as dens of iniquity, where drug dealers and criminals congregated, they were also a place of safety and a lively zone in which black business and 'the spirit of enterprise and entrepreneurialism' flourished, building an infrastructure and skills which would have a direct impact on the development of club cultures in London in the following decades (Monrose 2016: 83).

Just like their Jamaican models, the music Count Suckle and Duke Vin played initially was primarily American rhythm and blues, and jazz, but this was soon displaced as new genres emerged, more suited to the tone of life in both Kingston and London. There was already an indigenous music of the 'British' Caribbean – calypso in Trinidad, mento in Jamaica– some of which was being recorded, but domestic Caribbean production was only a cottage industry (Toynbee 2010). In Jamaica, the sound systems and the popular music production which supported them, previously reliant upon the United States, began to thrive in their own right in the early 1960s, with the evolution of the edgy, modern, urban form ska, a synthesis of mento and American rhythm and blues (especially the off-beat rhythm that can be heard in songs like Fats Domino's 'Be My Guest', from 1958) pioneered by guitarist Ernest Ranglin. Ranglin, along with trombonists Don Drummond and Rico Rodrigues, as well as dozens of other ska and reggae innovators, had attended the Alpha Boys School in Kingston, where they had been drilled in military marches, which, once 'Africanised' through hybridisation with West African drum traditions (something that had happened in New Orleans jazz at the turn of the century, as well as in Kingston in the 1960s), were one of the source codes of black musical rhythm (Baraka 1991: 145; Avanti 2013).

Count Suckle and Duke Vin maintained their sound system contacts in Jamaica, which gave them access to the newest recordings from sound system operators who had moved into music production in the early 1960s, like Prince Buster with his label Buster Wild Bells, and Clement Coxsone Dodd with Studio One.[17]

Initially, Jamaican music was relatively unknown outside the Caribbean and the small circuits of aficionados who had access to the limited supply of records, which were often carried over from Jamaican in luggage by new arrivals. This began to change in 1964, when Jamaican singer Millicent (Millie) Small (figure 1.2) was bought to London by her London-born Jamaica-raised manager Chris Blackwell, who ran Island Records, where she recorded a version of Barbie Gaye's bubblegum rhythm and blues song 'My Boy Lollypop', with an experienced band of jobbing musicians under the leadership of guitarist Ranglin. Released on Fontana Records rather than Blackwell's Island (which was too small at the time to adequately promote the record) it was a massive international hit, reaching number two in both the UK and the US charts, eventually selling six million copies. This simple ditty aimed squarely at the pop market had a distinctive Jamaican flavour: a jerky rhythm and Ranglin's distinctive down-stroke guitar announced a new force in pop. It was far from being the first ska record, or even one of the best, in that much of the rough and ready ska element was missing. But its success

Figure 1.2 Millie Small at Schiphol airport, Amsterdam, 1964. Harry Pot/ Netherlands National Archive

had huge ramifications for the Jamaican recording industry and the fact that it had been recorded in London, suggested the reciprocal relationship, and overlapping markets, which would drive the flourishing of Jamaican music's golden period over the next decade. 'Lollipop' (Small's version used a different spelling to Gaye's original) ushered in a period of ska fever, particularly in London, where white youth, especially the subcultural mods, skinheads and 'suedeheads', embraced it, and West Indians who had previously loved jazz and rhythm and blues were converted to Jamaican popular music almost overnight. As London sound system operator Duke Vigo told Lloyd Bradley:

Ska came in like a rush. I love my jazz, but when ska came along it just lick clean out of my head … because it was something from our own Jamaica, and that meant so much if you was living in England … it took the people back home a while to realise there was a market over here. (Vigo cited in Bradley 2000: 142)

In terms of the economic investment necessary to stimulate a domestic recording market with international ambitions, the impact of 'My Boy Lollipop' was dramatic. Although ska was already being played by sound systems in London – a lively mail-order business had sprung up to meet this UK demand – Small's radio-friendly record alerted both the wider British public to what Jamaica had to offer and Jamaican record producers to the growing market in England. In 1968 ska exploded as a dance genre in London and an at least moderately successful chart genre. In 1967 the Skatalite's 'Guns of Navarone', a ska tune past its sell-by date in Jamaica, had made it into the top ten in the British charts, another Island Records success. In 1969 Desmond Dekker and the Aces topped the UK charts with the sweet but authentically Jamaican anthem 'The Israelites', announcing not only the combined strength of Afro-Caribbean and white subcultural consumer power but also, in its biblical referencing and slower thrum, anticipating the direction of travel of Jamaican music towards reggae.

British labels emerged to meet the demand. Island (founded in 1958) and Emil Shalit's Blue Beat, founded in 1960, were the first to spot the potential of Jamaican music in the UK market, but they were soon followed by others, like Trojan in 1968, Greensleeves in 1975 and Virgin Records' reggae imprint Front Line in 1978 and numerous smaller independents, often based in the network of record shops which emerged in this period. By the mid-1970s, specialist reggae shops, like Peckings in Askew Road, Shepherd's Bush (founded in 1974 by Jamaican George 'Peckings' Price, a childhood friend of 'Coxsone' Dodd, who had started off selling Dodd's Studio One seven-inch singles from a suitcase), and Dub Vendor (founded by British reggae fans John MacGillivray and Chris Lane in Clapham Junction in 1976), had emerged to meet the demand for new Jamaican music.

Space invaders

By the early 1960s sound-system dances formerly confined within black colony areas – rent parties, blues, shubeens – had begun to extend across London from their local concentration in Notting Hill and Brixton into the West End at clubs like the Flamingo on Wardour Street and the Roaring Twenties at 50 Carnaby Street (site of Amy Garvey's Florence Mills Social Parlour in the 1930s), where Count Suckle became the first sound system operator resident in the West End in 1961. In these West End haunts, white Britons, West Indians, black Americans and African students mingled and danced. The Jamaican 'rude boy', the idealised image of the super-sharp stylish black mod conjured by ska and embodied by sound operator Prince Buster, became the dominant icon of late-1960s cool. Mick Jagger and the Beatles swung by and assimilated the style. So did a whole generation of white working-class men infatuated with ska and rude-boy cool, who innovated a 'rude' style of their own, with shaven heads, smart sporty shirts and Doc Martens boots, referencing in their skinhead style, according to Phil Cohen, the proletarian solidarities of masculine work rapidly disappearing with de-industrialisation (Cohen 1972).[18]

Jamaica gained independence in 1962. In Kingston, as ska became caught up in statecraft, which was attempting to project a respectable upwardly mobile Jamaican identity to fit the newly independent nation,[19] rhythms were changing. Uptempo ska had been slowing and thickening throughout the 1960s, becoming 'sticky' (Hebdige 1987); militant political messages combined with an Old Testament millenarianism began to dominate; dreadlocks were replacing the crop on the heads of Kingston ghetto youth; and prominent converts to Rastafarianism like Bob Marley and Burning Spear were transforming uptown and largely good-time ska into a slower, deeper, more confrontational 'rocksteady'. Marley's 'Steady Rocking' (1968[20]) and Spear's hit 'Door Peep' (1969) epitomise this change, as the great ska bands of the 1960s, the Skatalites, the Vikings, Prince Buster, gave way to the dreadlocked stars of reggae: Augustus Pablo, the Mighty Diamonds, Gregory Isaacs, Dennis Brown.

Once the Jamaican industry got off the ground, dominated by the strong-arm tactics of 'big men' like former policeman Duke Reid (who had usurped Tom the Great Sebastian's position as top Kingston sound), ex-boxer Prince Buster and future Prime Minister Edward Seaga, and their affiliated crews, there was no longer the need to go to America to buy records or to cede to America's cultural superiority. From the late 1960s onwards, the sound systems by which music was circulated and performed in Jamaica, and the UK, developed an almost exclusively Jamaican repertoire.

Reggae music and iconography galvanised resistant black identity in the name of the 'sufferer' against poverty and against racialised power geometry, and created the sound systems as the most significant force in Jamaican music and within black communities in Britain. Reggae's insistent bass culture, punched into the London atmosphere by increasingly massive speakers and increasingly powerful amplifiers driven by the wattage wars between sound systems, and the meticulous work of the sound scientists and dub tricksters, captured the heart of black British musical culture. This was a Jamaican take-over.

Black youth in London, although by no means all of them were from Jamaican families, received this music as something closer to their experience than American black music. It was something they could identify with, feel proud of, and something infinitely more beautiful, sweeter, more avant garde, more African, more exciting than the exhausted rock and pop of the late 1970s.

The sound systems mark the continuity (on the level of social form) across disparate black dance genres. The basic setup was not genre specific: turntable(s),[21] amplifiers, treble and 'tops' speakers, and most of all bass boxes, the construction of which saw a great flourishing of local wood and electronics craftsmanship. Sound systems like Sir Coxsone (which emerged in the late 1960s from Lloyd Coxsone's early career as the selector in a shubeen in Balham, and grew in size, wattage and reputation to become the champion London sound for fifteen consecutive years), Sufferers Hi-Fi operated by dub innovator Dennis Bovell, with his 1,000-watt amp and array of effects boxes, Neville the

Enchanter, and hundreds of others, were hand-made from salvaged wood from wardrobes and other discarded furniture or builders' cast-offs. Fathers and uncles mentored sons and nephews in the sonic and electronic arts. The extended families around the local set – which included women and children – helped build, maintain and promote the sound. Nevertheless, stringing up the sound system, selecting the records and keeping the dance going were all considered man's work. When the skills were available, the sound system benefited: local electricians and carpenters lent a hand. Metro, one of the technicians for the Shaka sound system in south-east London, had been an electrical engineer in the army. One of the technicians who helped develop the sonic design of the Sir Coxsone sound system worked on the air traffic control system at Heathrow Airport.[22]

Sound systems were arranged so as to create a 'field' of sound that enveloped, enclosed and entered the body of the dancing crowd (Henriques 2011). Though they were informal and unregulated, they were tightly organised units with a distinctive division of labour between the operator (who owned and managed and played the system live, as if it were a huge instrument), the engineer (responsible for the technical specifications and set-up for maximum volume and depth), the selector (who chose which records to play), the 'DJ' (who vocalised over a microphone, though not every sound system used one) and the 'box-boys' (responsible for transporting and placing the amps and speakers and humping the heavy record boxes). Sounds, all run by men, took on the form of the patriarchal family, where senior operators acted as sometimes strict father figures, guiding and training the younger generation and strictly enforcing the rules.

Sometimes, as for Nigel 'Jumping Jack Frost' Thompson, being a box-boy was merely the best way to get into a dance for free; for others it was the start of a career. Blacker Dread (Stephen Burnet-Martin), who joined the Brixton-based Sir Coxsone sound system after he ran away from home and was living in a squat on Brixton's semi-autonomous frontline area, started out as a box-boy for Coxsone, where he was expected to lift and carry the heavy set into the dance venue and lay out the cables, but was not allowed to plug them in – this was the job of more senior engineers, who had to ensure a reliable connection. For Blacker Dread, Coxsone was a revered and powerful local presence, 'the king of England' (Blacker Dread interview, 12 May 2017), and the opportunity to join his system provided a vital familial and educational structure for a young man estranged from his family and formal education, an apprenticeship, income and a future.

Sound systems established a network across the UK in the 1960s and 1970s, defined by performative competition; each area would have its own sound(s) (Michael La Rose interview in Harris and White 1999: 130) and local rivals would perform in the 'sound clash', where systems competed against each other on the basis of the volume and quality of the sound, and their access to unique recordings – produced individually on lacquer-covered metal discs known variously as 'lacquers', 'acetates', 'specials' or 'dubplates' – with which to win over the crowd, who were the final arbiters. Systems would travel all over the city, and between cities which had black populations – Birmingham, Leicester, Huddersfield, Bristol – building an intricately connected music and dance culture. These were the mobile nightclubs of Afro-diasporic culture, a substitute for the licensed clubs, bars and pubs from which the black population were largely excluded, which, because of their access to new music from Jamaica and the UK (British ska and reggae production, by artists such as Robert 'Dandy' Livingstone, developed in parallel with that of Jamaica), kept a constant stream of new musical ideas coursing into and around the city.

Although sound systems were based on the playing of records, the music was not reducible to a series of discrete commodities, and not just because the core commodity, the dubplate, was too precious to be sold. Rhythms would come into fashion and proliferate, countless 'versions' would appear of the same tunes, and dubs and special versions would be prepared. A sound-system session was a densely woven inter-textual panorama mediated by the voice of the DJ chatting over the microphone (Henry 2006). Even if these were recorded on tape, as many sound sessions were, they would be circulated for free (not sold) as promotion for the sound. Sound system was a live, ever-changing, antiphonal experience, with a sense of communal care at its core, as indicated by the language used to describe it. In Jamaican parlance, sound system operators do not 'promote', 'manage' or 'present' a dance, they 'keep' it. The dance, though it could be rude, was also a place of safety and social care. But it was also a business, providing precious and scare employment, training and inspiration: '[Sound system] gave me invaluable experience in business management', says Stan Zepherin from the Shock sound system, 'as well as inspiring me to study audio electronics' (Melville 1995).

Policing the sound

Reggae music and the sound systems and associated institutions through which it was disseminated became in the 1970s prime loci of racialised conflict. The Notting Hill area was not only the site of violent racist attacks in 1958 but the focus of continual racial antagonism throughout the following decades. With the creeping gentrification of the area, the black population was being pushed north through rent hikes, and the black institutions established in the area were under continual pressure. Mangrove Café at 8 All Saints Road, founded by Trinidadian Frank Critchlow in 1968 and soon an important hub for black politics and social life in the area, became a particular target: it was raided by the police twelve times in 1969–70 amid accusations of drug dealing and other illicit behaviour. A march to protest about this harassment descended into violence, which led to arrests and a widely publicised fifty-five-day trial in 1971, which eventually acquitted 'the Mangrove Nine' on all charges. The nearby Metro Youth Club on Tavistock Crescent, which regularly hosted sound system dances, also suffered frequent raids (Phillips and Phillips 1998: 175, 278). Elsewhere in the city youth clubs and reggae clubs like the Pastor Morris club in Tottenham, the Burning Spear in Harlesden and the Four Aces in Dalston found their dances frequently interrupted by police raids in a process Cecil Gutzmore describes as 'systematic brutalisation' (1983).

The musical frontline: carnival

Notting Hill Carnival, the annual two-day music festival which now attracts over a million people to north-west London on the last weekend of August, came about when two Caribbean-themed events merged: an in-door calypso event, first staged by the Trinidadian activist Claudia Jones in 1959, as a direct response to heightened racial tensions in the area; and the Caribbean culture street festival organised by the teacher Rhaune Laslett, inspired by the ethos of the progressive London Free School movement (which Laslett co-founded with the counter-culture impresario John 'Hoppy' Hopkins in 1966) (Busby 2014). By the late 1960s, these two had merged into the Carnival, an annual Caribbean event that featured decorated floats accompanied by extravagantly attired musicians and dancers, many playing steel drums, the improvised percussion instruments innovated in Trinidad from reclaimed oil drums. Kensington and Chelsea council began subsidising the carnival with small loans and the early period was characterised by an emphasis on culture across the West Indies but particularly Trinidad, which had the strongest carnival tradition. This was in the context of a liberal, and not exclusively black, coalition emerging in the area (Phillips and Phillips 1998: 276).

In the early 1970s the carnival expanded, with the increasing participation of West Indian activists, who organised costume and band competitions. The carnival attracted an increasing flow of West Indians from throughout the London area into Notting Hill, for what was to become the most important cultural celebration for London's black community. In the context of the spatialisation of race and the assaults on black leisure spaces in the area, Notting Hill Carnival began to take on the flavour of a black political demonstration, as policing of the event became more confrontational. Carnival 1971 saw serious clashes between carnival goers and police, and this marked the start of a grim pattern. Police would squeeze the crowds in a pincer movement as night fell, ostensibly to disperse people, but with the effect of confining carnival-goers in an ever-tightening space, which blocked escape and so ramped up tension. It proved, time and again, a volatile tactic. Carnival became 'a ritual battle' (Gutzmore 1993: 281).

By 1975, under the chairmanship of Trinidadian Leslie 'Teacher' Palmer, who that year had also joined Island Records to promote Chris Blackwell's reggae roster, the carnival emphatically swung towards Jamaican popular culture, as reggae music played by the sound systems dotted throughout the carnival route displaced the steel bands and calypso as the most significant musical attraction, just as reggae itself was entering its most fruitful and militant phase (Bob Marley and the Wailers had played a sold-out series of concerts that July at the Lyceum Theatre in London, recordings of which were subsequently released as the *Live* album, which included the militant classics 'Them Belly Full (But They Hungry)' and 'Burnin' and Lootin''). Palmer enlisted the support of local radio stations London and Capital to popularise the 1975 Notting Hill Carnival and a crowd of half a million attended. The unexpectedly large crowd was poorly catered for in terms of amenities, and free movement was blocked by barricades, with predictable consequences.

In 1976, Kensington and Chelsea council attempted to force the organising committee to stage the carnival at Stamford Bridge, the Chelsea football ground on the Fulham Road (an absurd proposal, given some Chelsea fans' manifest identification with racist politics), an idea that was abandoned only at the last minute due to safety concerns. A force of 1,600 police officers, many drawn from riot control squads, was placed around Notting Hill in patrols or in coaches parked down side streets in the heat of a legendarily hot summer, waiting for trouble. The carnival route was divided into six segments and passage between them was restricted. Pearl Boatswain was there, as she had been every year:

> There was this rustling in the air. You could feel it. There were lines of police up and down. I remember like it was yesterday. So I thought to myself, something's going to kick off. I just … you felt the tension. (Dubplate Pearl interview)

In the disturbances that followed, which saw the police officers with riot shields and batons charge the crowds, and the crowds charge back,

500 people were injured. Some, like Pearl, felt that the response of the crowd in fighting back against the police was justified:

> Well, they did get sort of like a hiding in a way because we just got so fed up with it and we thought we're not going to have any more of this and we didn't go down there with any intentions to cause this type of trouble. We just went down there to enjoy ourselves. But even enjoying ourselves we had been harassed – you know unnecessary arrests, sus – so we just thought we'd had enough and, you know, one thing led to another. (Dubplate Pearl interview)

Notting Hill Carnival was to be a focus of anxiety and confrontation for the rest of the decade, with policing increasing each year (by 1979, a total of 10,000 police officers were deployed).

During this period, young black Britons, even the well educated and aspirational like Pearl, turned their back on assimilation (Hall et al. 1978), and turned instead both 'inward' – to other blacks in Britain whom they might otherwise have shunned – and 'outward', to Jamaica and America, the nodes of an emergent black Atlantic consciousness (Gilroy 1993). Either way, it was away from 'official' British culture and its tepid pleasures, long denied, as Mike Phillips suggests:

> Sometimes … I hear a golden oldie on the radio or the television and it's like a gap in my memory. I don't recognise it and [my friend] would say 'How come you never heard of it? They were big in the seventies.' Right there is your answer, because for most of that decade I didn't hear most of the white bands, even by accident, which was a consequence of where I was and what I was doing, because I only ever heard the music of Jamaica or perhaps the USA. And that went on for a long time, starting with Desmond Dekker. (Phillips and Phillips 1998: 263)

Reggae became a vehicle of protest, affirmation and cultural cohesion during the period between its invention in 1968 and the death of Bob Marley in 1981. It sounded the rallying cry of a new international black identity and through the social form of the sound system, reggae became the dominant soundtrack for black London leisure. But it was not the end point of black British identity. Reggae was not a youth subculture, in the sense that punk was, but a cultural continuum, dominated by the older 'big men' who ran the sound systems and the complex and sometimes violent politics of turf and respect which characterised both its Jamaican origins (Bradley 2000) and its British urban manifestations (Gilroy 1987). It was not a free space for teens, but a sophisticated cross-generational hierarchy.

While reggae provided crucial resources for British black youth it also imposed limitations, in that a hegemonic Jamaican identity did not serve everyone and not all black youth were, or wanted to be, Rastas. Therefore, this was also the period of a search for other forms of black sociability, ones not defined solely by Jamaican revolutionary aesthetics, ones which better reflected the hybrid multicultural life worlds of London. One manifestation of this was the emergence of lovers rock, a London-made spin on reggae that blended reggae with an American soul feel. The first lovers rock tune, 'Caught You in a Lie', released in 1975, was co-produced by Dennis Bovell and Lloyd Coxsone, and featured a young singer, Louisa Marks, who had been identified at one of the many talent contests run by sound systems. Though many sound systems had been reluctant to play anything but Jamaican music up until this point (Asher Senator interview, 13 April 2017), times were changing and Lloyd Coxsone played it and other lovers rock tunes on his champion sound system from Brixton.[23] But beyond reggae and lovers rock there were other options, in the intercultural circuits of soul.

Black and white soul

Though the cleavage between reggae and soul can be exaggerated – many sound systems, like Count Suckle's nights at the Roaring Twenties, incorporated soul and funk into their sets and blues parties often featured a soul session alongside the roots, steppers and heavy dub – there was some antipathy between reggae and soul. Michael La Rose, who ran the People's War sound system and was determined to mix Jamaican music with soul and African music, has spoken about the difficulties this involved, when deviation from a Jamaican Rastafarian aesthetic could be interpreted as a betrayal: 'We had to physically fight to keep that [broad music] policy … there was a lot of competition and a lot of false nationalism and threats' (Michael La Rose interview in Harris and White 1999: 133). For some, committed to reggae and the militant anti-capitalist and anti-imperialist politics it articulated, American soul, with its apparently apolitical lyrics about love, its 'uptown' patina of sophistication and its accommodation of the rhetoric of assimilation, represented everything they opposed.[24] But others, though they recognised reggae's potency as a 'conscious music', chose other ways to self-identify. Femi Williams 'looked on reggae as a West Indian, a Jamaican thing. I was never against it, but I was never really in it. I was a soul boy' (Femi Williams interview). For people like him, nightclubs in the West End and the suburban periphery offered soul options to those looking beyond reggae. Here the racial composition was very different to the black sound system; indeed, it was mainly organised and run by white soul boys.

Soho and suburban white soul

The London soul scene was really an overlapping series of scenes connecting Soho to the southern and eastern periphery of London, incorporating a wide range of music from rhythm and blues and jazz to funk, which has its own diverse history (much of which is waiting to be told) which I have space to tell only in a much truncated version. It started in many ways as an extension of the mod culture of the 1960s, when white British youth were increasingly drawn to black American music, first modern jazz and then rhythm and blues and Motown, as a way to articulate their distance from the drab and austere world of post-war Britain. Mod clubs in Soho such as the Flamingo on Wardour Street, where you could hear Jamaican jazz musicians like Joe Harriot and Rico Rodrigues playing alongside British bands like Georgie Fame's Blue Flames, Tiles at 79 Oxford Street and the Scene in Ham Yard, which started as a jazz club but which had morphed into playing soul by 1963, became home bases for the burgeoning mod subculture.

At the Scene, DJ Guy Stevens[25] (who would soon be recruited by Chris Blackwell to run Island's Sue imprint, which specialised in re-leasing American blues and soul in the UK) played the original Chuck Berry or Fats Domino versions of songs popularised through covers by the Mersey Beat bands of the day. The Scene, particularly once the influential DJ and journalist James Hamilton took over from Stevens, tracked the emergence of American soul and ska on import records and UK labels like Sue and Bluebeat, from its bluesy R&B roots, on through Motown and into the late-1960s era of 'classic soul' (the Impressions, Marvin Gaye, Wilson Pickett, Aretha Franklin), mixing it with funky organ jazz, ska and pop.

The main movers of southern soul (as opposed to northern soul[26]) came of age during the mod period and took the influence of Stevens's and Hamilton's jazzy Soho back home to the suburban periphery of Essex and Kent. Chris Hill, the most influential figure in the soul subculture, started as a blues record enthusiast when he worked on the Ford pro-duction line in Dagenham in the early 1960s (Cotgrove 2009: 16). By the mid-1960s he was running a record shop in Westcliffe-on-Sea in Essex and started DJing himself. His first influential club was a long-running residency at the Orsett Cock pub in Grays in Essex, which started to build a substantial audience for soul in the area. In 1973 he started a new Monday night residency at the Goldmine in Canvey Island, in the Thames estuary, forty miles from London, at which he played only soul imports. Here, Hill (who had dabbled in repertory theatre) developed a distinct flamboyant style, talking on the mic, singing along to records and mixing 1970s glam with soul and funk records from America.

The Goldmine, which attracted large crowds, with many arriving on chartered buses from across the south and east, became the centre of a burgeoning soul scene. At the Goldmine, Hill played a wide selection of soul, funk and jazz, all organised around his manic end-of-the-pier schtick – he would dress up in wigs and funny hats and incite his crowd to do the same.[27] The Goldmine also became the site of a short-lived 1940s swing revival in the late 1970s, but through all this Hill's Monday night residency, dedicated to harder, less commercial forms of black dance music, kept the black American dance music flame alive on the Essex coast.

In 1976 Hill started a residency at the Lacy Lady in Ilford, east of London, alongside resident Tom Holland, where he played strictly 'black music' and his soul crowd grew, drawn both from the suburbs further east and from inner-city east London. Another Essex mod, Bob Jones, had started his own residency at a club called DeeJays in Chelmsford, Essex. Initially he played pop, but gradually he built a crowd who wanted to hear less commercial American soul. He worked in the local record shop, Pop Inn, where he would 'order anything that sounded black' (cited in Cotgrove 2009: 171) and by 1976 this was less the slower classic soul and more funk and jazz funk. In 1979 Jones moved up the road to the Countryman club, where he played on Monday ('pure soul') and Wednesday ('pure jazz'). The club pulled in dancers from across the south-east – Cambridge, Peterborough, Hertfordshire. Meanwhile, in the Kent commuter belt, Pete Tong, one of Hill's ardent fans, was establishing a Kent soul and jazz scene. By 1978 Tong was DJing all over Kent, at Kings Lodge in West Kingsdown, Hades in Margate, the Nelson in Gravesend and the Elizabethan Barn in Tunbridge Wells (Cotgrove 2009: 158).

By the late 1970s, the work of Hill, Jones, Tong and many other DJs (see Cotgrove 2009 for more details) had established a vibrant black music dance scene across Kent and Essex (there were parallel scenes throughout the country), supported by a network of record shops and magazines like *Blues & Soul,* all tuned in to DJ Robbie Vincent's hugely influential Saturday afternoon soul show on BBC Radio London, which by 1976 had evolved from playing pop to focusing on black American soul, funk and jazz. The only other regular source of soul on legitimate radio was the Soul Spectrum show presented by the Grenada-born New York-raised Greg Edwards on the commercial Capital Radio, from 1973. But unlicensed radio provided another vital outlet for the music.

Pirate radio had been a important method of circulating black music since the 1960s, when the ship-based commercial stations (hence the term 'pirate radio') like Radio Caroline and Radio London (not the BBC station) first circumvented Britain's restrictive licensing system and the

BBC monopoly by broadcasting on powerful transmitters from ships anchored outside territorial waters (Hebditch 2015). These early pirates are credited with challenging the stranglehold on taste and stimulating the market for soul music in the UK. The launch of the new pop station BBC Radio 1 in 1967, coinciding with a new Marine Offences Act which outlawed ship-based broadcasting, was a direct response to the threat pirates posed to the audience for official media, and it was former Radio Caroline and Radio London DJ Tony Blackburn (a lifelong advocate for soul) who played the first record on the new station. BBC Radio 1 also hired other pirate DJs, like Simon Dee and Emperor Rosko, but they were henceforth severely limited in what they could play by BBC playlist policies. A new generation of land-based pirate stations emerged in the late 1960s, like Radio Jackie and Invicta, the latter of which broadcast a diet of mainly specialist soul late at night from the Mitcham bedroom of Tony Johns, who founded the station with Peter St Crispian in 1969, using an old VHF transmitter recycled from a taxi office. Invicta provided a regular diet of soul to fuel the growing southern scene, and by 1978 some of the key southern soul DJs – Steve 'Froggy' Howlett (who ran a powerful soul sound system and had adept mixing skills picked up from America), Pete Tong, Steve Walsh and Hill himself – had regular Invicta shows.

The group of DJs around Chris Hill – Vincent, Tom Holland, Jeff Young, Sean French, Tony Munson (who as a record distributor kept DJs supplied with the latest imports), Chris Brown, Howlett and Walsh – acquired a name, 'the soul mafia', or 'the funk mafia', with Hill as the acknowledged 'godfather'. They built a strong network of clubs – Lacy Lady and Froggy's night at Ilford Town Hall, the Royalty in Southgate, Cheekee Pete's at the Castle in Richmond, the Barn in Didcot – and radio spots on the new soul pirate stations of the 1970s, like LWR and Horizon.

In April 1979 soul mafia DJs, copying a model that had been developed in the northern soul scene,[28] established the 'National Soul Weekender' at a holiday camp in Caister, outside Great Yarmouth in Norfolk, which attracted 3,000 in the first year and became a bi-annual meeting point for what Chris Hill started referring to as 'The Family'.

At Caister the ingredients of a typical working-class holiday camp – pick-up football games, beach fun and a treasure hunt – were combined with several rooms of music and dancing featuring a variety of black American genres, from 'classic' soul to jazz funk and jazz dance. Unlike the reggae sound systems, there were no toasters; instead, the DJs talked continually over the mic – introducing songs, wise-cracking with the crowd – betraying the origin of the soul DJ in the radio disc jockey.[29] The audience would respond enthusiastically to the DJ's cues and break out into coordinated dance steps as new dance fads like the hustle and the electric slide swept through soul. There were record stalls at which connoisseurs would search for the tunes they heard playing. When the main rooms closed at one in the morning it was back to the rudimentary chalets for after-parties.

This 'family' was composed of a myriad of small local soul 'tribes', on the model of football supporters, who would identify themselves with specially made banners and T-shirts representing their area and capturing the larky, ribald and blokey working-class atmosphere of the soul mafia events: the Larkfield Loonies, Dimwos, the Crawley Crumpets (an all-female tribe), the Streatham Virgin Eaters, Magnum Force, the Black Kidney (so-named because they met in a pub called the White Heart), Dartford Tunnel Moles, Medway Maggots, Sherwood Softshoe Shufflers, Welwyn Wobblers, the Stifford Sex Maniacs, the Enfield Perv Patrol and (one of the very few black soul crews) the Brixton Frontline. Soul sociality knitted these local allegiances into supra-local alliances and connections between the housing estates and new developments in Kent and Essex and inner-city working-class London.

Dedicated to the music of black America, the soul scene always aspired to racial mixture and a willed multiculturalism became part of its mythology. In *Soul Patrol*, a London Weekend Television documentary from 2003, Robbie Vincent describes the scene as 'one of the very early examples of where the black white thing came together'[30] and Chris Hill is introduced as 'one of the first British DJs to actively encourage race mixing'. Hill describes how he had to 'work with sympathetic club owners because I was encouraging these black people in'.

He recalls receiving hate mail for bringing 'coons' to Canvey Island (Cotgrove 2009: 17). Pete Tong claims in the same documentary that the soul scene was 'very, very integrated'. 'I was directly appealing to black kids', says Hill. 'For me it was a mark of success if there was 30 per cent black boys in there, this was exactly what I wanted.' This race mixing was underpinned by what DJ Mark Webster describes as a deliberate policy of non-violence that consciously steered clear of the tribalist violence that marked other forms of working-class leisure, like football, where fighting had become a ritual. 'We were a multiracial group of people', says Webster. 'It's not like we couldn't deal with a situation if it came up, but we were grown-up men who made a very conscious decision that we were not going to have that as part of our scene. Non-violence became the law' (Webster in *Soul Patrol*).

Though a large part of the southern soul audience was drawn from the relatively racially homogenous estates and suburbs of Essex and Kent, there was – as can be seen in the video footage from the Goldmine and Caister – a degree of race mixing, including, in the London clubs, Asian youth, for whom soul provided a route into multiculture (see Sharma et al. 1999).[31] Clubs such as Tiffany's in Wimbledon, Cheekee Pete's in Richmond, Cat's Whiskers in Streatham, Bogarts in South Harrow and Bentleys in Canning Town were popular with black as well as white youth, drawn mainly from residential areas in the south and north-east of the city. But soul dancers were also prepared to travel: like Marie, who would travel from Wembley in the north-west to Richmond in the south-west for soul nights at Cheekee Pete's and to the Lyceum in the Strand in central London, where Capital Radio's only black DJ Greg Edwards (an associate of the soul mafia who played regularly at Caister) presided (Marie Loney interview, 6 August 1998).

The scene was predicated on what the journalist Robert Elms argues is an obvious link between the white British working classes and the black working class in Detroit and Chicago who produced the music. It was good-time weekend party music for working people escaping the routines of labour, and though it was distinctly black music, it did not trade in racial exclusiveness: it was music, as described by Marvin Gaye biographer David Ritz, 'that wanted everyone to feel alright' (Ritz 1970: 46). As such, for black Londoners soul offered an alternative to reggae culture, or an addition. Many black dancers would move easily between blues parties, sound systems and soul clubs. Emerging from pubs and the working-class scenes of the south and east, this kind of soul was largely unknown to middle-class city dwellers. 'I never went to the soul clubs, Cheekee Pete's, Cat's Whiskers, Sinatras; I never contemplated going there – it was totally out of my universe', Jaimie D'Cruz, who grew up in a professional household in south London, told me. 'Our social life revolved around going to people's houses when their parents were out and having house parties', said Simon Payne, another interviewee. 'I never went to soul clubs. I was too middle class for that.'

But while the music was undeniably black and racial authenticity was a central value for the soul DJs, and the crowd achieved a degree of mixture, the reality of soul multicultural sociality didn't always live up to the aspiration. One comment posted under the *Soul Patrol* documentary on YouTube suggests the racial tensions under the surface:

> Some people seem very prone to remembering the scene as being more racially harmonious than it was (at times). I remember a group of black soulies being made very unwelcome at the Rio, Didcot and they left for their own safety. I also saw the same at other venues too. Black guys seemed to be accepted if they were with a tribe that had whites in it, but not in their own groups. I also knew a few of the mafia DJs quite well and the stuff they said privately was far from how some people remember the scene as having a lovey-dovey harmonious racial mix. ('Emadex' posted on YouTube, July 2017)

Others, like the sound system operator and activist Michael La Rose, felt that the soul mafia were deliberately exclusive and kept black DJs out: 'We used to call them the white mafia, because they used to keep black music, especially the soul … for themselves and would not allow any black DJs to come in' (Michael La Rose interview in Harris and White 1999: 144). In 1978 Norman Jay travelled across the city to Lacy Lady in Ilford to celebrate his twenty-first birthday at Chris Hill's soul night, but was turned away at the door. Trevor Beresford Romeo, aka Jazzie

B, from Tottenham, also fell foul of what he felt were rigid door quotas: 'It seemed so wrong that they were playing black music and not letting black guys in. I always wanted to ask the [soul mafia] DJs, were they aware of what was going on – they must have been'.[32]

Black Soho – Crackers

For black London soul boys and girls there were other options. One such was the club Crackers, a seedy basement gay club at the top of Dean Street on the northern edge of Soho. Owned by the Wheatley Brewery chain, Crackers was an unlovely dive, well past its prime, when, in 1972, Mark Roman, a young white DJ from Southend-on-Sea, who had started DJing at a Wheatley-owned pub in east London, was hired to play six nights a week in Soho, with Thursday off, for the princely sum of £63 a week. Roman was a determined lover of black music, the funkier the better, and was given complete control over the music policy. He quickly built the club into a mecca for dancers, attracting a crowd that mixed gay and straight, and he insisted that the door staff relax their quotas on black clubbers. With Roman on the decks Crackers began to break down racial barriers, to a soundtrack that foregrounded the sounds of American funk and soul alongside slick new jazz funk, all built around an emphasis on dance:

> It was the first London meeting place of black, white, straight, gay. The clientele originally was very gay. It wasn't a gay club per se, but it was hip and fashionable. Yes, the music was brilliant, but it was the coming together of different social groups and races. That was what was ground-breaking. (Norman Jay quoted in Titmus 2013a)

It was also free of the violence that characterised the heavy-drinking weekend rituals of British leisure. 'In all the years I was there', recalled Roman in an online interview with the website Six Million Steps, 'I never remember one fight'. [33]

In 1973 Roman revitalised a flagging Tuesday night by dedicating it to American import records, featuring music not released in the UK, creating a vital showcase for music that couldn't be heard on legitimate radio or in the chart-driven discos. In 1974 he introduced a Friday lunchtime slot (a continuation of the working-class mod tradition, based on the idea that little work would be done on a Friday afternoon – see Elms 2008) that attracted a young black working-class crowd keen to show off their moves. Tuesday night and Friday afternoon became the busiest sessions, jam-packed with black dancers. Roman instigated dance competitions in which the winners were selected by the crowd. Crackers attracted all the best dancers from across London, all of whom practised hard to compete in a fiercely competitive environment; some were even professionals, trained at dance studios like Pineapple in Covent Garden. The club only held a few hundred and it would get packed and sweaty as dancers competed for space and attention on the floor. Although Crackers achieved a degree of mixture in the make-up of its audience, race asserted itself in the competitive environment of the dancefloor, where graceful and athletic black dancers like Trevor Shakes, Horace Carter, Pinkie, Oily Baker, Clive Clarke and Shane 'Jabba' Henley ruled the roost (Farley 2017). Only the very best white dancers, like Tommy MacDonald, were brave enough to compete.

Terry Farley, who would go on to become a DJ and form the acid house collective Boy's Own, recalls the racial dynamics at work in the 'battling and burning' atmosphere, where humiliation awaited anyone who could not keep pace or didn't have the moves:

> The white-boys-stay-on-the-carpet rule was enforced quite strictly by the resident dancers who owned the wooden floor area, with only a handful of very good white boys having the skill and the chutzpah to put it on the line. The carpet at Crackers was rotten and sticky with all the spilt lager and fag butts from the straight-goers' nights and, on some occasions it was like dancing in sand. On quieter nights you could find a space on the edges of that hallowed wooden floor, do you own thing and be left alone. But most nights it was better to watch and learn. (Farley 2017)

For many black clubbers, Crackers was the first time they had found a central London venue where the black expertise of the music was matched by the black expertise of the dancers: 'It showed that young working-class black kids could be the best at something' (Norman Jay cited in Brewster and Farley 2017).

During the long hot summer of 1976 – the same year as the violence at the Notting Hill Carnival – Fridays at Crackers, which were free, became literally the hottest club in London, attracting long queues of young dancers. But in the autumn of that year Wheatley's brought in a new manager. Many among Roman's young black crowd chose not to drink alcohol or could not afford to, and instead perhaps nursed a blackcurrant and lemonade or drank water from the tap in the toilets. After turning off the taps did not increase bar takings, the manager made changes. 'He wanted the playlist to go pop', says Farley, 'which, reading between the lines, probably also meant less blacks, less weirdoes and homosexuals and more of the type of people he had just left at his previous job in Swansea' (Farley 2017). Roman was moved to another Wheatleys venue, Jaws in Leytonstone, in the insalubrious north-east of the city, taking much of his crowd with him, where he recreated the Crackers atmosphere, but, after only a few months, the night was closed down because of noise complaints from residents, though many detected in the manager's complaint that it was 'too busy' a complaint that it was too full of black people (Farley 2017). Meanwhile, punk had hit Soho[34] (the Buzzcocks, the Damned, the Clash, the Rezillos and the Slits all formed in 1976 and the Sex Pistols' first single, 'Anarchy in the UK', was released that November) and the new punk night (the Vortex) at Crackers had taken much of the funk club's trendy white crowd. It wasn't until later that year, with the hiring of George Power, a flamboyant north London DJ of Greek-Cypriot extraction, that Crackers reignited as a black dance venue (see the next chapter).

Conclusion

This long chapter has placed the emergence of the musical scenes of sound systems and soul in the context of the racialisation of space in London in the decades before the 1980s. Though it is important to resist the argument that the sound systems and reggae culture in London can be understood simply as responses to racism and exclusion – they were equally responses to the requirement for employment and friendship, fun and freedom – the founding of a mobile music and dance culture that provided lateral links across black London and between the city and other black populations in the UK, and sonic links to Jamaica, in the informal spaces of the shubeen, blues dance and sound clash, is shaped by the constitutive outside of the racialisation of space in the 1960s and 1970s. This mobility itself, given sus and other forms of limitations on movement, can be read as embodying a spatial politics, a desire to carve out the space for blackness in the liminal and municipal spaces of the capital, where 'the music, the poetry, the language all spoke of the shared experience of transformation and anxiety and defiance and hope' (Phillips and Phillips 1998: 295). Though an explicitly political response to power geometry was not the only content of sound-system culture, it constitutes an important part of its character and appeal. The developments in soul constitute a different way in which race and space were being worked through. Though many sound systems incorporated a soul element, Jamaican reggae was hegemonic, maintaining a primacy in the dance up until the early 1980s, when 'soul dances' run by black sound operators started developing new, post-Jamaican ways to keep a dance, where Jamaican music was incorporated into a wider palette of diasporic sounds.

Southern soul, with its origins in Soho mod culture, developed in different spaces, making over the spaces of white working-class leisure, pubs, suburban eateries, dance halls and holiday camps in east London, Kent, Essex and Norfolk, with an American soul-derived philosophy of fun, funk and assimilation, filtered through a British seaside playfulness and a reconfigured working-class tribalism that, partly through a self-conscious exclusiveness embodied in the notion of 'the Family' with Chris Hill as the paterfamilias, successfully dispensed with violence and hosted a degree of multicultural mixture unseen in British working-class culture hitherto. But there were limits to its racial tolerance: Chris Hill's ideal 30 per cent black (male) crowd represents both a distinct advance on racial exclusivity and a sense of the acceptable limits of black participation in white soul, just as the dominance of the white soul DJs, whether consciously or not, inhibited the full participation of black DJs and promoters.

The topological configurations of both reggae and soul emphasise that whether explicitly aimed at a political outcome – as 'Chant Down Babylon' reggae could be – or at apparently apolitical fun, where the only aspiration was to be 'the greatest dancer', 'space and politics remain mutually constitutive' (Iton 2008: 259). Both reggae and soul provided a gateway through which ideas and sensibilities from across the black Atlantic, but especially Jamaica and the United States, carried on records and through the licensed and unlicensed airwaves, could be annexed to the identity work of black and white Londoners and suburbanites, engaged in exploring the formation, and the limits, of multiculture.

These parallel streams, and the emergence of black West End clubs like Crackers, would meet and merge and be reconfigured in a variety of new scenes in the 1980s and 1990s. Reading backwards, jungle, arriving in the early 1990s, draws on sound system sonics, black Atlantic rhythms and some of the pathways of suburban soul that connected east London to Kent and Essex. Acid house, arriving in 1987, emerges from a split in the soul scene, where those converted to new kinds of black American music (house) break off from the soul classicists, and make use of new kinds of post-industrial space in the city and colonise the shires. But before the advent of acid house and the rave culture, a London music and dance scene emerges that is created by sound-system veterans with ambitions to step beyond both the racially circumscribed reggae scene and the restrictions of racialised space in the city. This is rare groove, which is the subject of the next chapter.

Notes

1 The term 'sound system' has multiple meanings. At a basic level it describes a collection of audio playback equipment – consisting of at least one turntable, amps and speakers – on which to play vinyl records, ideally at a high volume. In this definition, a sound system is a massive hi-fi (also known as

the 'set'). But 'sound system' also describes the group of people, engineers, selectors (those who choose the music to be played), operators (the person who owns the equipment) and associated helpers (known as box-boys and sound-boys) who run particular sound systems, such as the Tom the Great Sebastian sound system run by Tom Wong in Jamaica in the 1950s or Sir Coxsone Outernational, the south London-based sound system run by Lloyd Coxsone since the late 1960s. In reggae culture, sound systems are often referred to simply as 'sounds'. See Bradley (2000) for a detailed history of the development of sound systems in Jamaica, and Jones and Pinnock (2018) for a superbly detailed portrait of the 'collaborative artistry' of Birmingham's Scientist Hi Fi sound system.

2 See de Certeau (1984: xix) for a discussion of the difference between the strategies of the powerful and the tactics of the weak.

3 This period is beautifully recreated by S. I. Martin in his 1996 novel *Incomparable World*.

4 Though Rachman is infamous as a slumlord whose large property portfolio was legendarily substandard and overcrowded, and who used bully boys to intimidate his tenants, yet some in the black community acknowledged that at least he, unlike the vast majority of landlords, was prepared to rent to black tenants (see Pilkington 1988: 59–60).

5 Gilroy (1993: 82) writes: 'The cultural and political histories of Guyana, Jamaica, Barbados, Grenada, Trinidad, and Saint Lucia, like the economic forces at work in generating their respective migrations to Europe, are widely dissimilar. Even if it were possible, let alone desirable, their synthesis into a single black British culture could never have been guaranteed by the effects of racism alone. Thus the role in external meanings around blackness, drawn in particular from black America, became important in the elaboration of a connective culture which drew these different "national" groups together into a new pattern'.

6 The explicit intention of the National Front (NF) was (and is) to expunge Britain's multiracial society. Martin Webster, an NF national organiser, told the press: 'We believe that the multi-racial society is wrong, is evil and we want to destroy it' (*South London Press*, 5 August 1977).

7 A controversial reading of the entire text of the speech for a BBC Radio 4 documentary in 2018 marking fifty years since Powell's speech suggests that it continues to haunt debates around race.

8 Thirty years later, the *Guardian* (1 January 1999) revealed that according to secret intelligence briefings the march had been organised by right-wing extremists.

9 See Pilkington (1988: 71–7) for a detailed discussion of the background to the 1962 Immigrants Act, which had been under discussion since the mid-1950s.

10 Barbara Castle in *Playing the Race Card*, first broadcast 2 October 1999, BBC2.

11 In 1999 Callaghan admitted in a BBC documentary that this exemption was a serious mistake. *Playing The Race Card*, BBC2, first broadcast 2 October 1999.

12 See, for example, this definition of 'Negro' from *The Encyclopedia Britannica* of 1810: 'Vices the most notorious seem to be the portion of this unhappy race; idleness, treachery, revenge, cruelty, impudence, stealing, lying, profanity, debauchery, nastiness and intemperance, are said to have extinguished the principles of natural law, and to have silenced the reproof of conscience. They are strangers to every sentiment of compassion, and are an awful example of the corruption of man left to himself' (cited in Walvin 1982: 59).

13 One notorious incident involving SPG units came in 1979 when they were deployed to police an Anti-Nazi League rally in Southall, during which the anti-racist campaigner Blair Peach from New Zealand was struck on the head and killed. SPG units were widely blamed for Peach's death (Carr-Hill and Davis 1988: 37). Though no one was ever charged, leaked reports subsequently revealed that the Met had paid an out-of-court settlement to Peach's family (*Guardian*, 27 April 2010).

14 'Discretionary operation of police power [is] always something that's spatialised, it's always something that's localised, it's always something about keeping people in one area and excluding them from another' (interview with Paul Gilroy, in Phillips and Phillips 1998: 306).

15 'Shebeen' is an Irish word for an unlicensed drinking house. The West Indians who ran or used such establishments took the name from the earlier Irish migrants. Thus 'shubeen' is a black London twist on 'shebeen'.

16 Hinds writes: 'Of course the Saturday night disc jockeys were not partial to Tommy Steele and Marty Wilde, but favoured Shirley and Lee, Lloyd Price and Fats Domino, none of whom might have ever featured in the British charts' (Hinds 1980: 51).

17 Studio One, operated by Clement Coxsone Dodd, was the most innovative, radical and successful reggae studio and label of the late 1960s and early 1970s, recording such luminaries as the Heptones, Bob Marley, Burning Spear and Horace Andy. 'In Studio One Dodd established a brand identity and a reputation unsurpassed before or since' (Bradley 2000: 212).

18 See Cohen (1972) for a reading of skinhead style, and Hebdige (1979) on the 'fear and desire' underpinning the skins' complex attitude to black culture.

19 Jamaican Minister of Social Welfare and Economic Development Edward Seaga (later Prime Minister) managed Byron Lee and the Dragonaires, a popular 'uptown' show band who played mento and ska. His decision in 1964 to invite them to be the backing band for a showcase of Jamaican musicians, many of whom hailed from Kingston's ghetto areas, at the New York World's Fair is often cited as symbolic of the moment when the 'sufferers' of Kingston turned away from ska and developed the new, more militant sounds of reggae, less easily co-opted as a symbol of respectability.

Plates

Plate 1 Jazz dancer Cav Manning, Legends nightclub, Old Burlington Street, 1986. Photograph ©Dave Swindells

Plate 2 DJ Norman Jay, Starwash warehouse party, Islington, 1988. Photograph ©Dave Swindells

Plate 3 DJ Danny Rampling, Shoom, Fitness Centre, Elephant and Castle, 1988. Photograph ©Dave Swindells

Plate 4 Café Del Mar, Ibiza, 1989. Photograph ©Dave Swindells

Plate 5 Nicky Holloway's night 'the Trip' at the Astoria, Charing Cross Road, 1988. Photograph ©Dave Swindells

Plate 6 Street party outside the Trip, with Fabio (black bandana) and Grooverider (red bandana), 1988. Photograph ©Dave Swindells

Plate 7 Dancers at Soul II Soul at the Fridge, Brixton, 1989.
Photograph ©Dave Swindells

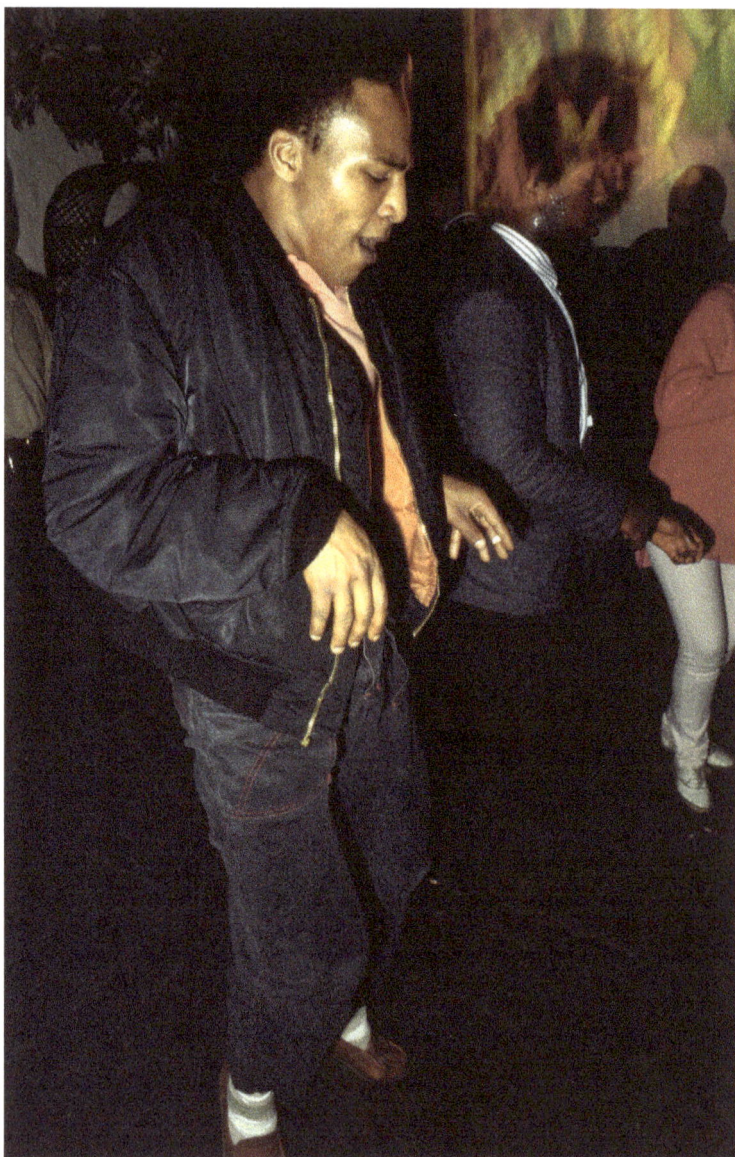

Plate 8 DJ and dancer Paul 'Trouble' Anderson, the Base at HQ club in Camden, 1988. Photograph ©Dave Swindells

20 Although this track is conventionally credited as being recorded in 1971 – as in the sleeve notes to the reissue album *One Love* (Heartbeat Records) – Ian McCann argues that, given that 'rocksteady' as a musical form and a dance style was already over in Jamaica by 1971, when Reggae had finally emerged, it is likely to be from a 1968 Studio One session. See McCann (1995: 21).

21 Original sound systems often only had one record player or 'deck' in place of the smooth deck to deck mixing of 'club culture'. To this day Jah Shaka still uses one deck, placed so high up on his set he has to drop the needle on the record way above his own head.

22 See Huxtable (2014) and Jones and Pinnock (2017) for detailed first-hand insider descriptions of the history, construction and development of sound systems and sound-system culture.

23 Reggae sound systems compete with each other at competitive events known as sound clashes or cup dances, where audience reaction, based on which sound system is deemed to have the best sound (a combination of volume and sound quality) or the most original records (hence the high value placed on dubplates or specials) dictates the winner. Lloyd Coxsone of Sir Coxsone Outernational claims to have been the London 'champion sound' for fifteen straight years (Lloyd Coxsone interview, 25 July 2017), through the 1970s and 1980s, and, though there are no official records to confirm this, few would dispute the dominance of the mighty Coxsone set in this period. On the emergence of lovers rock in London, see Bradley (2013).

24 This is brilliantly illustrated in Theodoros Bafaloukos's 1978 reggae film *Rockers*, which featured the cream of Kingston's reggae talent, including Winston Rodney, Jacob Miller and Gregory Isaacs. In a key scene, two 'downtown' Rastas, Leroy 'Horsemouth' Wallace and Richard 'Dirty Harry' Hall, playing themselves, stage a take-over at an uptown Kingston club where an apparently upper-class and effete crowd are dancing to American soul. They lock the DJ out of the booth and replace the soul record with the latest 'rockers' reggae tune, until the police are called to throw them out. Here reggae authenticity is cast against the inauthenticity of the American import. A clip of this scene can been seen at https://www.youtube.com/watch?v=G45UCqx9b_E (last accessed 25 June 2019).

25 Stevens was jailed in 1966 for drug possession, and while in prison his entire record collection was stolen. His career was marred by problems with drink and drugs, but he returned to music and in 1980 produced the album *London Calling* for the Clash. He died in 1981.

26 The southern soul scene was not the same as the northern soul scene, although there were links. The main difference, apart from geography – Northern Soul was centred on venues in the Midlands and the north of England such as the Eagle in Birmingham, the Twisted Wheel in Manchester, Wigan's Casino and Blackpool's Mecca – is the fact that northern soul fetishised music only from a very specific period, namely the late 1960s, whereas 'southern soul' scenes

played contemporary soul music (including house music). According to Tim Wall, 'the label "Northern Soul" was created in London, by the owner of Soul City records Dave Grodin, to refer to something taking place to the North of the definer's "map of meanings"' (Wall 2006: 441). See Wall (2006) and Cotgrove (2009) for a sense of how these scenes overlapped and diverged.

27 Hill became something of a star DJ during the 1970s when he had novelty pop hits in 1975, with 'Renta Santa', and 1976 with Bionic Santa, bizarre comedy mash-ups of current pop songs with his Goon Show style voice-overs. His 1978 release 'Disco Santa' was a flop.

28 Cotgrove identifies the dance party at the Top Rank Suite in Reading in August 1976 as the first influential 'all-dayer', kick-starting a series of increasingly large events that included the Purley all-dayers at Tiffany's, a Mecca dance hall, which ran until the 1980s (Cotgrove 2009: 19).

29 See Greg Wilson's article 'How The Talking Stopped' (2009) for a fascinating discussion of the transition from talking DJs to mixing, which came around at the end of the 1970s with disco and the innovative mixing of Steve 'Froggy' Howlett and James Hamilton.

30 The *Soul Patrol* programme is available at https://www.youtube.com/watch?v=atGnUf5vElQ (last accessed 25 June 2019).

31 Some footage of Chris Hill's Goldmine can be seen on YouTube, for example at https://www.youtube.com/watch?v=3DC43SCbTBc. Some footage of the early Caister weekenders is featured in the 2003 LWT documentary *Soul Patrol*, which can be seen at on YouTube https://www.youtube.com/watch?v=atGnUf5vElQ, accessed 25 June 2019.

32 Jazzie B interview, 26 May 2016, at https://www.residentadvisor.net/podcast-episode.aspx?exchange=303, accessed 25 June 2019.

33 The full three-part interview is available at http://www.sixmillionsteps.com/drupal/node/110, accessed 25 June 2019.

34 Norman Jay suggests that signs of punk were already around in 1975 and that punk was being innovated by many of the white clubbers who frequented Crackers' soul nights (Norman Jay interview).

Chapter 2

Warehouse parties, rare groove and the diversion of space

Summer 1986. Bankside

I'm not far from places I know, in a city I've lived in for twenty years – somewhere near the Thames, which I can smell – but I don't know where I am. I walk down a narrow unlit alley between two grey buildings, squinting at the map printed on the flyer in my hand. There it is: 'Bear Gardens'. This used to be part of the docks but they are long gone and now it just looks abandoned. But I can hear something. Muffled, somewhere up above, just recognisable as music.

Round the corner into a scruffy open courtyard. Two blue Portaloos sit against a wall; there're some steps, and an open doorway with someone standing at it. I climb the steps – I've come alone, but I know I won't be for long. Say my name. The bloke on the door, whose black flight jacket identifies him as a bouncer though he seems far too friendly, checks a list, finds my name and I'm in, thankful for a squeeze. Up a dusty concrete staircase, unlit except for one industrial light. Two flights up, mind the gaping hole in the floor, head towards the sound. Ducking inside a rough, concrete doorway and I'm in a large industrial space, windows blacked out with cloth, empty except for some more industrial lights, several stacks of speakers in the corners. Somewhere over in another corner behind a table, with metal barriers around it, a short black guy in a snazzy straw hat is concentrating on something. There are about fifty people in the room. And sound, a lot of sound, coming from the speakers; bass filling the space, high end bouncing harshly off the bare walls. What is the music? It's not familiar, but it's nice jazzy funk. A big bass sound booming from the eighteen-inch bins, crisp drum breaks, some kind of keyboard – Fender Rhodes? – and smooth jazz vibraphone over the top. Might be Roy Ayers.

The floor of this factory or storehouse or whatever this concrete building used to be is now a dancefloor. People arrive, in an unbroken

Figure 2.1 Flyer for the second Bear Wharf warehouse party, 12 July 1986. Courtesy Dan Benedict

stream. Soon there are hundreds. Not much later, thousands. Everyone is moving in the half-light. No one's talking much – how could you with the volume of this music? – but everyone is moving, engaged in non-verbal, physical conversation. The crowd are young, or mainly young, black and white and shades of brown, girls and boys, in groups, dancing in disorganised circles, looking inwards, swivelling to articulate the complex patterns of rhythm and bass, which seem to be getting faster, denser, more intense as the night moves on.

Time and space become deformed, elastic; time is quickened and slowed as the music chops minutes into fours and sixteenths, but the mix goes on forever; space is collapsed – we're in 'the ghetto', Nassau, New Orleans, on Mars, in the future, in a place where 'ain't nobody worried' – we are not where we are but where the music takes us. We must be three hours in – could be four – which means we've heard perhaps eighty tunes already, but we keep on moving, moving on up, moving in the right direction.

What time is it? No one cares. There is no time limit, no last call, no 'finish up at the bar now, please', no chucking out. The music won't stop until we do, we won't stop until the music does – suspended in a paradox we keep on moving, the DJ keeps playing. He drops another James Brown production, 'Cross the Track (We Better Go Back)' by the brilliant sax player Maceo Parker, our anthem. Followed by another that, over a driving organ and drum beat, encourages us to 'believe in miracles'. I'm not one for religion but everything seems possible.

Warehouse parties, rare groove and the diversion of space

The sun peeks over the top of the window fabric; people start peeling off and heading for the stairs. But they're not going home. Two floors up we reach the roof. We survey the city. The mutant synth strains of Kool and the Gang's 'Summer Madness' reaches us from the floor below. We've taken possession of London.

Eight-three years after the great black American sociologist, poet and philosopher W. E. B. Du Bois predicted that the problem of the twentieth century would 'be the problem of the color line' (Du Bois 1903: 209) the streets of London provided concrete evidence that he had been right. A colour line bisected the city space, and what were then called 'race relations' had become the defining social and political issue of 1980s London. Margaret Thatcher had swept to power as prime minister in 1979 promising to boost police resources and powers; policing had become increasingly politicised and racialised (Reiner 2000). As Stuart Hall pointed out in an influential essay, though Enoch Powell had been personally defeated, 'Powellism' and the far-right politics it inspired lived on in Thatcherism, through the 'magical connections and short circuits between the themes of race and immigration control and the images of the nation' which Powell had conjured (Hall 1979: 20). The Tory government pushed a 'law and order' agenda that posited immigration and blackness as inherent threats to an implicitly white British 'way of life'. Through this 'racecraft' – a term used by Karen and Barbara Fields for the toxic mixture of mystical ideas about race with public policy (Fields and Fields 2014) – the nation was inscribed as white space. The prospects for multiculture were hemmed in by these external pressures.

The 1980s was a period of intense experimentation and transformation in black music, which was reflected in the clubs and dances of London as reggae morphed into dancehall, disco and jazz funk into house, and the increasing availability of inexpensive digital production tools propelled electro and hip hop forward. Sound systems boomed throughout the city; soul clubs were packed in the suburban periphery; and the West End and Soho were entering a period of peak decadence (reaching a zenith at Leigh Bowery's high-fashion and low-morals nightclub Taboo, which opened in Leicester Square in 1985). Many of these scenes hosted encounters across the colour line, yet race still divided dance audiences. The reggae sound systems and blues parties had built semi-autonomous space in the black communities of Brixton, Lewisham, Notting Hill, Dalston, Hackney and Shepherd's Bush, playing roots and lovers rock to almost exclusively black audiences. As racialised policing became even more 'paramilitary' and tension between police and the black community reached boiling point, black social space became more contained, more militant, more dread.

The suburban soul clubs, though rightly proud of their commitment to non-violence and racial tolerance, remained largely white working-class spaces and racial tolerance had its limits. The West End, with some notable exceptions like Crackers, continued to operate various forms of discretionary colour bar. 'Knock-backs' from soul and Soho clubs remained a regular experience for black clubbers seeking alternatives to the reggae scene.

Across Britain, beleaguered black populations fought back. The year 1981 was pivotal. Community anger at a fire in January which killed thirteen black teenagers[1] at 439 New Cross Road in Deptford, south-east London (which may have been set intentionally, although, even now, the cause remains uncertain) led to a Black People's Day of Action in March when a large inter-generational black crowd (between 15,000 and 20,000) marched from Deptford to central London (despite attempts by the Metropolitan Police to halt the march at the river). The crowd chanted the title of the track 'Thirteen Dead (And Nothing Said)' by reggae singer Johnny Osbourne (produced by Aswad) and denounced the Thatcher government and the press for a callous disregard for black life.

In April 1981 the Metropolitan Police, responding to what they said were unprecedented rates of crime in Brixton, launched Operation Swamp '81, ramping up the presence of the SPGs. While trying to deal with the consequences of the stabbing of a young man, Michael Bailey, police were confronted by a large group who thought he was being arrested and pulled him from a police car. Tensions boiled over. Two nights of rioting broke out on 10 and 11 April, with crowds, mainly though by no means all black, openly confronting police in the streets, burning sixty-one private vehicles and fifty-six police cars, and widespread destruction of other property. There was more street violence in July, which spread beyond the capital to other areas of black settlement: Handsworth in Birmingham, Toxteth in Liverpool, Chapeltown in Leeds, Saint Pauls in Bristol and Hyson Green in Nottingham. In his memoir *The Life and Rhymes of Benjamin Zephaniah* (2018) the dub poet argues that what were called riots are better understood as uprisings, driven by anger at decades of humiliation and mistreatment at the hands of the police.[2] Paul Gilroy (1987: 324) calls them 'riotous protests' and Linton Kwesi Johnson 'Di Great Insohreckshan' (a track on his 1984 album *Making History*).

Follow the diversion

The previous chapter examined some of the conditions under which informal and organic relations across the colour line were formed in London in the 1970s – in the soul scene, West End club culture and the sound systems. This chapter focuses on the mid-1980s and explores how new forms of multiracial club culture emerged in London from the spatial and musical disruptions of the early 1980s. The focus here is on the emergence of a new kind of displaced club culture that broke with both the white soul mafia clubs and the Jamaican-centred roots reggae sound systems, and formed new alliances between disparate groups of soul fans from the suburban scene, West End trendies and black funk fans. It highlights in particular the series of funk-driven warehouse parties that sprang up between 1982 and 1987 in the city in the empty, 'dead', spaces of the becoming-post-industrial city.

Warehouse parties like this ran in London for about five years before house music and rave culture swept in in 1988. They involved the participation of no more than tens of thousands of people, though it is impossible to say for sure since no records were kept except in the memories of those who were there. Illicit gatherings around music were hardly unique in London. Socialising in the black public sphere had been taking place in the city for decades in alternative and unlicensed venues, shubeens, blues parties, municipal halls, squats. From 1968, when a group calling themselves the London Squatting Campaign occupied the rooftop of a luxury block in east London, a loosely organised squatters' movement emerged in London that occupied empty housing and commercial buildings throughout the 1970s and early 1980s (Reeve 2009).[3] Here, anarchists and libertarians, artists and bohemians, hippies, drug addicts, homosexuals and other social outliers created their own alternative zones of housing, politics and sociality and staged art shows and parties beyond the purview of official regulation.

But here I want to argue that the warehouse parties of the mid-1980s are distinct, and have a greater significance. They represent a series of ruptures to the racial power geometry of the city. This cultural activity of young Londoners, a racially mixed group of young people working collaboratively if not always harmoniously, exploited the possibilities offered by industrial decline, turning the carcasses of dying imperial industry, manufacturing and trade, left empty during the shift to the competitive marketisation and service-driven neoliberal economy that starts to take hold at the end of the 1970s (Davies 2014), into new spaces of multiculture.

Warehouse parties also ruptured London nightlife, which had become separated into, on the one hand, the white space of licensed clubs of the West End and the soul clubs of the suburban periphery, and, on the other, the black space of the sound systems. Warehouse parties offered new opportunities to black and white Londoners, and particularly to those whose involvement in leisure was constrained by the norms of race and gender. Club culture was male-dominated across genres – with very few exceptions the promoters and DJs were all men – and women's participation was mediated in the reggae dance by strict Caribbean parenting, which often prevented girls from attending dances (DJ Ade and Junie Rankin interviews, both 5 June 2017), and, inside the dance, by the gendered norms of Rastafari, which accorded women a subordinate status (Iton 2008).[4] Meanwhile, the soul clubs, which offered some space on the dancefloor for women, were still cross-cut with the norms of male performance and the masculine codes of working-class leisure. The black jazz funk scene, such as that at Crackers, though it opened up new possibilities for alliances between straight and gay, placed forms of male competition and display at the centre, to the exclusion of women. In terms of multiculture, white participation was heavily mediated[5] in reggae sound systems, while informal colour bars continued to limit black participation in soul clubs in the suburban periphery and the West End, which were dominated by white DJs.

The warehouse parties of the mid-1980s broke down some of these barriers. They brought the sonic practices of bass culture into new kinds of relatively unregulated space with a soundtrack drawn from the rich history of (mainly) American black music, offering new space for the articulation of 'new ethnicities' (Hall 1989). Warehouse parties 'diverted' space (Lefebvre 1994) and opened up new, albeit fragile and temporary, aesthetic and social possibilities where the 'old boundaries' of race, gender and class might be challenged (Bakare-Yusuf 1997: 92).

In the self-made cultural spaces of the warehouse party that this chapter foregrounds, the dancing body finds new space 'to make itself known', where 'rhythms reclaim their rights' (Lefebvre 1994: 384). The sonic texts made available by the DJs, manifesting the connections between black music of different periods and from different parts of the black Atlantic, often drew explicit attention to and critiqued the complex geography of racial power, and offered imaginative ways in which it might be overcome. These were spaces unhitched from 'the fixed mapping of the social order' (Smith 1997: 520), in buildings with no known name or identity (often partygoers had no idea where they were, which is why flyers often had maps printed on them), beyond the reach of spatialised forms of power, be it of the police or of competitive neighbourhood or gang affiliation.

These parties were not a utopian moment beyond race or a multicultural idyll but the product of distinct histories and intentions, of tactical alliances between different communities with a shared desire to produce their own culture. Unlike the events staged by Rock Against Racism in the late 1970s, they had no explicit political or anti-racist agenda; they were everyday 'repositories of anti-racist feeling' (Gilroy 1987) primarily dedicated to music. But this does not mean that those who ran them did not recognise that what they were doing had a politics. Like all gatherings of young people, they were about fun, display and sexual frisson. Yet they had political and social effects where the aesthetic resources of the black Atlantic were deployed by black Britons defining and representing themselves alongside and in collaboration with non-blacks.

This chapter explores these issues through a number of different ways of thinking about space. In the first instance, this is the space of official leisure – the nightclubs of central London – and how the emergence of a new generation of freelance promoters introduced a new fluidity to club culture, breaking the hold of club owners and (on the model of sound systems) staging dance clubs in new kinds of space. This meant a move away from the established, corporate-owned venues of the soul scene – the Royalty, the Lyceum, Cheekee Pete's – and the rise of independent promoters and their club brands, which moved between venues, throughout the city, opening up space for a new generation of clubbers. Here I explore the emergence of new spaces for black music in the city centre and the parallel emergence of the 'soul' sound system, as roots reggae gave way to new mixes of Afro-American and Jamaican popular music in the semi-autonomous zones of sound system culture and in the renegade frequencies of pirate radio. These streams fed into the development of the warehouse party, which took place beyond regulation and racialised door quotas and offered new potential for multiculture.

Musical genres, as I have argued, can also be thought of spatially: here I will consider the real and imaginary spacings of 'rare groove', the composite genre inspired by hip-hop sampling, involving the recovery of black American (and other diasporic) music of a previous era, which rose to prominence through the warehouse parties. Finally, in the light of the new space of the warehouse and the spacings of the rare groove text, I consider the space of the warehouse dancefloor and the novel possibilities it offered, particularly to black women.

Keep on movin' – reggae, soul and Soho

Warehouse parties built on the developments pioneered by sound systems. Reggae sounds systems are essentially mobile forms of leisure, where the name and reputation of the sound system are always more important than the geographical place where any particular dance is happening. From the small and local to the large and celebrated, sound systems play in all kinds of places and spaces, many of which were not originally designed for dancing. These have included squats and blues parties in private houses, youth clubs and church halls to the town halls of Lambeth, Hackney and Acton and other municipal buildings, which could be hired relatively cheaply, or where 'West Indian caretakers would make premises available after hours' (Bradley 2013: 215). Sound systems always pushed against the fixed hierarchies of place.

In terms of the music, as we saw in the previous chapter, from the mid-1970s British sound systems had begun to move away from the strictly Jamaican model of Rasta-inspired roots reggae with the development of lovers rock, which was more in step with the tastes and aspirations of London's young black British population (Bradley 2013: 210). As Bob Marley and the roots and culture artists who followed in his wake – Burning Spear, Max Romeo, Black Uhuru – promoted by record labels like Island, were parlaying reggae's renegade reputation into big sales to international markets of rock consumers, sound systems incorporated a lighter, more soulful British sound predicated less on tales of sufferation in the yard. The death of Marley in May 1981, exactly a month after the worst night of unrest in Brixton, symbolised the end of an era.

The Jamaican election of 1980, later described by the *Jamaican Observer* as 'the wickedest election' (30 October 2012), which saw Michael Manley's Popular National Party administration swept aside by Edward Seaga's Jamaican Labour Party amidst violence that claimed more than 800 lives, signalled a transformation in the Jamaican political landscape that was registered in sound: it was a political reordering, Paul Gilroy writes, that had 'cataclysmic effects on the relationship between music and politics' (Gilroy 1987: 188). The Rasta ideology which had held together the dual musical cultures of sound systems, on the one hand, and musicians, songwriters and independent producers and labels, on the other, was waning, as roots reggae was supplanted by the altogether more secular, rougher and 'slacker' (sexually aggressive) sounds of dancehall. By 1985, when Prince Jammy and Wayne Smith released 'Under Mi Sleng Teng', featuring the first ever computerised bassline in reggae, the shift away from organic roots music toward the digitised dancehall sound which foregrounded gunplay over 'one love', cocaine use over marijuana and 'anti-women jive talk' (Gilroy 1987: 189) over depictions of African queens,[6] was complete. Though Rastafarianism still provides one pole in a 'conscious' versus 'slack' debate which continues to play out in Jamaica's music, where 'roots' revivals periodically emerge to challenge dancehall dominance,[7] it was never again to achieve the hegemony over Jamaican and Jamaican-derived musical expression it enjoyed during the 1970s.

What Bradley describes with only slight exaggeration as 'Jamaican tyranny within the UK reggae scene' (2013: 246) was being challenged by new configurations in sound system culture. There was a lessening of Jamaican influence over London's disparate Afro-Caribbean population – who, during the 1970s, had largely claimed affiliation to the island's powerful music-political culture, whichever island their families actually came from[8] – and the concomitant shift to the United States with the arrival of potent new strains of American black music: electro and hip hop. Reggae purists resisted the change, but younger generations of London sound-boys, like rapper Rodney P (Rodney Panton), threw themselves into the emergent, and racially mixed, breakdancing and rapping scenes, centred in the mid-1980s in the outdoor market in Convent Garden (Rodney P interview, 2 October 2017).

Change was also afoot in the suburban soul and jazz funk scene, where the dominance of the soul mafia DJs grounded in series of identifiable suburban venues – Chris Hill's Goldmine, the Royalty in

Southgate, Frenchies in Camberley, Lacy Lady in Ilford, Cheekee Pete's in Richmond – was being challenged by a new generation of promoters. Promoter-DJ Nicky Holloway expanded his Special Branch franchise from the Royal Oak pub in London Bridge to a wider range of venues, displaying a flair for PR as he built his crowd through a mailing list, and innovating mobile functions in exotic locations like the 'magical mystery' tours to the Chislehurst caves[9] and one-off nights at London Zoo ('Doo at the Zoo') and the Natural History Museum ('Doo at the Dinosaur'), in addition to running an annual soul weekender, at Rockley Sands caravan park in Poole, Dorset.

Holloway did not originate the soul weekender, which started in the northern soul scenes in the north of England and spread south in the late 1970s, embodied in big events like the jazz funk all-dayer at Alexandra Palace in 1978, which had 6,000 in attendance, and the bi-annual Caister weekender in Norfolk. Since the late 1970s, other DJ-entrepreneurs had been running coach trips to other venues, like Paul Murphy from the Lacy Lady (Cotgrove 2009: 24–6). But Holloway provided new energy and marketing savvy in the early 1980s. He was in tune with the media and the style magazines (Gilles Peterson interview, 3 August 2017) and reached out to a new style-driven crowd beyond the usual working-class soul audience addressed by magazines like *Blues & Soul*. Holloway employed a younger generation of white soul, funk and jazz DJs, Pete Tong, Danny Rampling, Johnny Walker and Paul Oakenfold (who, with Holloway, would become the pioneers of acid house later in the decade – see the next chapter) and his peripatetic soul clubs began to prove the concept of the club brand and demonstrate that the reputation of the promoter and the DJ with access to the newest music was more important than that of any given venue.

A similar fluidity began to emerge in Soho, where the established pattern, with club owners or in-house promoters dictating music policy and hiring DJs, who sometimes played six nights a week, was giving way to a new model, where small collectives of promoters would bring their club concept, music and crowd to clubs on a temporary basis. This early version of the 'pop-up' concept took a hold, as it made good economic sense for club owners at a time when nightclub income was threatened by economic recession and mass unemployment (in 1982, unemployment in the UK reached more than 10 per cent, the highest since the 1930s).

Early innovators of the 'pop-up' club include the promoters Rusty Egan[10] and Philip Salon, whose branded club nights, Blitz and the Mud Club respectively, built their own identities and crowds, and moved from venue to venue, depending on capacity, relations with owners and the shifting sands of fashion. The multistorey nightclub at 69 Dean Street, on the corner of Meard Street in the heart of Soho, provides a good example of this larger process. Part of Soho's oldest intact Georgian terrace, dating from the 1730s, the building had been part of West End club life since the early twentieth century. Upstairs in the 1930s was the theatrical-political Gargoyle Club, which boasted Noel Coward and Tallulah Bankhead among its members and an art deco staircase designed by Henri Matisse.

In the basement was Gossips (formerly the gay club Billy's), owned by the larger-than-life Jamaican Vince Howard, at the time the only black owner of a Soho venue. The club at 69 Dean Street symbolised the heady mix that defined Soho in the popular imagination, a mix of outsiders, bohemians and thrill-seekers from across the spectrum of class and race, where, to quote a feature from the February 1983 issue of *The Face* magazine (number 34), you could 'find underage Wembley mods Doing the Dog beside young Lady Cosima Fry'. The venue led the way in the shift from owner-operated nightclubs to one-off nights promoted by ambitious young scenesters. In 1978, Welshman Steve Harrington, who worked at Gossips and styled himself 'Steve Strange', and his flatmate Rusty Egan, started a Tuesday Bowie look-alike night. Though it ran for only three months, the night has gone down in pop history as a way station in the transition from punk and new wave to the New Romantics, which continued at Egan's Blitz nights (Haslam 2015: xii). Alongside the synth pop and Bowie, DJs played jazz funk, soul and reggae, a musical influence that can be heard in the early releases by the bands that emerged from this scene, like Spandau Ballet and Culture Club.

Warehouse parties, rare groove and the diversion of space

By the early 1980s every night of the week at Gossips was one of these 'one-nighters', promoted by different groups of DJs and promoters with distinct music policies and crowds, which suited the owners, who were keen to attract fresh crowds of drinkers but unable to keep up with the swiftly shifting tastes of music audiences. A typical week at Gossips in 1983 featured the Afrobeat Gold Coast club, a straight-ahead jazz night, Gaz's Rocking Blues,[11] DJ Steve Walsh's jazz funk Friday night, and a roots reggae and soul night hosted by Radio London DJ David Rodigan and Papa Face, the last two nights hosting much more racially mixed crowds than were usual in central London. Upstairs, the Gargoyle hosted the 'weirdoes and freaks' goth club night Batcave, a moviemakers' showcase, a 1960s soul night, the Lift, a funky gay club which welcomed straights (see figure 2.2) and Don Ward's American-style Comedy Store, where British alternative comedy was incubated.[12] Such one-off nights became a staple of central London's clubbing in the 1980s, with specialist dance nights hosted at pubs and wine bars throughout Soho: Munkbery's in Jermyn Street, Le Beat Route in Greek Street, Upstairs at Ronnie Scott's in Frith Street, Spats in Oxford Street, Legends in Old Burlington Street (see plate 1), the 100 Club on Oxford Street and Fouberts in Fouberts Place. These often featured DJs who had been schooled in dance and DJing at Crackers, like Trevor Shakes, Paul 'Trouble' Anderson and Steve Lewis.

This form of outsourcing ensured that West End nightclubs could keep step with rapidly shifting trends, and instead of being permanently associated with just one genre like many discotheques were, could remain profitable even on traditionally hard-to-fill weekdays and Sundays (the nights to which black music was often relegated). But although the one-nighters provided an alternative to the owner-controlled nights, they remained subject to restrictive and often racist door policies. The 1965 Race Relations Act had explicitly outlawed colour bars in licensed venues but even the overhauling of the legislation in the 1976 Race Relations Act, which established the Commission for Racial Equality to field complaints about racist policies, did little to prevent everyday racial exclusion (Haslam 2015: 222).[13] Even in those clubs that

Figure 2.2 Flyer for the mixed/gay club the Lift at the Gargoyle, Soho, featuring the club's signature statement 'all human beings welcome'. Courtesy Steve Swindells, https://steveswindells.wordpress.com

were championing black music, young black men, especially in groups, were routinely denied access, or subjected to humiliating quota systems or dress codes that were deliberately targeted at the exclusion of black youth ('no jeans, no trainers, no hats').[14]

The Wag (a revamp of the former Whiskey A-Go-Go) in Wardour Street, Soho, for example, which was taken over in 1982 by the Welsh jazz dancer, DJ and journalist Chris Sullivan with Ollie O'Donnell (who had presided over the famously restrictive door policies of Le Beat Route), became the central London base for many genres of black music, with a busy Monday jazz night and specialist nights for funk, soul and electro. But the Wag also became notorious as a place where black men were routinely turned away at the door, by Winston the formidable head bouncer (Trevor Nelson interview, 7 August 1998). Sullivan denies that the Wag door policy was explicitly aimed at black clubbers: 'We were racist', he admitted to jazz dance historian Mark 'Snowboy' Cotgrove, 'about badly dressed people. It wasn't a club for passer-by people – also, there was a bit of handbag stealing and "steaming" going on so we had to tighten it up on the door. We'd turn away Black, White, Chinese, Triads, Football hooligans, casual sportswear…' (Cotgrove 2009: 201). Despite his disavowal, Sullivan's words suggest how easily the connection was made between black clubbers and crime (Hall et al. 1978).[15] 'Knock-backs' from these central London clubs were a routine experience for black clubbers like Trevor Beresford Romeo (Jazzie B): 'you'd get to the front and the bouncer would take one look at you and say "Sorry Mate, it's not your night"'.[16] Because the Wag did achieve a degree of race mixing, and white patrons did not experience anything like the exclusion rate of black clubbers, many of the Wag's white patrons were unaware of the exclusion of black youth from black music nights (as one Wag regular told me many years later).

Black clubbing in the West End

The DJ George Power had taken over Mark Roman's intense jazz funk dance club at Crackers in 1976, and revitalised it as a venue for black dance, especially during the Sunday and Friday lunchtime slots. Power, from a north London Greek Cypriot family, started out as a mobile disco DJ playing weddings and pubs, and an occasional Radio 1 Roadshow, as a warm-up for 'personality' jocks like Alan 'Fluff' Freeman and Jimmy Saville, but he preferred more obscure black American dance music than he was able to play in these places. He developed a rapport with a new younger generation of Crackers dancers. 'George would work with the dancers', says Terry Farley. 'He would use them to break certain records and focus upon them during the session, made them feel special and they stayed loyal' (Farley cited in Titmus 2013a). As punk siphoned away the fashionable white crowd from 1976 onwards, Power's crowd became blacker and more male: Farley estimates it was typically 80 per cent men, taking on the gendered competitiveness that characterised the 'shuffling' contests in the roots reggae scene. The musical accompaniment to the dancing, where only the very best could keep pace, was the fast-paced and complex Latin-tinged sounds of US jazz funk – Herbie Hancock, George Duke, Dexter Wansel, Idris Muhammad, Norman Connors and Chick Corea.[17] Some of the black dancers, like Trevor Shakes and Horace Clarke, were trained in modern dance and ballet, while others were still at school or unemployed. All of them devoted long hours to practice, and they evolved potent new styles combining ballet and modern dance, fast jazz footwork and kung fu[18] into a new kinetic art form known as 'fusion' (Cotgrove 2009: 24).

When Crackers closed in 1981 (it was replaced by a Stringfellow's strip club) Power went on the move, playing gigs in other central London locations like the Whiskey A-Go-Go (just before it was renamed the Wag). He started a new night, Jaffas, at the Horseshoe, a bar adjacent to the Horseshoe Hotel at the southern end of Tottenham Court Road (figure 2.3). Using the 'Jazzifunk club' mailing list he had developed, he rapidly built an audience large enough to fill the spacious purpose-built dancefloor in the hotel, which could accommodate at least 600. At the Horseshoe, Power innovated his 'jazz funk double disco' idea, with two sound systems in different rooms playing simultaneously: jazz funk and boogie in one room, and 'hard' jazz dance in the other (a two-room format that became a staple of UK club culture). Here he was joined by other soul and jazz DJs, including Chris White, Peter Christian, Mehmet 'Boo' Bulent, Colin Parnell and Paul 'Trouble' Anderson, the first black DJ – outside the reggae scene – to DJ regularly in Soho, who, as a dancer, had ruled the dancefloor at Crackers.[19] In contrast to the tight space and sticky carpet of Crackers, the Horseshoe had a sprung wooden floor for dancers to express themselves on (Bulent cited in Nurse 2010).

The Horseshoe cemented Power's reputation as a DJ who considerably widened the parameters of what music could be played to London

Jazzifunk CLUB
EVERY FRIDAY
9pm till 2am

AT THE HORSESHOE, TOTTENHAM CT. RD., W.1.

Jazz Funk Double Disco !

GEORGE POWER
Chris White · Peter Christian
Paul Anderson · Leslie Grant

GARY WOODFORD'S & THE AMBASSADORS' ROADSHOWS

Admission £2.00 before 11pm - £2.50 after 11pm.

Figure 2.3 Flyer for George Power's Jazzifunk night at the Horseshoe. Courtesy George Power

dancing crowds while insisting on a door policy that did not restrict black entry. Soul DJs like Steve Walsh, Steven Howlett (aka Froggy)[20] and David Rodigan (who played soul alongside reggae) had always managed to attract mixed crowds but Power was the first to establish a central London club where black dancers, crowd and music predominated. Power had a complex relationship with the powerful white soul mafia who dominated the soul clubs and the soul pirate radio stations like JFM and Horizon. He was never fully welcomed into the fold: 'George had two taboos', says Norman Jay, 'He was friend of the gays and friend of the blacks' (quoted in Titmus 2013a). 'George should get real credit', says Bulent, 'for catering for a predominantly black crowd when others could not or would not' (quoted in Nurse 2010). 'The London Jazz/funk scene', writes journalist and pirate radio DJ Lloyd Bradley,[21] 'was the first manifestation of black and white youngsters being comfortable with each other, in an English-created black milieu' (Bradley 2013: 283).

99

Figure 2.4 The Electric Ballroom in Camden, 2001. Photograph by Andrea Rocca

After only a year, the Horseshoe was sold and Power moved the Jazzifunk club to the Saturday night at the Electric Ballroom (see figure 2.4) on Chalk Farm Road in Camden, north London (after a while it shifted to Fridays), along with Paul 'Trouble' Anderson and the other Horseshoe DJs. He and Anderson played jazz funk, soul and boogie[22] in the main room, while Bulent and Parnell played hard jazz in the smaller bar area. The venue had been a nightclub since the end of the war, originally catering to the large Irish migrant population who worked in Camden's engineering and metal factories. A decline in manufacturing and Caribbean immigration displaced the Irish population and gentrification brought new middle-class Londoners to Camden, where a lively youth-orientated food, clothing, antiques and bric-a-brac market (based in the former industrial buildings adjacent to the Grand Union Canal that had been refurbished in 1973) brought a steady stream of young consumers to the area, looking for cheap fashion, records and a good time at the bar and music venues (McRobbie 1998). These changes were registered in the Electric Ballroom crowds.

After a few months, Bulent and Parnell left and were replaced by jazz DJ Paul Murphy and the Special Branch regular Gilles Peterson (learning the jazz-dance ropes which would help him create the 'acid jazz' scene of the late 1980s[23]). For a self-described nerdy white kid from suburban East Sheen like Peterson, Crackers was an intimidating experience. The jazz dancers were competitive and uncompromising, unafraid to reject a DJ whose selection failed to meet their exacting standards. Peterson's debut, in the intense atmosphere of the upstairs jazz room, was 'disastrous'. The good dancers voted with their feet the next week, and followed Paul Murphy to his new club residency at the Titanic club in Soho. But, because of the colour bar, many of them couldn't get in. Peterson used his connections with Jerry Barry, the leader of I Dance Jazz (IDJ), one of the premier dance crews (Peterson had given him a lift home after his inauspicious debut), to persuade the dancers back and he quickly learnt the ropes of the hyperfast and competitive upstairs room (Gilles Peterson interview).

The Jazzifunk club ran at Electric Ballroom for five years, until 1986, attracting a mixed but mainly black crowd from across London. For a new generation of dancers and DJs like Trevor Nelson from Hackney, who had grown up with blues parties and reggae dances and who had been 'knocked back' from the Wag (he told journalist Lloyd Bradley the first time he had been able to get in to the club was when he was asked to DJ there: Bradley 2013: 286), the Jazzifunk club was 'the first real nightclub' they attended. It felt different from the Soho clubs and southern soul clubs,: 'It was really mixed and the people were from all over London, but it was a black club in feel' (Trevor Nelson interview). For those who had grown up on reggae, where blues parties and sound systems needed to be hidden and were always subject to being raided or shut down, the Jazzifunk club, in a large purpose-built nightclub, on a busy and trendy north London high street, offered a new sense of visibility. For black youth used to unwanted police attention when they congregated in any numbers[24] the queue before the club and the journey home held a symbolic importance: 'I remember coming out of there and the amount of black people, it was mad. We walked there all the time; it was part of the night' (Trevor Nelson interview).

At the time, an infrequent night bus service ran through London via Trafalgar Square. With few cars and no money for the cab home (even if they could get one to stop for them) black clubbers from south, east and west London would walk through the central thoroughfares to get the bus home while the city was asleep. For Roger Drakes (DJ Dodge), from south London, 'the journey home was as big as the club' (Roger Drakes interview, 4 August 1998). The route from Camden to Trafalgar Square traverses the heart of London's commercial and entertainment district – south down Eversholt Street, right on Euston Road, left on Tottenham Court Road, right on Oxford Street, left into Soho and down through Leicester Square – areas where black youth were particularly vulnerable to police surveillance. By night, racial power geometry was temporarily remade.

Soul sound systems

Crackers and the Electric Ballroom announced new possibilities for black DJs who were trained in sound system culture but wanted to move beyond reggae and had effectively been locked out of the suburban soul scene and the circuits of Soho soul. Mark Roman, George Power and Paul Anderson had proved the concept of a black-oriented club in the city, and it was graduates of Crackers and the Jazzifunk club who made the next moves. This combined both a savvy economic imperative – mixed clubs which reached out to white as well as black clubbers could be lucrative – and a commitment to transcending the confines of the local. They practised a commitment to multiculturalism and actively sought cross-over. Though the scene that developed warehouse parties involved the cultural labour of dozens of promoters and DJs, flyer distributors and dancers, I focus here on the two most prominent figures: Norman Jay, from west London, and Jazzie B, from north London, indicative of a generation of black Londoners who wanted something more from the city than they had been given.

Norman Jay, whose parents had migrated from Grenada, was born in 1956 in Paddington and grew up in the area of high West Indian settlement in Notting Hill. His father was a music lover with a wide collection of black music – jazz, swing, ska – and, as in many West Indian households, a Blaupunkt 'Blue Spot' radiogram took pride of place in the front room on which to play the records. There was a continual flow of new music into the house, especially at parties and Christmas. From age eight, Norman would be given a fiver and sent down to Webster's record stall under the railway arches in Shepherd's Bush market to buy the latest forty-fives. Initially it was American jazz and rhythm and blues but then, from the mid-1960s, Jamaican music, as bluebeat, ska and rocksteady took hold in the sound systems and blues parties of the area, and found an audience both in the black community and in the new white youth subcultures of mod, skinhead and suedehead (Norman Jay interview, 22 November 1999).

Living on a mixed estate, Norman had a lot of white friends, steeped in the subcultural styles of the day, and Jay's early role models were Tubs and Barry, two mods from the neighbourhood with scooters and a taste for Caribbean music. 'I've always been into fashion,' Norman says, 'I wanted to be a mod'. Though he loved reggae, he was more into soul. The spaces he aspired to were not the Kingston yard or mythical Africa but the spaces of British working-class leisure: football, soul clubs and Soho. 'I always had [an] aspiration for the West End; you knew that was where the big people went.... The West End was the mythical place' (Norman Jay interview).

His younger brother Joey was more interested in sound technology. He took the Blue Spot apart to see how it worked. 'My Dad was furious, but he put it back together, and from then on if it ever broke, he knew how to fix it.' In 1979 Joey and Norman built their own sound system and called it 'Great Tribulation', after Hugh Mundell's 1978 deep Rastafari track, using wardrobes and old planks, with Joey doing the soldering and emblazoning the speakers with 'GT' in big white letters. Joey grew dreadlocks and found his home in reggae, but Norman wanted something different.

Diving into white working-class culture (except the pub – 'I'm not a drinker') he and his west London mates used their street fighting skills to get themselves accepted on Tottenham's White Hart Lane terraces[25] and made trips to the soul weekenders at Caister, where the soul mafia decamped in May and September. On a trip to the citadel of northern soul, Wigan Casino, he was 'totally baffled by the realisation that I was the only black person in the place' (Jay cited in O'Hagan 2002). Jay was a regular at Crackers, where he was inspired by George Power's music and the punk movement he saw emerge in Soho from the mid-1970s.

Jay took his knock-back from Chris Hill's Lacy Lady soul night on his twenty-first birthday as a challenge:

> When you're faced with that kind of oppression and racism you can take one of two paths: you can be bitter and resentful or you can be inspired to do your own thing. I chose the latter. (Norman Jay interview)

Jay regularly visited his grandmother in New York. On one trip in 1979 he discovered that his uncle ran one of the biggest Soca sound systems in the city and he got the chance to play at a block party, where he saw hip hop being born: DJs manipulating forty-fives that had been taped to albums to make them easier to manipulate on clunky Hoehner turntables.[26] Further New York trips took him to the clubs, including the members-only New York gay club Paradise Garage (which opened in 1977 and ran for a decade), where DJ Larry Levan[27] was refining the continuous beat mixing and thumping four-to-the-floor beats of house, which would transform club culture at the end of the decade (Lawrence 2003).

In 1981 Joey and Norman renamed their sound system Good Times (no need to repaint the 'GT') and retooled it as a soul and funk system. That year Jay began a thirty-year association with the Notting Hill Carnival, breaking the unwritten rule that sound systems play only reggae by selecting a wide selection of soul, funk and disco. In contrast to the militant dread selection of the reggae sounds, Jay's uplifting soul and disco attracted a mixed crowd dedicated to the dance of such size that he was forced to move his pitch from the centre out to Southern Row on the northern tip of Carnival to accommodate them.[28]

Combining mod style, the DIY ethos of punk and sound systems, and his archive of American soul and funk, Jay started to hold parties of his own around west London, in any venue he could find. His aim was to reclaim soul from the Essex soul boys.

> I wanted to do parties where everyone was welcome regardless of race or gender. I grew up a black working-class kid in Notting Hill; my best friends were white and Asian and Jewish. I had friends who were gay, lesbian; my parties were about welcoming and celebrating all of that. (Norman Jay interview)

Parallel developments were happening in north London. Trevor Beresford Romeo, whose parents had migrated from Antigua, grew up in Hornsey, north London. As a teenager, Romeo and his mates had built a sound system of their own – Jah Rico – using woodwork classes at school to build the bass bins, and carting it around in a shopping trolley because they were too young to drive. Just like Norman, he and his friends were regulars at Crackers' Friday afternoon sessions. He got a job working as a tape operator in a London studio, working for the song and dance man Tommy Steele and learning the basics of sound design, recording and cutting dub plates. He started his own business, a clothes and records stall in Camden market.

Jah Rico morphed into a different kind of sound as Romeo, the operator, took note of the new electro, soul and hip hop arriving in the UK via the import stores, pirate radio and clubs. They renamed themselves Soul II Soul[29] and coined a new term, funki dread,[30] an identity which captured the idea of a nascent black Britishness, as Jazzie B recalled:

> [In reggae] everyone was trying to be Jamaican, but for me I was like we're not in Jamaica we're in England. That was my driving force. I always tried to use what was known as Great Britain, fantastic engineering, a

melting pot. I tried to take those traditional things and combine it with our love of soul and jazz.[31]

With his Soul II Soul sound system Jazzie B and his gang of Funki Dreads (Jazzie Q, Aitch B, Daddae Harvey) started to hold their own parties in north London and to gain a name for himself as a DJ. Through Norman Jay and Jazzie B and dozens of others, a new form of club culture began to coalesce.

Birth of the warehouse party

By 1982 there was a revolt against restrictive licensing hours, door quotas, weak sound systems and stale music policies in the West End. Informal, self-organised parties started popping up in unlicensed locations, drawing crowds away from the West End, using the networks built between promoters, DJs and crowds. There is no agreement about who held the city's first proper warehouse party: Chris Sullivan, the promoter of the Wag club, claims his 1979 party was the first (Brewster and Farley 2017); Steve Swindells, promoter of the Lift, held one on a Stockwell housing estate in 1978. But arguably the first successful warehouse brand was Dirtbox (run by Phil X, Rob Milton and DJ Ian Whittington). The first Dirtbox was in summer 1982 in a Jamaican shubeen above a chemist in Earl's Court. Their crowd was a trendy Soho mix of the post-punk and style generation, who gathered around the second-hand markets and young designer shops like DeMob in Soho and Rock-a-Cha in Kensington market, where young designers were blending American rockabilly, classic English tailoring and punk into a new kind of affordable street style (McRobbie 1998). The music policy was as eclectic as the clothing: rockabilly and tango with hip hop, funk and go-go. Here, Jay Strongman, who was to become the first star DJ of the scene, got his break:

> I was there as a punter when the DJ got drunk and passed out and they asked me if I would take over. I grabbed a taxi home, picked up my old 1970s funk collection, my rockabilly records and a few hip-hop 12's and

came back and DJed from 11pm until 5 in the morning. (Strongman interviewed by Will Sumsuch, in Sumsuch 2016)

Dirtbox held a series of parties across London over the next few years – London Bridge, King's Cross, Stockwell, Wandsworth. Other Soho types were getting in on the act, including the Welshman Chris Brick, who had founded the young designer clothes shop Demob[32] in Beak Street in 1981, which became the scene of many after-hours parties. Demob also ran club nights like Substation, which started at the Electric Ballroom in Camden but soon moved to a new, illegal, venue in Roseberry Avenue in Clerkenwell. Maurice Watson, who worked at Demob as a tailor, and his brother Noel were the DJs. A decadent, druggy, punk-funky affair, Substation often ran until 10 a.m., until it was closed due to a local protest led by campaigning *Daily Mirror* journalist Paul Foot on behalf of peeved residents.

The Watsons had moved to London in 1975 to escape the sectarian gang violence of Belfast; they had initially been attracted by the punk scene but had been drawn into London's black music nexus via the New Romantic clubs, nights at the Wag and DJ Steve Lewis's nights at the Le Beat Route. In 1982 they started a new night with Sean Oliver (from the post-punk-funk band Rip Rig and Panic), in a disused school in Battle Bridge Road among the goods yards, dilapidated Victorian terraces behind King's Cross Station, an area notorious at the time for the sex trade and drug dealing. Singer Neneh Cherry, another band member, ran the bar. Many of London's soul and funk clubbers passed through Battle Bridge Road. Jazzie B was there and so was Norman Jay:

> Battle Bridge Road gave me the inspiration to do my own. If black guys were having a party like that we'd have had every Old Bill [police] in London on us. They were white kids, they could fucking do anything … and they did! Illegal parties … that ran for months. (Norman Jay cited in Brewster and Farley 2017)

Jay partnered with west Londoner Femi Williams (aka Femi Fem) to form a new promotion outfit, Shake and Fingerpop (named after a

Junior Walker song). Jay's concept was not to focus on musical genres, or DJ names, but to present the whole thing as a celebration: a party. More than 1,000 people turned up to the first Shake and Fingerpop party, in an old carpet warehouse in Acton, west London, on New Year's Eve 1985. Promotion was done using hand-printed flyers, distributed at clubs, and by word of mouth, but they also used the airwaves.

Pirates of Charlton High Street[33]

Two months before the first Shake and Fingerpop party the unlicensed 'pirate' radio station Kiss FM made its first broadcast. As discussed in the previous chapter, pirate radio had boomed in the early 1980s with the launch of soul stations like Horizon, JFM and LWR and the reggae specialist DBC, providing a vital channel for new kinds of black music that had been largely ignored by the BBC and the commercial stations. But soul pirates were largely dominated by the soul mafia, locking other DJs out. Kiss FM filled the gap. George Power, who had already set up the community station London Greek Radio, and his friend Tosca Jackson, also a DJ with connections across the club scene, wanted to launch a new station. They approached the DJ Gordon 'Mac' McNamee, who programmed the busy Peckham High Street soul club Kisses (formerly the reggae club Bouncing Ball), owned by entrepreneur Emperor Ken, and who knew most of the top London DJs because he booked them to play. The Communications Act 1984 had just come into force, stiffening the penalties for illegal broadcasting and removing the loopholes that had allowed pirates to operate from private premises with relative impunity.[34] The Act offered pirates the opportunity to bid for a legal 'community licence' on condition that they cease broadcasting illegally.

Mac was presenting the drive-time show on the soul pirate JFM at the time but had been told by the station manager, Brian Anthony, a veteran of 1960s pirate Radio Jackie, that he didn't have a future as a radio jock – 'he said I needed speech therapy – I was pissed off about it', says Mac (Gordon Mac interview, 22 February 2017). When JFM was forced off air following a Department of Trade and Industry (DTI) raid on its transmitters,[35] Mac threw in his lot with Power and Tosca Jackson. Jackson contacted Norman Jay, whom he had met when Jay organised a meeting of black DJs to discuss how they could break into the soul scene. Jay seized the opportunity to push his 'pro-black' agenda by creating a station that gathered London's top black music talent in one place.[36] With an experienced engineer, Pyers Easton, who had worked at Power's LGR, and Mac's book of DJ contacts, Kiss FM was formed with a racially mixed roster of (all male) DJs from across London, including Jay and his brother Joey, Jazzie B, Paul 'Trouble' Anderson, Tim Westwood, Trevor Nelson, Jonathan Moore and Matt Black (Cold Cut), Manasseh and Gilles Peterson.

From October 1985 Kiss began broadcasting five days a week across the capital and soon gained a large audience. As more established stations like Solar and Horizon went off air while they bid for a community licence, Kiss had a free run. Its operators knew how to avoid getting busted by the agents of the DTI, with whom pirate operators played a continual game of cat and mouse: 'because we was up on top of this rickety old building on Charlton High Street the DTI couldn't get up because it was against health and safety' (Gordon Mac interview, 22 February 2017). But it didn't last. Kiss was raided several times before the end of 1985 and forced off air. But it came back in early 1986 as a three-days-a-week station and soon reclaimed its position as the most popular pirate station in London (though, judging by the lively debate which ensued after the premier of the BBC film on pirate radio, *Last of the Pirates*, in 2017, this is still disputed by the DJs and owner of LWR).

Norman Jay took the coveted Saturday afternoon slot, branding it 'Norman Jay's Original Rare Groove Show', a device by which he was able to play right across his record collection, from 1960s soul to 1970s funk and 1980s boogie. The show served as a platform for introducing a wide range of black music to a new audience and communicating, covertly, information about upcoming parties. In the second-hand markets and independent designer shops of Camden, Soho and Kensington, every radio would be tuned to Kiss. Jay used his new platform to build the Shake and Fingerpop party audience:

I did a huge one in a big empty school on Hampstead Heath we called Amityville, the House on the Hill. It was the first time the Hooray Henrys, Sloaney girls and middle-class white people turned up. We had three white public schoolboys – Ed, Bill and Nick – who became [reggae sound system] Manasseh. [DJ and rapper] Derek B played on the top floor, doing new stuff, Manasseh on the middle floor playing dub reggae and us downstairs.... Over 2,000 people turned up. The next day it was in the *Sunday Times* with them declaring it an 'all-night sex and drugs party'.... During this time I was doing the Rare Groove Show on Kiss FM on a Saturday afternoon. I'd give coded messages about where the next party was. (Norman Jay interview, 15 December 2015)

Jay was acutely aware of the racial and class politics of party promotion. Though he had the musical knowledge and the sound system to stage parties alone for a local black audience, he made a conscious decision to seek white collaborators who could diversify his audience and mediate with the police. Jay's partner, Femi, was studying in central London and had come across a group of white DJs and promoters putting on parties for a student crowd at a grubby Soho restaurant called Sol Y Sombra (see figure 2.5).[37]

Figure 2.5 Flyer for Family Affair at Sol Y Sombra (an early incarnation of what would become Family Funktion). Courtesy Dan Benedict

Norman went to investigate the DJ Julius O'Riordan:

> Femi said he had a good crowd. The main thing was, he was white. His crowd would help the racial mix of the crowd, to make it more socially acceptable to the police. I went down to check him out one Friday, and as sure as Femi's word, he played abysmally. He was crap. But his heart was in the right place. I approached him about doing parties and he said he was doing something with Soul II Soul the following week in King's Cross. Jazzie was astute: get in with some white dudes and your party won't get busted. (Norman Jay interview)

An alliance was formed between Shake and Fingerpop and Family Funktion – DJ Judge Jules[38] (Julius O'Riordan) and promoter Dan Benedict, friends from the private University College School in Hampstead, designed to broaden the audience and to head off the police attention which conventionally accompanied black parties:

> I said to Jules, 'The only way around this is if you front them.' I gave him a script, telling him what to say, and I said, 'When you're talking to them, use an Oxbridge accent on them and don't look away'. And it worked. We never got bothered after that. (Norman Jay, personal communication, 21 September 2017)

A further benefit of the connections provided by working with middle-class white promoters was that their networks included people who worked in commercial real estate: one of Dan's friends from school helped run his dad's agency and he proved more than willing to provide tip-offs about empty spaces, and on occasions even the keys. The first fruit of the new alliance was the party at Bear Wharf in the summer of 1986 with which this book began.

A new cartography of the city

Between 1985 and 1987, warehouse parties remapped the city. A new informal economy emerged, as it had in sound systems in the 1970s. 'Sourcers' would scour abandoned parts of the city – places like the goods yards behind King's Cross Station, the concrete warehouses in

Paddington Basin, boarded up cinemas, abandoned bus garages, areas that had 'escaped the notice of the map maker' (Bey 1985: 103) and pass the information on to sound systems, for a fee and a 'squeeze' on the door (i.e. guest-list). There were paid jobs for door staff and people to run the rudimentary bar, and tax-free profits to be made by promoters, who would not have to pay venue fees or deal with profit-hungry owners or moody bouncers and their racial quotas. In Paddington Basin, Family Funktion and Shake and Fingerpop found some empty storage warehouses built into the base of the 1950s A40 flyover – the Westway – where they staged a series of 'Subway' parties in 1986 and 1987.

Health and safety provisions were rudimentary – one partygoer remembers the ventilation was so poor that he struggled to light a match (Norman Rosenberg, personal communication, August 2000) – but promoters were not blind to the dangers and did not consider themselves criminals:

> If it was quite evidently somebody's space and they were utilising it we would leave – we had morals. If the space was empty and there was nothing happening with it – often it was up for sale – you'd have a look around and 'spec it up', physically think about how many people you could get in, what loos have you got, how can you accommodate people, how do you get them in quickly, get them off the street quickly, how can you run it effectively. Because, you know, the police will turn up but they will be able to see that it's being run fairly effectively so it's not total mayhem. (Dan Benedict interview, 12 August 1998)

The two parties at Bear Wharf in 1986, in an ideal if dangerously dilapidated location, both close to the centre and hidden from view, alongside the jugular vein of empire, ran unhindered by the police[39] until well after dawn and attracted a crowd of (according to the organisers) more than 2,000. They set the tone for hundreds of parties over the next few years. For many of the people I interviewed, these parties have become symbolic of the whole period. Blurred memories of parties in vacant space throughout London from Chiswick to Hackney, Hampstead to Richmond, are collapsed into this one event,[40] which seemed to the participants to connote some kind of triumph over Thatcherite 'authoritarian populist' policies and the racial power geometry it enforced. 'For us it felt miraculous' (Simon Payne interview, 4 July 1998).

For those charged with organising the party, the memories are bitter-sweet: 'What I remember most', says Femi Williams, who had to clean the site beforehand, 'is the pigeon shit' (Femi Williams interview, 8 July 1999).

Since the riots of 1981 and 1985, the London police had been wary of shutting down parties once they had started for fear of inciting crowd trouble (though this did not stop them raiding reggae sound systems[41]).'The police were always reactive, not proactive', says Dan Benedict (interview 12 August 1998). 'The main thing is that usually the police never found out about our gigs until they were already happening.' The facts that these parties were being held in hidden space outside of the localised strategies of London police (Keith 1993) and that they brought together young black and white youth in a way they did not expect posed problems for police seeking to close them down.

One example illustrates the way in which police discretion in the case of warehouse parties operated differently from how it did in relation to black sound systems. For New Year's Eve 1986, Family Funktion and Shake and Fingerpop planned a party in an empty office at Bell Wharf (see figure 2.6), the former corporate headquarters of Beefeater Gin on the north bank of the Thames, east of Southwark Bridge. The flyer proclaimed 'New Year's Eve at the Riverside' and had a map and directions from Bank tube station. It made no mention of DJs or music policy: the logos of Shake and Fingerpop and Family Funktion, backed by coded PR on Kiss FM, were sufficient to ensure a large crowd.

At about four in the afternoon, as the promoters were setting up, the City of London Police, whose jurisdiction covers the square mile of the City of London north of the river, arrived. A constable informed the promoter that the party would not be allowed to take place. Benedict told the policeman that there were a lot of people expected, implying a troublesome night for the police. After a few moments' thought, the policeman pointed over Southwark Bridge towards an empty office block on the south side (Riverside House). 'You can't have the party in the City

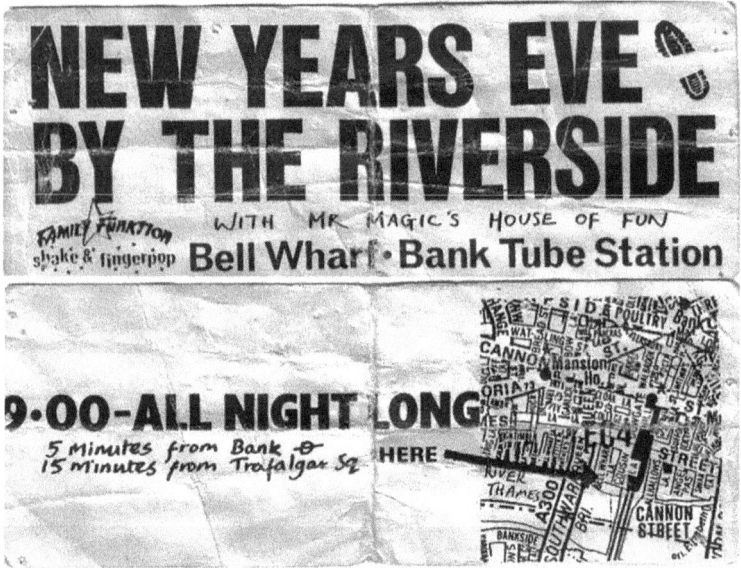

Figure 2.6 Front and back of the flyer for the warehouse party at Bell Wharf, which was hastily rearranged on the other side of the river, New Year's Eve 1986. Courtesy Dan Benedict

of London', said the policeman, 'but over the river is Metropolitan Police territory. Why not do it there?' 'It seemed to me that they had no policy at the time', says promoter Femi, 'because it was such a new thing; they would come along and assess, and it wouldn't be a hierarchy decision, this is just the guys on the street who come along and say there's nothing really happening here, there's no trouble' (Femi Williams interview). The sound system was stripped down and reassembled in the office block on the south side of the Thames, whose previous function could still be discerned in the cubicle dividers and office furniture; it felt like it had only recently been abandoned. There were special pleasures for the crowd dancing in an environment more associated with the strictures and boredoms of office work.

Norman Jay counted down the last ten seconds of 1986, and then at midnight played the record that had become the anthem of the warehouse party scene: 'Cross the Track (We Better Go Back)',[42] by Maceo and the Macks (1974), produced by James Brown and released on his own People label.[43] Its popularity owed much to the driving horns, New Orleans breakbeats and insistent two-note whistle refrain traded between the electric keyboard and Maceo's soaring alto sax, but it also had something to do with its theme of space. The lyrics address American racial segregation through the image of the railroad tracks that bisect American towns, dividing space along class and race lines into good (respectable, white) and bad (poor, black) sides of town. It conjures the notion of 'the wrong side of the tracks', the literal and symbolic place to which black populations are consigned by what Jared Sexton calls 'the built environment of segregation and the mythos of Jim Crow' (Sexton 2015).

The act of 'crossing the tracks' evokes the symbolism of racial containment. Describing life in the American South, cultural theorist bell hooks describes how black domestic workers would be allowed on the 'good' side of town to work but 'we had always to return to the margin, to cross the tracks, to shacks and abandoned houses on the edge of town' (hooks 1984: ix). 'Cross the Track' plays with this idea – the song's subtitle is 'We Better Go Back' and the song counterposes a male chorus asking 'tell me what it's like across the track' and a female vocalist responding 'I never cross the track, baby, cos I know what it's like' – signifying racial division (see Munson 1994: 291–2) and asserting the dignity of life on the 'wrong side' of the race–space divide.

Rare groove

'Cross the Track', with its bed of New Orleans breakbeats and Bootsy Collins's insistent melodic bassline, counter-punching horns and keyboard stabs, is emblematic of the genre that is most closely associated with the warehouse parties: rare groove. Rare groove is not really a genre at all but a term that emerges retrospectively to describe the funk and funky jazz and soul made in America between 1968 and 1975, before the arrival of disco. Used, as we have seen, by Norman Jay as the title of his Saturday afternoon slot on Kiss FM, the term had been circulating within reggae sound systems for many years to identify the 'oldie' soul sessions that would punctuate the roots reggae at sound systems dances (also called 2step). This was not entirely novel. Some younger sound systems, like Funkadelic, founded by Dennis Lewis (DJ Scanka) and Antony 'George Small', and Touch of Class, as well as DJs like Mistri and Desi G, had developed a style based on playing contemporary 1980s soul (Luther Vandross, Evelyn 'Champagne' King) alongside older 'rare' funky cuts by Milton Wright or Aaron Neville, presented in a sound system content with ragga-style toasters, dubbing effects and rewinds. They coined the term 'soul blues' to describe this hybrid and played widely around south-east London from the mid-1980s, to mixed but majority black crowds well versed in sound system sociality.[44]

Jay's concept of rare groove drew on these models but moved it away from the reggae inflections and downplayed the smoother contemporary soul for rawer funk, allowing him to make the music more acceptable to a hipster white audience unfamiliar with sound systems and generally resistant to smoother modern forms of soul. Jay's use of the term was something of a marketing masterstroke, as it allowed him to play from across his large collection, which he had been accruing since 1964, outside the generic limitations imposed by categories such as soul, disco or funk. The concept was deliberately capacious and vague enough to accommodate his desire for eclecticism, a defining feature of his DJ style. And though rare groove inspired generations of collectors, dancers, DJs and wannabe-DJs to scour the shelves of second-hand record shops for vintage music, this, for Jay, was an unintended side-effect ('The only way to buy old records', according to Norman Jay in interview, 15 December 2015, 'is to buy them new').

The idea was to introduce new generations of listeners to music they would not have heard when it was made. The 'rare groove' tag allowed DJs like Jay, Jazzie B and Trevor Nelson to play music that could not find a home in clubs dedicated to contemporary 1980s soul or those which placed a premium on chart music that was already popular with the audience. It was a moment of openness inspired by the music that was being rediscovered and redeployed within hip hop sampling, which, as Richard Iton writes, rearranged the 'geography of black life' in America (2008: 129).

Jay was the face of the rare groove, but there were many other DJs involved, including those who were making the Wag club the centre of Soho funk: Paul Guntrip, Lascelle Lascelles and Barrie K. Sharpe, an obsessive east London record collector. Primarily a collector, Sharpe had seldom DJed live when he was recruited by Rene Gelston, owner of Black Market records, for a new night at the Wag in 1984. He in turn recruited his neighbour and fellow funk fanatic Lascelles. Sharpe's connections in the DIY fashion industry – he founded the Duffer of St George label, which started as a Camden stall – fuelled the hip credentials of rare groove. Sharpe's Blackmarket night was a key site of musical discovery: 'Barrie was the one who was pulling out Barbara Randolph and Ann Sexton "You're Losing Me" and "Sad Chicken" by Leroy and the Drivers, and bands like Mickey and the Soul Generation; he was a digger, hard' (Gilles Peterson interview). Sharpe left the Wag after a year, citing problems with the door policy – 'we were playing black-oriented music, a lot of my friends were black and a lot of them were not getting in' he said on camera to filmmaker Geoffrey Pheasant in 2013 – and opened his own night, Cat in the Hat, at the nearby Comedy Store in Leicester Square, which continued to provide a crash course in 1970s American funk for the fashionable uptown racially mixed crowd who also flocked to the warehouse parties. He recruited Paul 'Trouble' Anderson, who was happy to play from his collection of funk forty-fives which he had had since his early days of DJing at youth clubs (Farsides 2018).

Though Cat in the Hat was the key rare groove club in Soho, Sharpe was scornful of the rare groove tag – 'We didn't call it rare groove at the time; in fact, by the time it was called rare groove it was already dry to us' he later said on film – and has accused Norman Jay of cashing in and turning an underground music scene into a pop scene, revealing the kind of bitter rivalry which often comes with success. But Jay's tag stuck and at the rare groove warehouse parties the different scenes – Soho's funky fashionistas, east London soul boys, and those who had come up on the reggae–funk–boogie tunes of the north and west London sound systems – coalesced into a discernible community.

Lying behind the renewed interest in 'old' music was the new genre of hip hop. The release of the first clutch of hip hop singles – Sugarhill Gang's 'Rappers Delight' in 1979, 'Planet Rock' by Afrika Bambaataa and the Soulsonic Force in 1981, 'The Message' by Grandmaster Flash and the Furious Five in 1982 – ignited the London club crowd, especially in the more avant-garde clubs of the West End, where DJs were encouraged to experiment. Canny punk impresario Malcolm McLaren had been quick to exploit the new sound with his 'Buffalo Gals' (1982), which featured the New York breakdancing crew the World Famous Supreme Team, whom he brought over to London for demonstrations in nightclubs. Hip hop was initially taken up more enthusiastically in the trendy West End – by Mud club DJ Mark Moore and Dave Dorrell at Raw – than it was in sound systems or soul clubs. Rapper Rodney P, from Battersea, says that a lot of his black friends from the south London sound systems rejected hip hop as too alien and too American, in contrast to Jamaican reggae. For Rodney and his youthful inter-racial crew of breakdancers and beatboxers who met up in Covent Garden to dance, practise and earn money from the tourists, the arrival of hip hop signalled a new orientation of black London youth away from Jamaica and towards America (Rodney P interview, 2 October 2017).

Hip hop reintroduces music of black America as a source material for the reconfiguration of the present. The fact that hip hop is made by assembling samples from older records – a practice adapted from the live block party mixing of Kool DJ Herc, Grandmaster Flash and Grand Wizzard Theodore, and then extended through the use of a new genera-tion of samplers and drum machines – stimulated interest in the source of these samples, and among a generation of would-be producers the feverish desire to find copies of the obscure records sampled by the New York producers (like 'Apache' by the Incredible Bongo Band and 'Take Me to the Mardi Gras' by Bob James) and track down fresh breakbeats. What hip hop discovered – and DJs like Jay, Power and Trouble had known all along – was a rich but largely untapped seam of dance music, the fruits of the golden age of American music production spanning the period from the late 1960s to the rise of disco, when major labels fed off the innovation and creativity of a wide range of specialist black music independents, which in turn fed off the incredible pool of musicianship, song-writing and rhythmic dynamism that was the legacy of the incessant touring and performing which characterised the American black music economy of the time. To give just one example, during a career that started in 1958 when he was fifteen, James Brown's saxophonist Maceo Parker played an average of 290 live shows a year, which means he has played somewhere in the region of 17,500 shows over sixty years (Parker cited in Stillman 2013). He would already have played more than 4,000 live shows by the time he recorded 'Cross the Track' in 1974.

Similar levels of musicianship characterise many of the creators of the 1970s rare groove canon. We know that James Brown was the self-styled 'hardest working man in show business' but jazzmen like Donald Byrd, Roy Ayers, Henry Gibson and Herbie Hancock, all of whom started their careers in the post-bop jazz scene of the 1950s, and soul veterans like Curtis Mayfield, Eddie Bo, Leroy Hutson, Martha Wash and Eddie Kendricks, alongside the many members of forgotten funk bands like African Music Machine, the Vibrations, the Skull Snaps and the Mighty Ryeders, were similarly veterans of the punishing touring schedule of the 'Chitlin Circuit'. Once DJs discovered this music and saw how potent it was on the dancefloor, the treasure trove of forgotten music – only a very small proportion of which ever made it into the pop charts on either side of the Atlantic, or got a UK release – was ripe for the picking. As the DJ and music journalist Dean Rudland attests, London record stores had 'tons of funk records just waiting to be stumbled across for a couple of quid'.[45] A network of record stores which sold second-hand as well as new imports, including the Record and Tape Exchange, which had branches in Camden and Notting Hill, where acres of old records were sold at bargain prices and perseverance could uncover rare dancefloor fillers, was there to meet the demands of a new buying public. The market was supported by specialist dealers – Des Parkes, Tony Munson,

Gary Dennis – who spent their hours unearthing lost gems and supplied the DJs always hungry for new and unknown grooves (mirroring the reggae sound system emphasis on dubplates).

Not everything played by the rare groove DJs was rare – floor fillers like James Brown's 'Sex Machine' (1970) and 'I Want You Back' by the Jackson Five (1969) had been substantial hits – but the majority of what the rare groove DJs played was entirely unknown to their crowd, with the exception of the experienced black dancers, who knew much of it from Crackers, the Electric Ballroom and sound system soul sessions. The key for the younger crowd was that this music made sense juxtaposed with the new hip hop which was sampling these very same cuts – Bobby Byrd's 'I Know You Got Soul' (1971) was mixed into Eric B and Rakim's 'I Got Soul' (1986), which samples it. The older cut, recorded in a good studio and released as a thick-vinyl seven-inch single with a high dynamic range, did not sound outdated by comparison. Sound systems built to reggae specifications, like Good Times and Soul II Soul, that were relentlessly tinkered with to elicit the best combinations of 'cris' tops, full mid-range and sonorous bass frequencies brought out the best in this music, which had been recorded in technologically sophisticated studios with the meticulous care of experienced engineers working to the, often despotic, sonic principles of producers like James Brown.

Though the funk of James Brown and the hip hop which rode on its rhythms are both strongly associated with assertions of black (American) specificity and racial pride (Vincent 1995), this music was often produced through inter-racial collaboration (see Back 2000). Late-1960s America politics with the rise of both the Black Panthers and white counter-cultures and the pan-racial protests against the Vietnam War and Richard Nixon's corrupt administration had fuelled the emergence of inter-racial funk bands like Sly and the Family Stone, Funkadelic, the Headhunters, Blood Sweat and Tears, the Brecker Brothers, Tower of Power, War and Sun (Vincent 1995). Many white rock bands and artists of the era – Chicago, Rare Earth, Foxy, Herbie Mann, Archie Fairweather, Kenny Rankin, José Feliciano and Britain's Brian Auger and his Oblivion Express – experimented with funk. DJs scoured the archive looking for those album cuts that might work on the dancefloor.

Keen 'crate diggers' unearthed funk breakbeats in surprising places: jazz singer Ella Fitzgerald's version of Led Zeppelin's 'Sunshine of Your Love', big-voiced Welsh singer Shirley Bassey's reworking of the Doors' 'Light My Fire', white bluesman Boz Scaggs's version of the Neville Brothers' 'Hercules'. This was pre-eminently the music of cross-over, often made by veteran jazz and soul acts accommodating themselves to then current taste for rock in search of a career revival, the kind of music disdained by the jazz establishment and often ignored by the audience too. These kinds of jazz–funk–rock experiments had largely been abandoned by the American recording industry with the rise of disco (Lawrence 2003) but once it was archived on vinyl the information stored in the grooves could be recombined and amplified through the booming sound systems for an entirely new, inter-racial audience. Rare groove also unearthed music from across the black Atlantic that incorporated funk motifs with other musical influences. The Equals and Cymande, British bands made up of Afro-Caribbean musicians blending reggae and funk, the Beginning of the End, from the Bahamas, Puerto Rican pianist Eddie Palmieri's Afro-Cuban funk band Harlem River Drive, the Afrobeat of Nigerian Fela Kuti, the Afro-funk of Manu Dibango from Cameroon, and Mandrill, a conglomerate from the Spanish and Anglo-Caribbean, from Panama via Brooklyn, all featured on the rare groove playlist, though since the records were rare and generally bought second hand anyway, the artists will not have seen any bump in their royalty cheques.

The political rhetoric of funk – drawing on civil rights, black power and internationalist forms of black politics and embodying an aspirant entrepreneurial spirit – 'I don't want nobody to give me nothing; (open up the door I'll get it myself)', as James Brown put it in his 1969 hit – which dovetailed with Thatcherite narratives of bootstrapping entrepreneurial self-sufficiency – suited the temper of London in the mid-1980s, dealing with its own forms of authoritarian governance, racial intolerance and economic recession. Funk's resources of black resilience and aspiration, which critiques the present in the interests of a better self-made tomorrow, defined the rare groove dancefloor both as a space that was alive to racial inequality and the spatial politics of ghettoisation and as a space where these could be imaginatively overcome. In the same DJ set, apocalyptic narratives like 'Slipping Into Darkness' (Ramsey Lewis) could be juxtaposed with optimistic calls for pan-racial unity like Funkadelic's 'One Nation Under a Groove' and for self-realisation like Charles Wright's 'Express Yourself', and statements about the binding transcendent qualities of music like Gary Bartz's 'Music Is My Sanctuary'.

None of this was exactly new – many of the rare groove dancefloor hits[46] had been staples of Crackers and soul clubs, which Norman Jay acknowledges: 'The whole rare groove thing was predicated on that [Crackers] era; I just reinvented it for the times. Even my playlist in the early days was based on my memory of Crackers' (Norman Jay interview). But it sounded new to a younger generation, consumed in unregulated space where dancing feet were scuffing out the colour line: '[Rare groove] was the first time I'd really mixed with white people', recalls the Arsenal striker Ian Wright in his autobiography. 'It didn't make any difference to how I felt about myself. If anything, living in London, it made far more sense' (Wright 2016: 202).

Women ain't going for that no more: gender on the dancefloor

James Nott's history of British dance halls in the first half of the twentieth century, *Going to the Palais*, argues that they offered women 'opportunities and a freedom of expression often denied them at work and at home' (2015: 160). In providing an opportunity to enter the public sphere ostensibly on equal terms with men, and to participate in an activity – dancing – in which they were frequently more experienced, more skilled and more numerous than men (especially during wartime), the dance halls of mid-century were a 'predominantly female space' which offered women new social opportunities. But, though new forms of freedom were on offer, patriarchy would always reassert itself. Anxieties about the untrammelled female sexuality which dance connoted are threaded through the discourses around dance which Nott examines, from debates over the wartime relaxation of the rule that only men could initiate dancing (a rule which was firmly reintroduced soon after the end of the Second World War), to the attempt by professional dance organisations to legislate acceptable dance steps, were frequently expressed in concerns about inter-racial dancing (Nott 2015: 179). Moreover, despite the degree of freedom the dance hall offered women, it continued to emphasise heterosexual coupling – expressed through couple dancing with the man leading – which reinforced gendered societal norms.

Couple dancing as a mass phenomenon was largely killed off in the 1960s, when Nott's study ends, by the pop counter-culture and the rise of the discotheque, where non-couple dancing was the norm. To address this, many of the dance-hall chains rebranded their dance halls as discos – Locarno ballrooms became Cat's Whiskers, Mecca ballrooms were rebranded as Tiffany's – or made them available for hire by promoters offering these new kinds of dance, soundtracked by pop, rock and soul. Although dancing and clubs continued to offer women forms of freedom not necessarily available elsewhere and women continued to make the space of the dancefloor their own, masculine dominance continually reasserted itself across dance cultures, especially through spatial organisation.

With a purpose-built dancefloor surrounded by seats and a bar, the nightclub was a gendered space where women could take their place on the dancefloor but often under male gaze (the origin of the notion of the conventional nightclub as a 'meat market') where boys 'on the pull' circled the dancefloor and scoped their prey, swooping in to ask for a dance during the 'slow dance' sections which punctuated the night (and which club owners mandated in order to give dancers a break and get them to the bar). The space of the warehouse party provided a contrast with that of the West End nightclub, or the pubs and wine bars and dance halls used as venues for staging clubs. Unlike the spatial rationality that divided venues into distinct zones – the bar, the dancefloor, the lounge – and reinforced social hierarchy through door quotas, VIP zones and other forms of regulation, the warehouse party dancefloor was everywhere within the aural space defined by the sound system speakers (Henriques 2011).

This spatial democratisation reduced the conventional function of the club as a space of heteronormative coupling. In sound systems, dancing had always been about far more than finding a sexual partner, but conventional nightclubs, partly due to the reluctance of many white men to dance, were often defined by gendered spatial divisions between the female space of the dancefloor and the male areas of the bar which conformed to the norms of British pub culture. Gender continued to divide even those clubs more obviously dedicated to music: jazz funk and jazz dance clubs from Crackers to Gilles Peterson's Dingwalls sessions in the late 1980s were spaces of masculine competition which could break out into open physical confrontation (Cotgrove 2009), just as the northern soul clubs placed male performance at the centre. Lacking rigid spatial organisation, warehouse partygoers were freer to organise their own spatial practice.

Competitive jazz dancers, like Jerry Barry's IDJ crew, did go to warehouse parties, and impromptu dance battles could break out wherever dancers could find an appropriate space, but the emphasis on the easier-to-dance-to bass-heavy James Brown funk rather than the hard and heavy Latin and Brazilian rhythms which defined the jazz dance clubs (Cotgrove 2009) lent the dancefloor a less competitive character. Thus warehouse parties provided new opportunities for women to make space for themselves. Without a designated bar area, dancefloor or anything but rudimentary lighting, the scopic gave way to the sonic, and new forms of gender practice were opened up. With little to see and nothing to do other than dance, warehouse parties reoriented the night away from the pick-up and towards the dancefloor – as underlined by Jazzie B's dictum 'If You're Not Dancing Then Fuck Off', made famous at the Soul II Soul Sunday night residency at the Africa Centre in Covent Garden from 1986.[47] Dancing, for men and women alike, became the primary form of consumption and interaction with others – the music was too loud for people to talk anyway – lending the dancing an enhanced role in expressing eroticism, but in a context removed from one-to-one heterosexual coupling. Sex, or the possibility of sex, remained, of course, on the agenda of the young rare groove crowd, but the conventional rituals of the chat-up and the slow dance were subsumed into the requirement to express yourself through your competence, and stamina, on the dancefloor.

The soundtrack of the warehouse parties, combining dance-oriented soul, mid-1970s funk and the uptempo orchestral soul of labels like Philly Soul and Salsoul that marks the early transition to disco from around 1975, offered new ways of expressing sexuality through dance. In his much-anthologised essay 'In Defence of Disco' (1979), cultural theorist Richard Dyer describes how the 'all-body eroticism' of disco moves beyond both the disembodied eroticism of popular song – whose strict musical structure evokes a sense of 'security and containment', which stops the music 'entering the body' – and the phallic eroticism of 'grinding, thrusting' rock, which confines 'sexuality to the cock' (Dyer 1979: 4). The vehicle for moving beyond these two unsatisfying options, Dyer argues, was black rhythm, which 'leads to the expressive, sinuous movement of disco dancing' (Dyer 1979: 4). This pervasive all-body eroticism breaks with those dance traditions that are focused on hetero-sexual contact dancing to offer collective ways in which to experience the erotic self and the body communally. Tim Lawrence describes the character of dancing that is both individual and collective:

> Dancers, however, didn't get a rush from dancing in isolation: there was no fun to be had if you were the only person in the club. Rather dancers got high because they were in a room with other dancers and a DJ, and this meant that their experience was simultaneously individual and collective. The pleasure was at its most intense when individual motions came into synergistic sync. (Lawrence 2003: 320)

Dancers can create a proto-community that in principle can include, on an equal footing, anyone who wants to join in, and this has special pleasures for those populations routinely denied such equality outside the club. For those who had been subject to the gendered topology of the disco, where women danced and men watched them, and those of the sound system and jazz funk, where male display and competition limited female participation, warehouse parties were liberating. This, as Bibi Bakare-Yusuf (1997) argues, is particularly the case for black women, who are doubly entrapped, by virtue of race and gender, within defensive structures that encourage them to strictly regulate their own sexuality (Nava 1999: 71).

Patriarchal authority often entirely prevented black girls accessing the night-time economy (Junie Rankin interview, 5 June 2017) but even if they could get out the strong masculinist codes of the reggae sound system[48] or the soul club inhibited their sense of full participation (Bakare-Yusuf 1997). Black music writer and dancer Joy White describes the difference between the reggae dances she grew up with and the space of the warehouse: 'at the dance it was, like, stand in a corner with your backpack on and shuffle a bit. The blokes ran it. In the warehouse parties I could let myself go' (personal communication, 2017). Contrasting soul with reggae's 'rigidities of sex and race', filmmaker Isaac Julien suggests soul 'challenged some of the structure of black masculinity' and 'opened up a less fixed and more fluid space' (cited in Iton 2008: 277). For Rachael, a white soul girl from south London, compared with the soul clubs she frequented, the warehouse parties were 'much freakier, much freer' (Rachael Bee interview, 10 August 1998).

Bakare-Yusuf argues that the chance to socialise beyond the reggae scene and mix with people from a variety of social and racial backgrounds proved a particular draw for young black women: 'The multi-cultural character of the rare-groove scene attracted black women who felt confined by ideas of black and female activities and roles'. Here they could 'reinvent themselves without adhering to the fixed racial regime' (Bakare-Yusuf 1989: 89, 94). These new possibilities were sonically facilitated by the dissident proto-feminist spirit of 1970s funk, especially the singles produced by James Brown (no feminist himself) for his trio of funky black divas Lyn Collins, Marva Whitney and Vicki Anderson and other female soul singers influenced by Brown's late-1960s funk sound. On tracks like Lyn Collins's 'Think' (1972, People) and Jean Knight's 'Mr

Big Stuff' (1971, Stax) wayward fellas who 'go out and stay out all night long, and half the next night' and overweening men who 'think they are higher than every star above' are put firmly in their place – 'who do you think you are?' – and the tough funk rhythms are put in the service of female freedom and self-determination: 'Women ain't going for that no more', Lyn Collins declares in 'Think'. Marva Whitney 'It's My Thing (You Can't Tell Me Who To Sock It To)' (1969, Polydor) expressed the right to female sexual self-determination, while Vicki Anderson's 'Message from the Soul Sisters' (1970, King) is a proto-feminist warning to a man that if he doesn't give Vicki what she wants she 'gotta get it some other place'.

This kind of sexual assertiveness and freaky Afro-feminism can also be found in the string of tracks by Betty Davis (née Mabry) – who had a tempestuous year-long marriage to Miles Davis in 1968[49] – like 'Your Mama Wants You Back', 'Anti-Love Song' and 'If I'm In Luck I Might Just Get Picked Up', where, as ethnomusicologist Cheryl Keyes has written, Betty Davis 'subverts gendered arrangements of social power by unabashedly dictating her sexual desires with seemingly little to no emotional attachment' (Keyes 2013: 46). Artists like Davis, who confounded the racialised divisions of American music (according to Keyes she was 'too black for rock, and too hard for soul') and had consequently struggled to find an audience in the United States in the mid-1970s, found a new receptive audience in 1980s London. This rediscovery by rare groove of narratives of black politics, including black female empowerment, consumed collectively by a mixed crowd including black women, black men and white men and women of different classes, is what leads Bakare-Yusuf to argue that the rare groove scene was a 'liberatory space' that enabled black women to 'affirm their cultural identities and if need be, relinquish the restrictive code of racial essence and acceptable femininity' (1997: 88, 94) (see plate 7).

At the same time, this music made available to white Londoners ideas and experiences with which they were unfamiliar, presented in the context of black self-determination within which black female experience and autonomy were given space. But what are the social effects of exposure to these kinds of meanings? Writing about the centrality of the figure of the black diva in white gay discos, cultural critic Walter Hughes argues that although many of the disco diva narratives reproduce stereotypes associated with 'powerless' black womanhood (think Thelma Houston's pleading version of 'Don't Leave Me This Way', originally by Harold Melvin and the Blue Notes), nevertheless, there is also the potential that (relatively) privileged white men might come to identify with the plight and experiences of a population hitherto hidden from them. Disco diva music, for Hughes, offers a kind of dare: 'can a man, even or perhaps particularly a white one, possibly identify with this supposedly degraded subject position?' For Hughes, the persistent throb of the beat works here to compel the dancer to 'abandon the privileges attendant on masculine identity … and occupy the position of the racial or sexual other' (Hughes 1994: 152). Using Hughes's terms, a similar case could be made for what was happening in the warehouse party, where white people were guided through a set of black experiences and attitudes that allowed them to identify with diasporic experience, both the harsh realities of racism and the counter-narratives of black joy and self-empowerment.

From narratives which normalise black people and black life –as depicted in Stevie Wonder's paean to Southern US black childhood 'I Wish' (1976) – to the dispatches from the grim battlegrounds of black working-class life – Marlena Shaw's 'Woman of the Ghetto' (1974), Cymande's 'Brothers on the Slide' (1974) – to statements of black self-empowerment and aspiration – Steve Parks's 'Movin' in the Right Direction' (1974), 'Move On Up' by Curtis Mayfield (1970) – to the ecstatic articulations of black hope – 'I Believe in Miracles' by the Jackson Sisters (1976) – the rare groove canon enabled white dancers to develop a picture of diasporic life on the 'wrong side of the tracks', unavailable in any other medium, by which they could rethink race, in the company of those they had been encouraged to perceive as the other. Here a generation of black and white became accustomed to the sharing of social space with people who were (not so) different.

The dangers of romanticising these kinds of temporary alliances across the colour line are evident. They could be seen to stand in for, rather than presage, genuine social or political transformation. The structure of racism and race thinking has always accommodated, indeed has fetished, inter-racial desire. Cultural theorist Coco Fusco warns that 'interracial or intercultural desire … in and of itself does not disrupt historically entrenched inequalities' (Fusco 1995: 76–7). Within the racial economy of rare groove, where blackness had significant cache and black physicality was on display, race could be subject to its own forms of fetishisation. Indeed, Bakare-Yusuf (1997) suggests that the erotic lure of sex across the colour line – 'forbidden fruit' – was part of the appeal of rare groove, where relationships especially between black men and white women were, unlike in wider society, both acceptable and commonplace.

Nonetheless, we shouldn't lose sight of the wider political potential of such scenes. As Les Back has argued, too often the relationship between white people and black music, and the human relationships that might ensue, 'are reduced to the binomial of pernicious envy and vicarious exoticism' around a series of 'prototypical images of love and theft' (Back 2002b: 229). Though such relationships could not exist completely outside the reach of the 'sliding signifier' of race, which over-determines all relationships across the colour line, the normalising of multiculture to which rare groove contributed did chip away at assumptions, stereo-types and typifications through everyday – everynight – social activity.

Black popular cultural, like all popular culture, is contradictory, a space of struggle over social meaning (Hall 1992). Black music creates spaces that can 'draw attention to ethnic [gender and class] divisions' even as those spaces 'demonstrate how ethnic differences might be transcended' (Lipsitz 1994a: 119) and, as Mica Nava has argued, we should acknowledge that relationships of all kinds across the colour line can be expressions of a social and political commitment to equality (Nava 1999: 71). If the rare groove moment was one of the 'conduits of crossover' by which the rules of black music and dance could be taught and learnt, and potentially exploited, it also provided the resources for the creation of new communities, where 'collective sensibilities' across race and class 'could be shared and new ones forged' (Back 1996: 187).

The warehouse party, by this view, could be imagined as the grounds for what Bakare-Yusuf (1997) calls 'a politics of affinity' across the lines of race, class and gender.

Conclusion

Warehouse parties and rare groove represent a moment of ambivalence. This was when the protocols, skills and knowledge of the black underground became available beyond the confines of racial difference: rare groove was part of the process by which dance music displaced rock as the centre of affective politics for British youth and through which new generations of white Britons acquired the cultural capital – as DJs, dancers, producers and promoters – which they could parlay into new forms of economic capital and cultural power, without, necessarily, remembering or repaying their debt to black Atlantic culture, or retaining the commitment to multiculture the rare groove moment implied.

The very same processes and motivations which open up the possibility of new forms of post-racial communalism can prove to be the route by which competence in the forms of and style of the (always desirable) other are parlayed into profit, a process within which blackness itself can be commodified (Gilroy 2000). As we have seen, it was in the mid-1980s that entrepreneurial Londoners started developing club brands and PR strategies allied with a style culture that was keen to exploit the idea of club culture as a fashionable new economy. By the end of the decade, many of the top pirate radio DJs had been lured away by legitimate radio. Tim Westwood moved to the commercial station Capital and Kiss FM DJs like Danny Rampling and Trevor Nelson shifted to Radio One. The commodification of club culture starts here.

But it was also a time when cultural activity around music brought Londoners together and undermined the racialised power geometry of the city. Though it is entirely possible to maintain both a racist mind-set and a love for black music (as Les Back has shown in his study of racist skinhead ska-lovers – see Back 2000), racist sentiments and suspicions which assign black people only negative value or assume all black people are the same are difficult to sustain once you have some experience of sharing space, a drink, a dancefloor or a life.

The affective alliances of rare groove and the warehouse parties established a dialogue between 1980s Britain – defined in part by race riots, authoritarian policing, unemployment and recession – and an America of the 1970s suffering under the same kinds of social and political conditions. When rare groove audiences danced to Maceo Parker's 'Soul Power '74', which 'samples' Martin Luther King's 'I Have A Dream' speech, or Keith LeBlanc's electro reworking of Malcolm X's 'No Sell Out' speech, the gap was bridged between late 1960s America and 1980s London, and the desire for freedom and racial justice which animated the civil rights and black power movements was placed in the service of establishing racial solidarity in the here and now of multicultural London. For young Londoners, black as well as white, rare groove served as a crash course in black Atlantic politics and art, signalling the contours of a still to be realised politics of justice and breaching the borders between different London populations who were part of the architecture of injustice. In this way, rare groove and warehouse parties opened up the historical possibilities of desire in relation both to human intimacy across the colour line and to political desires for unity and racial justice. Then, in 1987–8, it all changed.

Notes

1 The fire claimed another victim when one of the partygoers committed suicide eighteen months later, unable to live with his traumatic memories of the fire.

2 Zephaniah (2018) suggests the direct link to policing. He describes a policeman explaining to him why 'Rastas are always suspicious': 'If they have their locks down they're probably high on marijuana; if they have a hat on they probably have a gun hidden under it.' Zephaniah went straight from this encounter onto the streets to vent his anger.

3 Though accurate numbers are hard to come by, Wates and Wolmer (1980) estimate that there were in the region of 50,000 people squatting in the UK by 1975, and a large proportion of these would have been in London.

4 Richard Iton describes the ambivalent politics of Rastafari, which 'enabled

some of the most potent forms of resistance available in the second half of the twentieth century' but was 'underpinned by an Old Testament misogyny' which 'never really transcended the dichotomous (queen/whore) dynamic characteristic of most nationalist movements' (Iton 2008: 265–6).

5 The impact of external forms of racism on relations between white and black youth in sound-system culture is brilliantly illustrated in Franco Rosso's 1980 film *Babylon*. The group of young men who run the Jah Lion sound system includes a white man, Ronnie. He is part of the group but not a central figure, acknowledging the priority of the black men and Jamaican character of sound system. When the sound system is vandalised, one of the sound-boys, Beefy, rounds on Ronnie suggesting it was 'his people' who did the damage. Ronnie leaves with a bloodied nose, symbolising how inter-racial friendships and collaborations are made impossible by the external pressure of racism.

6 Although the highly sexualised and often misogynistic lyrics of dancehall would appear to be the polar opposite of the respectful gender codes of Rasta-infused 'conscious' reggae, Richard Iton makes a compelling case that they represent 'flipside expressions of what is essentially the same philosophical orientation towards gender issues and roles' (2008: 268).

7 Since the emergence of dancehall in the mid-1980s, with its hyper-sexual and often violent lyrics – a combination known as 'slackness' – as opposed to the spiritual and politically 'conscious' themes of Rasta-inspired roots reggae, the two styles have defined two poles in a tussle over Jamaican popular culture. Dancehall has remained dominant, but roots reggae saw a revival in the early 1990s and again in 2014. See Katz (2014).

8 Many of the pioneers of Rasta-oriented British reggae, though they sported locks and perfected a Jamaican patois, were not in fact from Jamaica. Dub producer Dennis Bovell, for example, was born in Barbados, and Asher Senator, a pioneer of UK chat, in Guyana.

9 'We'd meet at the Royal Oak, bundle into a coach and turn up at some weird place with a sound system' (Gilles Peterson interview, 3 August 2017).

10 Rusty Egan was also the drummer in the 'new wave' band the Rich Kids, with Steve Matlock of the Sex Pistols and Midge Ure from Ultravox.

11 The February 1983 *The Face* article noted that Gaz's Rocking Blues was, at three years, already the longest continuously running club night in London. After some four decades, Gaz's remains London's longest-running club night, an accolade it is unlikely ever to lose, given the fast pace of musical fashion and generic change.

12 *The Face*, no. 34, February 1983. The Gargoyle closed in late 1983. The building was sold in 2007 to be redeveloped, and reopened the same year as a boutique hotel, the Dean Street Townhouse.

13 Race relations legislation required clubs to allow a certain number of black punters in, and on some occasions bouncers would very publicly count off

the number, and when the quota had been reached stop any more from coming in (Brewster and Farley 2017).

14 Research by May and Goldsmith (2018) in nightclubs in three Texas cities in 2016 reveals the way that dress codes – including bans on 'hoodies' and 'sagging pants' – served to limit African-American participation in leisure spaces. My argument is that similar racial codings of clothing underpinned black exclusion in London in the 1980s.

15 See Hall et al. (1978) on the construction of the figure of the black youth as 'mugger'. In the 1990s these themes re-emerged around anxieties over 'steaming' – youths moving in large groups on buses or trains, indiscriminately robbing and causing mayhem – media depictions of which reproduced the racialisation of crime which Hall et al. had identified (see Nayak 2003).

16 Jazzie B interview, 26 May 2016, at https://www.residentadvisor.net/podcast-episode.aspx?exchange=303, accessed 25 June 2019.

17 Most of these fast and furious jazz records had not been made as dance records – there was no equivalent jazz dance scene in the United States. As Mark Cotgrove reports, when Chick Corea heard that young Londoners were dancing to his track 'Central Park', he was shocked (Cotgrove 2009: 24).

18 Paul 'Trouble' Anderson, the 'king of Crackers' in the late 1970s, practised the weng chung form of kung fu, which he folded into his dance style (personal communication, 21 September 2017).

19 Anderson is widely known as Paul 'Trouble' Anderson or just 'Trouble'. He says this stemmed from his days as 'a bit of a hooligan' (Anderson in private conversation, June 1996), though he has also said it is a tribute to the US go-go band Trouble Funk. Anderson was a Kiss FM radio DJ and a well known advocate of US garage music (as opposed to UK or 'speed garage') since the late 1980s (Brian Wheeler, manager of the Electric Ballroom from 1981, in private conversation, 24 July 2000). He died after a long struggle with cancer – during which he continued to DJ – on 2 December 2018.

20 Howlett was a sound engineer with a powerful system of his own, and one of the first London DJs to beat-mix following his trips to New York to watch the mixing DJs like Larry Levan and Frankie Knuckles in action at the Paradise Garage.

21 Bradley, using the name Dark Star, had a soul show on JFM, along with his wife, Diana.

22 'Boogie' describes the kind of uptempo post-disco soul which was coming mainly out of New York in the early 1980s, exemplified by the Universal Robot Band's 'Barely Breaking Even', produced by Leroy Burgess. Norman Jay uses this term to distance himself from the white soul boys. 'I was not an Essex Soul Boy. I was a London boogie boy' (see Titmus 2013b).

23 In 1986, Peterson started an influential Sunday afternoon jazz dance session with Kiss FM DJ Patrick Forge, 'Talkin' Loud and Saying Something' (a riff on the title of a James Brown single, which served, in truncated form, as the title

of his Phonogam imprint label Talkin' Loud, launched in 1990) at Dingwalls, down the road from the Electric Ballroom. He pioneered the concept of 'acid jazz' in the late 1980s (the term, coined by DJ Dean Rudland, was originally meant as a joke, riffing on then-dominant acid house) (see Titmus 2013b).

24 'There were day-to-day battles with police over where we could play our music, where we could be, where we could congregate. Because if black youths congregate anywhere, there was a big problem' (Michael La Rose interview in Harris and White 1999: 124).

25 Though he is from west London, Norman chose to support Tottenham, to distinguish himself from the local Queens Park Rangers supporters, because he liked the strip and their deadly striker Jimmy Greaves.

26 Technics 1200s, which became the go-to decks for scratch DJs, had been on the market since 1972 but were prohibitively expensive for hip hop DJs until the 1980s.

27 Frankie Knuckles and Larry Levan grew up New York together. They started out as dancers, and frequently attended David Mancuso's loft parties. They learnt their trade as DJs at the Continental Baths and other New York gay clubs where disco was born and DJs like Francis Grasso and Nicky Siano were innovating beat mixing. In 1977 Levan became the DJ at the Paradise Garage. Knuckles moved to Chicago in 1982 to become the main DJ at the Warehouse, where he presided over the development of house music (Lawrence 2003).

28 In 2014 Jay quit Carnival after organisers failed to find another space to accommodate his ever-growing crowd.

29 Though many London sound systems take the name of systems in Jamaica – Coxsone, Duke Reid – the fact that there is also a Soul II Soul system in Jamaica is a coincidence, says Jazzie B. He only heard about the Jamaican Soul II Soul years later.

30 Jazzie B explains the origins of the funki dread style as coming from the fact that growing up in a Christian household he was not allowed to grow dreadlocks, so he would wear a hat to cover them, and shave the sides of his head so that he had locks only on the top of this head, concealed by the hat. See https://www.youtube.com/watch?v=1rjcN1Z2q04 (accessed 1 July 2019).

31 Jazzie B interview at https://www.residentadvisor.net/podcast-episode.aspx ?exchange=303 (accessed 1 July 2019).

32 Among the young design talent at Demob was Sade Adu, who become one of London club lands break out pop stars as Sade.

33 Because of its elevation, Charlton High Street was a perfect place to put illegal radio transmitters for maximum range. One strip of the High Street became known as 'pirates' alley' because of the concentration of radio antennae. See *The Last Pirates: Britain's Rebel DJs*, BBC 4, first broadcast 29 September 2017 (director Jaimie D'Cruz).

34 Before the 1984 Act came into force, while aerials on top of tower blocks

or other public spaces could be seized at any time, those on top of private houses could be removed only with a court order.

35 Pirate radio stations were locked in a cat-and-mouse battle with the Department of Trade and Industry enforcers who sought to shut them down but relations were not always antagonistic: through frequent raids, DTI inspectors got to know many of the pirate operators, with whom they were sometimes on friendly terms. See the BBC4 programme *The Last Pirates*.

36 As Norman Jay told Lindsay Wesker, in the promotional video for Wesker and Dave VJ's book on London pirate radio *Masters of the Airwaves: The Rise and Rise of Underground Radio* (VJ and Wesker 2012), which is available at https://vimeo.com/61412151# (accessed 1 July 2019). Jay had organised a meeting of black London DJs at his mother's house a few months previously, to discuss how they could ensure a place for black DJs in the burgeoning black music market then dominated by the soul mafia.

37 A sometime gay club, the Sol Y Sombra gets a mention in Alan Hollinghurst's 2017 novel about underground gay life in London, *The Sparsholt Affair*.

38 Julius was studying law at the time, hence the nickname given him by Norman Jay: 'Judge Jules'.

39 'When the police would come [to a warehouse party] they would see enough white faces not to freak out. At the time, the police would come along to assess and, nine times out of ten, Dan and Jules would do the middle-class number on them. They knew, the police, that it wasn't a real problem, especially as they were so hidden, you know, in some industrial scenario; it's a case of the old bill thinking "what's the point?"' (Femi Fem interview, 8 July 1999).

40 This suggests that the actual geographical location of the parties was relatively unimportant compared to what they contained – informants recall of the music played was frequently far clearer than where the parties were.

41 Lloyd Coxsone tells of one night in the mid-1980s when the police raided a dance in Brixton at 2 a.m. and tried to grab his decks. He punched an officer, and it descended into a serious brawl, following which Coxsone spent six months in prison for affray. After this, he claims, police became more reticent to shut down reggae dances once they were going (Lloyd Coxsone interview, 1 November 2017).

42 Due its popularity on the rare groove scene, 'Cross the Track' was re-released in 1987 in the UK on the Urban label, and reached number 1 in the dance music charts.

43 Maceo Parker was James Brown's lead alto sax player, a founder member and hugely influential figure on Brown's backing band the JBs. He recorded several albums produced by Brown under a number of different names – Maceo and the Macks, Maceo and All the King's Men, the Horny Horns – and played in George Clinton's Parliament (see Brackett 1992; Vincent 1995: 72–6; Neal 1998).

44 I should credit the Essex sound veteran and criminologist Kenny Monrose for pointing this out to me (personal communication, 18 July 2018).

45 From a Dean Rudland post on the Soul Source discussion forum, 28 January 2012, accessed at https://www.soul-source.co.uk/forums/topic/220629-rare-groove-2-step-thread on 15 July 2019.

46 Songs such as Lonnie Liston Smith's 'Expansions', 'Life on Mars' by Dexter Wansel, Gil Scott-Heron's 'The Bottle', James Mason's 'Sweet Power Your Embrace', Eddie Kendricks' 'Girl You Need a Change of Mind' and MFSB's 'Love Is the Message' had been played on London and southern soul dancefloors since their release in the 1970s, but found a new audience through rare groove. These same songs had also been big hits in the mixed gay clubs of New York, like the Gallery, Paradise Garage and David Mancuso's the Loft, from which London clubs drew their inspiration (see Lawrence 2003).

47 The Africa Centre was a not-for-profit African arts and cultural centre which opened in 1964, housed in a former banana factory and auction house, bequeathed by the Catholic Church to 'the people of Africa'.

48 When asked about the involvement of women in his sound system, Lloyd Coxsone replied 'We never let our women become involved in the sound system. They were there to support us' (Lloyd Coxsone interview). DJ Jumping Jack Frost described the competitive 'shuffling contests' he participated in at Shepherd Youth Club in Brixton in the early 1980s as an all-male affair (Jumping Jack Frost interview, 27 March 2017).

49 Though the marriage was short-lived Miles Davis has credited Betty with being a big influence on him musically, introducing him to the music of Jimi Hendrix (Keyes 2013: 35–6). Betty memorialised her former husband in 'He Was a Big Freak' from her 1974 LP *They Say I'm Different* (Just Sunshine Records).

Chapter 3

From Ibiza to London: Brixton acid and rave

June 1988. Clink Street

We've come late, after a shift at the restaurant, but there's no rush – it doesn't get started until midnight. We walk under the railway arches – the train line that crosses the Thames north to Cannon Street is above us – and find a blue door. Unlit, unmarked, except for a couple of blokes standing outside. We push it open and hear the music. At the bottom of the staircase are a makeshift desk and a girl taking the money. We pay our fiver and up we go, into the dank heart of the building. The night is called RIP, which feels appropriate: there is something ominous and dreadful about the building, and the music we can hear from above (later I find out that the building is on the site of a notorious prison, its location, Clink Street, is what has given us the slang term for prison). I've been to loads of warehouse parties but I feel apprehensive. I've been told that this is something new, possibly dangerous, and I'm going to try a new drug – ecstasy – assuming we can find any. My adventurous Spanish friend is sorting it out; she knows people. We pass the first room, booming bass-heavy funk, and I can see the familiar figure of Soul II Soul's Jazzie B behind the decks. So far, so familiar. But in the next room it changes. The room is sparse, with a massive sound system, but this time there is a lot of smoke – dry ice? – a strobe, and a seething mass of people moving in strange ways to the sound of machines. There's a beat, a very insistent thumping beat, no discernible instruments, and no singing, just snatches of words – 'said rock to the beat', a sinister distorted voice asking 'where's your child?' and laughing like a robotic Bond villain, as well as snatches of screams, and every now and then someone talking over the mic, exhorting the crowd to get into it. It's strange and unsettling and I don't like it. Is this black music? Is it even music?

My friend slips away. I back into a corner and watch. The smoke is un-pleasantly heavy, the music oppressively fast. No soul. When she comes back she holds something out to me, a pill. I put it in my mouth and swallow.

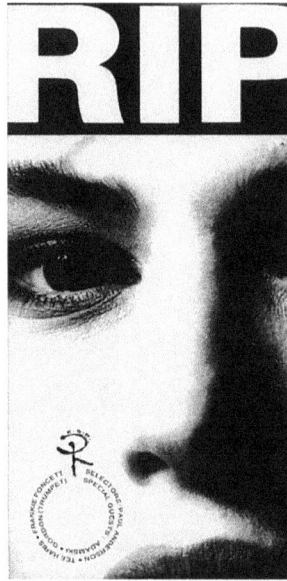

Figure 3.1 Flyer for Revolution in Progress (RIP) from 1990, after RIP had moved from Clink Street to 313 Holloway Road, where the resident DJs were Paul 'Trouble' Anderson and Frankie Foncett. Courtesy Paul Stone

There is no chronological order to what happens next: just a series of strobe-lit impressions. I can remember thinking that nothing was happening, I still wasn't feeling it, then I was. It was like they said – something warm creeping up your body, tingling your fingers. Something that made you close your eyes and feel … what? A great sense of – surprise, surprise – rising euphoria. I don't remember deciding to dance, but I was dancing. Not as I usually did, though I was moving. Everyone, everything was moving. I had to move. I looked at my friend. She was beautiful, her eyes great glittering saucers. I looked around. Everyone was beautiful, something I had not noticed when I arrived. Boys and girls, black and white, mostly young but not all. All beautiful. And the music, the thumping machine babble, starting to make sense, not as songs but a ceaselessly shifting landscape on which my twitching body was riding. It was calm and frenetic at the same time. I look down. I was half naked. Where did my shirt go? Doesn't matter.

Later, perhaps an hour or two hours – or two minutes, who can tell? – I take a walk. Everyone looks sinister and seductive at the same time. It's moody but also if not exactly friendly then, I don't know, tolerant, a sense of tentative unity and liberation. Someone is digging a hole in the wall with a screwdriver. I don't ask why. In the Soul II Soul room it's sweaty and funky but I don't have sufficient command over my limbs to dance the funk basslines and breaks. I need a drink, water. I have a cigarette. Every drag brings another surge of contentment. Soon I'm back with the machines, where the DJ has changed. I recognise this guy from the Africa Centre, Kid something. He's not playing funk but more of this deranged machine music. I hate it. I love it. Every now and then a burst of something recognisable, some heavy Latin percussion, a hip hop voice, a snatch of soul, but the machines always win in the end. The dancefloor – we – are going crazy, arms up punching the air – 'the sounds in the air will make you move and groove'– Sweat drips from the ceiling. It's madness, collective fucking madness. Can you feel it?

By late 1987 rare groove, which had been the dominant London music scene for at least the last three years, was waning, and a new kind of music was bubbling up on the fringes of club culture, with very different cultural associations and modes of behaviour. This was acid house, a dance scene soundtracked by a new kind of electronic dance music from America, mixed, with that London talent for recombination, with mod peacockyness and punk negation, and sprinkled with sun-drenched hippie sentiments picked up from Ibiza. Acid house arrived in late 1987, erupted in 1988 in London clubs and warehouse parties, and then swept the city, the suburbs, the shires and eventually the whole of the country in the guise of the 'rave' phenomenon.[1] This chapter covers the period between the dawn of acid house in 1987 and the emergence of jungle in the early 1990s, one of rave's many offshoots and arguably the first entirely original black music to emerge from London (which is the subject of the next chapter).

Acid house and the rave scene it spawned have been the dance music most discussed, debated and commemorated in academic and popular accounts of club culture. These accounts accord acid house a founding role in club culture and treat it as a fundamental break with what came before (Redhead 1993; Thornton 1995; Rietveld 1998). On the shelves alongside academic discussions of the technologies (Rietveld 1998), gender politics (Pini 1997), 'vitality' (Malbon 1999) and discourses of dance cultures which originate with acid house (Gilbert and Pearson 1999) sit a slew of journalistic accounts of 'ecstasy culture and acid house' (Collin 1997), 'generation ecstasy' (Reynolds 1998), the 'crazy days of acid house' (Bussman 1998) and the 'true story of acid house' (Bainbridge 2013) which further establish acid house and rave as the ground zero of club culture, a wholly novel cultural form that got the nation dancing.

These texts emphasise the world-shaking novelty of the acid house moment, which, it is claimed, ushered in a 'rave new world'[2] of political possibility, and offered solutions to the intractable social divisions of class, race and gender which bedevilled life in the late twentieth-century city. Rave promoter Wayne Anthony's memoir *Class of 88: The True Acid House Experience* (2002) typifies these political claims made for the impact of acid house:

> Ecstasy united black, white, yellow and brown people as one. At any big dance party there was an across-the-board mixture of races holding hands and giving out total love and respect for one another. The hysteria whipped up by people going to dance parties caused a massive surge of positive energy. The E generation became the We generation. We were making history. (Anthony 2002: 50)

Perhaps participants can be forgiven for such hyperbole, as the social and political impact of acid house and rave is well documented. By the early 1990s raves had spread from the cities to every part of the country and been discussed by ministers at the highest levels of government, who were determined to stamp them out. Musically, too, acid house left its mark on every genre that succeeded it. Yet we should treat claims for the world-changing nature of acid house and rave with caution. They can burden club culture with a political and social significance that they are not necessarily able to support. Taking rave's claims to novelty too literally also obscures the hybrid origins of acid house and its connections with bass culture and the black music and dance traditions that I have been exploring in this book.

This chapter critically examines these claims and connects the history and development of rave to the histories of black Atlantic music.

Might we uncover an alternative history of rave, one that pays more attention to the multiple pathways by which house music entered the space of London club culture? What might this do for our appreciation of London dance culture as a multicultural space? This involves consideration of how house music and rave were received, understood and transformed by black Londoners and their collaborators, a focus on the racial politics of rave and an enquiry into the black cultural producers who made rave what it was and took it in new directions in the 1990s.

But I want to start with a brief consideration of what happened to rare groove. Music, and dance music perhaps most of all, is a site of continual change and innovation, of fads, generic fracturing and the application of established traditions of rhythmic intelligence to new technologies, yielding new forms. A key push factor in the development of new genres is the process by which innovation from the margins is appropriated within the circuits of the corporate music industry, ever alert for new ways to boost its bottom line. Running parallel to this is the restless form of Afro-diasporic creativity, which innovates partly to stay ahead of commodification (Gilroy 1987). This is not a simple binary. Commodification can be enabling as well as constraining (Saha 2017: 23); there would be no disc-based dance cultures without the studios, records and circuits of commerce that brought vinyl from Jamaica and the United States to London. We need to remain critical, as David Hesmondhalgh and Leslie Meier argue, of the narrative of 'heroic outsiders challenging powerful incumbents' (2018: 1558) and recognise that commodification is a fundamentally ambivalent. After all, marginal cultural producers are not necessarily happy to be marginal, and the lure of record deals, fame and cultural status understandably persuades many to participate in, and benefit from, the selling of the culture they produce. The fate of rare groove can tell us something about the dynamics of these processes.

Rare groove: movin' on up

It was far from obvious in 1987 that rare groove was in decline. Funk-oriented warehouse parties and central London club nights at venues

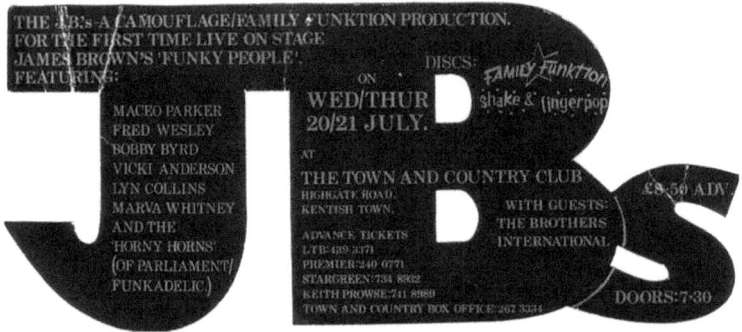

Figure 3.2 Flyer for the 'Return of the JBs' gig at the Town and Country Club, Kentish Town, 20 and 21 July 1988, promoted by Family Funktion and Shake and Fingerpop. Courtesy Dan Benedict

like the Wag, Dingwalls and Soul II Soul's Sunday night at the Africa Centre were packed with dancers. In the summer of 1987, promoters Shake and Fingerpop and Family Funktion brought two prominent members of James Brown's musical family, husband and wife team Bobby Byrd[3] and Vicky Anderson, to perform at the 1,800-capacity Town and Country Club in Kentish Town, north London, to a large enthusiastic audience who knew their records from the rare groove dancefloor. Capitalising on the success of this first gig they arranged an even bigger show for the following summer. Promoted as 'the return of the JBs', this show, which played for two nights, both sold out, on 20 and 21 July 1988 (figure 3.2), starred an eighteen-strong funk orchestra comprising original members of James Brown's late-1960s and 1970s bands, including 'the Horny Horns' – Fred Wesley, Maceo Parker and Pee Wee Ellis – and Brown's trio of powerhouse singers Vicki Anderson, Marva Whitney and Lyn Collins, with Bobby Byrd as leader. Anderson's twenty-year-old daughter, Carleen Anderson, already a seasoned performer on the Southern gospel circuit in the United States, sang backing vocals and took the lead on a version of Deniece Williams's 'Free'. The set-list,[4] designed with advice from the rare groove DJs, was tailored to the rare groove audience and featured a string of London dancefloor hits, including Lyn Collins's 'Think (About It)', trombonist Fred Wesley's 'House Party' and a Maceo Parker medley of 'Soul Power '74' and 'Cross the Track'.

These gigs offered the chance for London club audiences to experience music they had been dancing to for years played live by the original artists, who had lost none of their potency (although several had stopped making music altogether or had careers that were a pale shadow of former glories). It also demonstrated the status of the rare groove promoters, able to attract American funk aristocracy while showing the musicians that though they may have been largely forgotten in their own country they were revered in London. The players were visibly moved by the enthusiasm of a crowd that danced non-stop and knew every word and rhythmic nuance of the music. One of America's great black bands, performing to an adoring, racially mixed London audience suggested a different kind of 'special relationship' across the (black) Atlantic.

These shows gave a shot in the arm to London's live black music scene, which, with the rise of the (far cheaper) DJ and decks set-ups, had been relatively dormant since the Afro-funk craze of the mid-1970s and the Brit-funk era of the early 1980s (Coester 2014; Bradley 2013). London-based bands like Incognito, formed in 1982 from the remnants of Brit-funkers Light of the World, Brand New Heavies (formed in 1985) and Push (1987) were energised by the revival of interest in live funk embodied by the James Brown shows. The formation of the Young Disciples, one of the most critically acclaimed of this new generation of bands, was a direct consequence of the concert: Shake and Finger-pop promoter Femi Williams and musician Marco Nelson had been so impressed by Carleen Anderson that backstage they suggested working together. When Anderson moved permanently to London in 1989, the trio formed the Young Disciples, becoming one of the first acts signed to Gilles Peterson's Phonogram subsidiary Talkin' Loud in 1990, whose debut (and only) album, *Road To Freedom*, was released in 1991. It reached number 21 in the album chart and earned the band a prestigious

Mercury Prize nomination (even as the band disintegrated). In 1998 Anderson told the journalist Cole Morton that the main reason for her move to London had been the relative lack of racial tension compared with her home town of Los Angeles: 'I haven't seen anybody looking at me like they wish I was dead'.[5]

Meanwhile, Jazzie B's Soul II Soul collective, which had been incorporating elements of live performance into their sets at the Africa Centre, coalesced into a fully fledged band. Signing to Virgin Records in 1988 they released a cheekily titled debut album *Club Classics Volume 1* and a string of increasingly successful singles that charted on both sides of the Atlantic. 'Back to Life', the fourth single, which the cultural theorist Richard Iton described as achieving 'a provocative fusion of R&B/Lover's Rock feminism and sound system masculism' (2008: 278), topped the UK chart in June 1989 and reached number 4 in the US top 100. A series of colourful MTV-friendly videos packaged the band's 'funki dread' persona and its optimistic vision of hybrid black British identity for a US audience and the band won Grammys in 1990 for best R&B performance and best R&B song. As their performing career took off, Soul II Soul shelved their Sunday night Africa Centre sessions to concentrate on touring and recording. Thus the centre of gravity of the rare groove scene moved from clubs and pirate radio to legitimate media, recording studios, label offices and global circuits of the corporate music industry.

The underground circuits by which rare groove knowledge had circulated – club nights, second-hand records stores, pirate radio – had circumvented the major record labels and music industry gatekeepers, but by the late 1980s they were catching on. New imprints like Talkin' Loud, often run by DJs, were keen to sign new funk talent and the established majors were cottoning on to the lively market in hard-to-find vinyl and to the expertise of DJs whose proximity to the clubs ensured they (usually) chose the right songs to reissue. In 1986 Polydor had started reissuing music from its neglected back catalogue through the Urban Classics imprint, curated by the Liverpool DJ Steve Proctor.[6] *Urban Classics Volume Four*, from 1989, included the rare groove staples 'Cross

the Track', 'I Believe in Miracles' and 'I Know You Got Soul'. Other labels
followed suit: Charley started the 'Got to Get Your Own – Some Rare
Grooves' series, which drew on DJ expertise, including Femi and Marco
of the Young Disciples, to find and release previously hard-to-find cuts
by Reuben Wilson, Ripple, African Music Machine, Cymande and
Eddie Bo. Reissues and compilations compiled by DJs proliferated and
1970s albums by James Brown, Roy Ayers and the JBs were reissued by
the original labels, which were seeking to compete with the unlicensed
'bootlegs' which had circulated for many years.

This new availability undermined the clubs as the site of discovery,
and the ubiquity of these tracks was lending the clubs an air of predict-
ability. Crowds, and DJs, were getting bored. Norman Jay, the presiding
godfather of the scene, had seen change coming. At midnight at the
New Year's Eve Shake and Fingerpop party in 1986 at Riverside House
(discussed in the previous chapter) he played, as was expected, 'Cross
the Track' followed by 'I Believe in Miracles'. But as he introduced them
and counted down to 1987 he told the crowd this was the last time he
would ever play them. The funky breakbeats and soulful vocals, and
the possibilities of multicultural unity they had evoked, were about to
get radically remixed up by the frenetic machine beats of acid house,
whose proximity to Afro-diasporic traditions and its cultural and racial
meanings were far less easy to read.

The acid origin myth

At the centre of the acid house story is a mythological journey to Ibiza
that has become a central part of club folklore (Cavanaugh 2016). According to this story, it all began in September 1987 on the small Island
of Ibiza in the Balearics, when four English DJs discovered the holy
trinity of electronic dance music, all-night dancing and the dance drug
ecstasy. On returning to London, so the legend has it, they transformed a
stale club culture, crippled by its own cool, into an everyone-is-welcome
psychedelic pleasure dome of uninhibited abandon and *jouissance*,[7]
where distinctions of race, class or gender were washed away in a

collective surrender to the technologies of electronic beats and psychoactive drugs (Gilbert and Pearson 1999). The 'road to Damascus' overtones of the Ibiza myth are reinforced by the witness of original participants, like DJ Johnny Walker, who described the Ibiza trip as 'a religious experience' (Collin 1997: 53).

By calling this story a myth, I do not mean to suggest that it is false. As Vincent Mosco has argued in a different context, 'myths are more than fabrications of the truth' and what matters is not so much whether a myth is true but whether it is 'living or dead' (Mosco 2004: 28). Citing the anthropologist Claude Lévi-Strauss, Mosco suggests that myths function as stories that help people deal with contradictions in their lives that can never be fully resolved. The resilience of the Ibiza myth, which reappears, for example, as the centrepiece of the first episode of Sky's four-part oral history of UK club culture broadcast in 2017,[8] and which has played a significant part in Ibiza's tourist economy ever since[9] – can be read in part as an index of the genuine desire to overcome divisions of race, class and gender that continued to structure social relations in London. But though it is based on real events, the repetition of this story also serves an ideological function. It has facilitated the 'whitewashing' of rave,[10] analogous to the way that the 1977 film *Saturday Night Fever* functioned to conceal disco's origins in the black gay clubs of New York. Just as *Saturday Night Fever* attempted to neuter the implicit threat disco posed 'to [white] heteronormative late capitalist masculinity' (Hughes 1994: 147) by focusing on white-suited hyper-heterosexuality of Tony Manero (played by John Travolta) and the vanilla Bee Gees in place of the unsettling sexual and racial ambiguity of disco divas like Sylvester, so the Ibiza myth fixes the unstable histories of house music in the image of four white working-class lads living it large in Spain. The politics and constituencies of acid house and rave are not identical to those of disco, but the way in which they have been historicised suggests some of the same mechanisms of historical racialised amnesia.

The facts of the story are not in dispute. In September 1987 Paul Oakenfold, a London-born soul, funk and hip hop DJ who had lived in New York and worked as an A&R (artists and repertoire) man for the hip hop and funk indie Champion Records, did indeed celebrate his twenty-fourth birthday in Ibiza with some of his DJ mates, including Nicky Holloway, Danny Rampling and Johnny Walker.[11] The lads rented a villa in St Antonio, where locals retreated to escape the British tourists and set out to sample the illicit pleasures of the 'White Isle', a staging post for illicit drug smuggling along the hippy trail. Their mates Trevor Fung and Ian St Paul (Holloway's cousin) had been DJing regularly on the island for several years, and the entrepreneurial Holloway had already organised several Special Branch trips to the island, bringing over 300 of his soul and funk crowd in 1985, but this was going to be different. Fung and St Paul knew of an after-hours club that was the new spot on the island. Amnesia, located in an old *finca* out of town, reopened at 3 a.m. after the regular Euro-disco night was over, for a clued-up bunch of locals, under the orchestration of Argentinian DJ Alfredo Fiorito (who had come to Ibiza to escape the military dictatorship). Alfredo mixed a range of musical styles, disco, pop and Spanish folk, with the new sounds of house music from Chicago. Such an eclectic mix of music was novel enough – London clubs were marked by strong generic distinctions and discourses of authenticity (Thornton 1995) that militated against the mixing of underground black music with pop – but it was the drugs that made the real difference. In this case, the friends all took 3,4-methylenedioxymethamphetamine (MDMA), known as ecstasy (or simply 'E').

There is a long history of the relation between dance music cultures and drugs. Various forms of cannabis, hashish from Pakistan and Lebanon and weed from Jamaica and Thailand, were widely available and ubiquitous in the reggae sound system scene and South American cocaine and Afghan heroin were available to those with the right connections, especially around the West End nightclubs. Since the rise of the mods in the 1960s, various forms of amphetamines, from Benzedrine to the infamous 'purple hearts' and 'black bombers', had acquired a strong association with all-night dance culture, a music–dance–speed cocktail inherited by and refined in the northern soul subcultures in Manchester and Wigan. The psychedelic hippies had their LSD. But in the 1980s in

London no single drug could be said to predominate in the clubs, other than alcohol. Many black London clubbers were anti-drugs, especially the dancers at Crackers (many of whom, much to the venue owners' consternation, did not even drink alcohol), the Electric Ballroom and warehouse parties, where physical coordination and grace were highly valued. The suburban soul scene, as an extension of working-class pub culture, was a drinking crowd. Gilles Peterson, who DJed at many of Holloway's nights, recalls that Nicky Holloway and his crowd were 'beer drinkers' and Holloway was generally against drug taking in his parties for fear of losing his licence (Gilles Peterson interview, 3 August 2017). But on this Ibiza night, Holloway set his reservations aside and swallowed a pill along with his mates. 'We all did ecstasy for the first time together', Holloway told journalist Luke Bainbridge, 'and then it all made sense…':

> Alfredo was playing [Chicago house labels] Trax and DJ International next to Kate Bush and Queen, all the white English acts we'd turn our noses up at. But on E it all made sense. Half an hour or so after you necked a pill you'd feel this euphoric wave got though you … and you suddenly felt that everything in the world was alright. If we hadn't had the Es we'd have thought it was shit. (Holloway cited in Bainbridge 2013: 71)

This mixture of pop, rock, hard electronic house rhythms and European disco with Spanish guitar flourishes – a mixture that became known as 'Balearic', after the islands – along with the ingestion of ecstasy, hit the Brits as a 'revelation' and led to a 'conversion'. On their return to London this group of soul and funk DJs began to proselytise.

They turned away from the black music – soul, funk and hip hop – on which they had built their DJ careers and started to recreate the Balearic vibe in London. First was an Ibiza reunion – with the new music and drugs – held one Friday after Paul Oakenfold's regular hip hop set at the Project club at Ziggy's in Streatham, south London. This rapidly developed into a weekly after-hours club, running until 6 a.m., and became a gathering point for a nascent group of 'ravers' converted to the new acid house/ecstasy cocktail. Many soon-to-be influential acid house

From Ibiza to London: Brixton acid and rave

DJs, black and white, including Colin Dale, Fabio (Fitzroy Heslop), Andrew Weatherall and Carl Cox, got their first taste of the Ibiza vibe in to the less salubrious surroundings of Streatham High Street, where the notorious boxer and stuntman Nosher Powell presided over the door (see Petrides 2016). The Ziggy's Balearic sessions lasted only a short while before a police raid forced the club's closure, but by then, so the story goes, the spark was lit.

These Ibiza reunions spawned a series of new club nights in the capital, run by 'the Ibiza four' and affiliated DJs like Pete Tong, which spread the Ibiza formula. Based on a new eclecticism – though considerably less daring than Alfredo's, with no Queen or Kate Bush – this scene foregrounded the new futuristic sounds of Chicago house, which often featured an oscillating bassline made with the Roland TR 303 bass synthesiser. This sound began to be called 'acid house' after the release of 'Acid Track' by Phuture on the Trax label in 1987 (though it was recorded several years earlier – see Cheeseman 1995: 4), which had been popularised by the DJ Ron Hardy at Chicago club the Muzik Box (formerly the Warehouse).[12] Alongside this new music, the scene introduced a number of other innovations: a disorientating dancefloor awash with dry ice and strafed with strobe lights; a new uniform deploying colourful baggy clothes, a mix of sportswear and hippy motifs; all pivoting round the central acid house bio-chemical technology ecstasy, which became readily available in high-dosage pills supplied by a network of dealers, many of whom evidently ignored the traditional injunction not to get high on your own supply (Collin 1997; Chester 2016).[13]

In November 1987 Danny Rampling and his wife Jenni started Shoom, an invitation-only affair at the Fitness Centre, a shabby gym in Elephant and Castle, south London (see plate 3). With its love and peace ethos and relentless, drug-enabled positivity – embodied in the smiley face logo that Rampling nicked from an iconic 1970s design for one of his flyers, which rapidly took off as the logo of the entire scene – Shoom crystallised the 'luvved up' acid house formula. From the old soul stomping grounds of Streatham and Elephant and Castle, acid house swept into the West End. Two weeks after the launch of Shoom, Paul

Oakenfold started Future, at the Soundshaft, the small venue annexed to the 1,500-capacity gay nightclub Heaven in the arches beneath Charing Cross Station. Starting as a haven for Ibiza insiders, soon both nights were overflowing. By March 1988 Shoom had moved to the YMCA in Tottenham Court Road and then to the larger Busby's on Charing Cross Road. The next month Oakenfold took over the main dancefloor at Heaven on a Monday night, renaming the night Spectrum. Also in March, promoter Nicky Holloway staged his annual soul weekender at Rockley Sands caravan park in Poole, Dorset, where the shift in club culture became clear. 'It was on the cusp of change', recalls Terry Farley, 'when the crowd split between the black music purists and the kids who had been to Ibiza and took gear [ecstasy]' (Farley cited in Brewster and Broughton 2018). In May that year, Holloway opened the Trip, at the Astoria on the Charing Cross Road, already an established nightclub venue where Family Funktion had been running a Friday night rare groove club for several years, and the proto-house club Delirium had been running since 1986 (see plate 5). That month both *The Face* and *ID*, the leading style magazines of the day, ran flattering features on acid house.

The Balearic boys had succeeded in bringing their Ibiza acid house concept into central London but it did not stay confined to the city.[14] By November 1988 acid house and the rave ethos were sweeping even those suburban soul dancefloors whose dedication to black music authenticity and disdain for digitised rhythm had appeared so secure just a few months previously. Dean Cavanaugh recalls his visit to the annual soul weekender in Prestatyn, North Wales, when 'it all kicked off':

> Nicky Holloway, Paul Oakenfold, Frenchie and Pete Tong took over a big room, renamed it The Reactor and threw an acid house party…. It was strange for me to watch it all grow from the sidelines. A lot of our gang would have no truck with Acid House – the same ones who had been resistant to Hip Hop, and chose to spend the weekend listening to Robbie Vincent and Jeff Young dropping 'classics' in the main arena – but it wasn't long before they too were 'getting on one'. You just couldn't help but get sucked into the vortex. (Cavanaugh 2016)

During the ensuing long 'summer of love' (which really covers the period from summer 1987 to late 1988) the acid house phenomenon spawned a fully blown countrywide youth and music subculture known as 'rave',[15] after its primary social form, complete with its smiley logo, a catchphrase – 'acieed' – a new style of dress and a new form of dancing, eschewing complex dance steps beyond the competence of a raver 'coming up', big on wavy hand gestures, all organised around the tell-tale saucer-eyed gurn of the ecstasy taker, barely able to contain the rising rush of speedy euphoria. As Cavanaugh and Farley suggest, the spaces of soul, funk and rare groove, and the diasporic imaginary they conjured, were invaded with a new fast-tempoed technological soundscape and new ways of occupying space.

What had started in nightclubs and small venues began to super-size, precipitated by the first mega-rave, Apocalypse Now at Wembley Studios in August 1988, promoted by the soon-to-be moguls of rave Tony Colston-Hayter[16] and Wayne Anthony (soon joined by Paul Staines[17]), who, unlike the members-only underground elitism of Rampling's Shoom, consciously sought a mass audience and courted media exposure by inviting ITN News to film the event. The ensuing news report, which cut out the DJ interviews in favour of shock footage of drugged up youth 'gone wild', caught the attention of the tabloid media, who initially embraced acid house as 'the latest dance craze' and offered their own 'groovy and cool' version of an acid house T-shirt (*The Sun*, 12 October 1988). But following the first reported ecstasy casualty in October 1988 (Janet Mayes, who collapsed at the Jolly Boatman pub in Hampton Court on 2 November after taking two ecstasy tablets) *The Sun* rapidly changed tack, running a double-spread with the headline 'The Evils of Ecstasy' on 19 October. The newspaper withdrew its T-shirt giveaway offer and replaced it with a 'Just Say No To Drugs' badge and the headline 'Shoot These Evil Acid Barons' (see Lynsky 2014). That November the BBC banned any reference to 'acid' from the airwaves (*Dummy Magazine*, 20 December 2012). The mechanisms of a full-blown moral panic,[18] reminiscent of the coverage of the mods and rockers, were in place (Collin 1989), with the media engaged in what

Stan Cohen defines as 'deviancy amplification' (Cohen 1972: 198) with the new the folk devil of the 'pill potty' raver at its centre (see plate 4).

As well as winning public consent for a crackdown on raves, this publicity significantly increased the profile and subcultural cache of the nascent rave scene and drew legions of neophyte ravers to the rapidly growing circuit of 'orbital' raves sprouting beyond the city (Thornton 1995). Acid house events grew bigger and spread outwards beyond the city, into fields, farms, studios and abandoned airfields in the commuter belt, announcing their electro-chemical-hippy ethos at mega-raves with names like Biology, Sunrise, Energy, Raindance, Perception, Kaleido-scope and Brainstorm.

Acid as spatial threat

Government papers released by the National Archive in 2016 reveal the rapid expansion of the acid house party phenomenon and the anxieties it triggered at the very top of government.[19] According to Home Office figures (which we have no reason to believe are comprehensive) by October 1989 there had been 223 illegal acid house parties in London and the south-east of England alone, and a further ninety-five had been stopped by 'pre-emptive police action'. Ministers were considering in-creasing fines and surveillance to combat what was becoming, in their view, a nationwide threat (Home Office letter to Geoffrey Howe, Lord President of the Privy Council, 2 October 1989). These papers suggest the way that acid house was considered to represent a new kind of spatial threat. The earliest document in the National Archive dossier, which seems to have triggered the government's anxiety about acid house parties, is a letter, dated 22 August 1989, from Gerald Coke CBE, a local magistrate from Bentley in Hampshire. Addressed to the MP Michael Mates, Coke's letter expresses his concern following an acid house party in Hampshire on 19 August. Coke's letter (which he copied to his nephew, the MP Archie Hamilton, former parliamentary private secretary to Margaret Thatcher, in the hope it would get to her, as indeed it did[20]) views raves as an explicit threat to the ordered village life of the English shires. Decrying the 'invasion of privacy' which raves represented – materialised in 'noise' that 'kept the whole village awake' – Coke warns of the danger that the crowd of several thousand – 'consisting of mainly undesirable characters' – might 'go on the rampage and break up the village'. He suggests that if the government fails to respond, justifiably angry villagers might be forced to take matters into their own hands, which 'could end in bloodshed'.

Coke's barely veiled threat of vigilantism, and the ministerial discussions which ensued, do not cast the problem in explicitly racial terms, but in terms of the invasion of rural space by urban youth, the 'undesirable characters' who are an illegitimate presence in the English village (Coke does not seem to countenance what the rave promoters knew: that a high proportion of these ravers would have been from these same Hampshire villages, the sons and daughters of the squirocracy). Rave represented a defiling of the English countryside. Ravers were literally out of place, just as their music, the invasion of the aural space by illegitimate sound, was conceived as 'noise', the sonic manifestation of 'matter out of place' (Douglas 1966).

This is reinforced in a report from the Association of District Councils, also included in the dossier, which notes that 'pay parties have existed in various forms for some years' but have not presented a problem because 'they have mainly been confined to inner city areas'. Thus in the response to rave we see anxieties about the way that dancing to amplified music characteristic of bass culture had escaped confinement in the city and posed a sonic and moral threat to the harmony of the suburbs and the shires. What had apparently been held in place by spatial forms of discipline and containment had overflowed the borders. The Secretary of State for Scotland, Malcolm Rifkind, commenting on possible methods to suppress raves, in a letter dated 5 December 1989, makes the point that any legal restraints would need to be 'carefully drafted so as not to catch entirely innocent events such as a barn dance'. Thus although rave audiences were racially mixed, the response to them can be read in the tradition of responses to what Tricia Rose has termed 'black noise' (1994), conceived as the sonic articulation of otherness, announcing the presence of 'undesirables' in the white space where authentic Englishness resides.

Ministerial discussions illustrate the development of strategies to contain and stamp out the growing rave threat. The initial plan was to strengthen the provisions of existing licensing and noise-abatement laws by increasing fines (from £2,000 to £20,000) and enabling profits from raves to be seized. These provisions proved entirely inadequate, as rave culture continued to spread countrywide into the early 1990s, and so they were eventually enhanced with the passing of the infamous Criminal Justice and Public Order Act 1994, which specifically targeted outdoor raves, defined as 'a gathering on land in the open air of 20 or more persons (whether or not trespassers), at which amplified music is played during the night'. Notoriously, it attempted to single out acid house by defining music as 'sounds wholly or predominantly characterised by the emission of a succession of repetitive beats' (Criminal Justice Act 1994), a designation that could in principle be applied to any form of dance music based on black rhythmic traditions of repetition (Snead 1984).

The early 1990s saw the increasingly efficient application of authoritarian methods of suppression. The Kent police force was among the first to be faced with raves beyond the city, and its Pay Party Unit, under superintendent Ken Tappenham, gradually became expert in tracking and preventing raves. It learnt how to track the rave promoters' innovative use of telecommunications – flyers would not advertise addresses but give a telephone number to an automated message which would release venue details at an agreed time – and subsequently it shared its expertise with other regional forces. Police tactics became increasingly aggressive. Rave DJ Optical (Matt Quinn) recalls the impact of the new policies in 1994: 'That year instead of parking cars which they were doing the year before and, like, friendly they were suddenly coming with sledge hammers and smashing my records and putting the speakers in while the kids were watching' (interview by Chris Christodoulou, 2 March 2017).

Meanwhile, the government had found a more successful tactic than attempting to suppress outdoor raves. In 1990 Turnmills, a huge dance club in Clerkenwell, became the first UK club to be granted a twenty-four-hour licence, followed in 1991 by the Ministry of Sound, a purpose-built nightclub on the model of New York's Paradise Garage, with a high-spec sound system, in a disused bus garage in Elephant and Castle. Both clubs courted rave crowds. 'The concept of having rave clubs in London', says Quinn, 'was encouraged by the government because it was a way of keeping it under control'. Between the increased powers and emerging competence of the police deploying aggressive tactics and the new leniency in the granting of late licences, by 1994 rave was moved (back) into licensed venues. This explains the only slightly tongue-in-cheek notion that circulates within dance music circles that 'Maggie Thatcher created the club scene'.

An alternative history of acid house

Undoubtedly acid house represents a potent cultural phenomenon, a disruption of club culture within which the soul-trained Balearic DJs were first movers. Well connected with London-based journalists and fashion leaders, the Balearic DJs spearheaded a new model of clubbing which grew rapidly: clubs like Shoom and Spectrum provided the template for the explosion of raves which followed. Acid house, gestated in the same period at the Manchester club the Hacienda, reshaped the landscape of London dance culture and eventually that of the whole of the UK. This is what has led dance music historians to suggest that rave was a fundamental break with what went before. But this is to overlook the continuing influence of sound systems, soul clubs and warehouse parties. And the subsequent lionisation of Oakenfold, Rampling and the other Ibiza DJs similarly obscures the work of black DJs who drove the house explosion. Despite the rave rhetoric of inclusiveness there is a contested racial politics of rave that has been largely ignored, as some critics have acknowledged.[21] This section presents an enquiry into these politics, with an emphasis on space. It asks whether rave – so routinely identified with Ibiza, and celebrated as the moment when the nation, especially white men, shuffled off their social inhibitions and got down on the dancefloor – can be considered part of a black Atlantic musical continuum.

Compared with the substantial literature on the relationship between hip hop and race (Rose 1994; Perkins 1996) there is disappointingly little academic writing on the racial politics of house music (Albeiz 2011: 44), or the relationship between hip hop and house or techno. Scholars of rave seem to have taken literally the claims made by acid house that it represented a new beginning, so there was no need to enquire into its historical origins, and the claim of rave ideology, that it successfully transcended the boundaries of class, race, gender and sexual identity, has generally been taken at face value. On the other hand, those working within black studies and on black musical traditions have neglected house and focused their attention on hip hop instead, a genre that, in its emphasis on black space and the African-American experience, foregrounds and thematises its racial particularity in a way that house music refuses.

Even Richard Iton's otherwise wide-ranging study of 'the black fantastic', which places an analysis of black cultural production and especially music at the centre of the discussion of black politics after the civil rights movement, covering soul, R&B and the complex re-lations between reggae and hip hop, contains only a frustratingly brief, if suggestive, passage on the 'antagonistic' relations between hip hop and house. This pivots around the notion that, in the context of hip hop and reggae-derived projections of conservative versions of black heterosexual masculinity, disco, house and its offshoots were perceived as 'problematic … as sponsoring and subsidizing unappealing, unfixed and indeterminate conceptions of sexual identity' (Iton 2008: 280).

Despite their shared origins in 1970s New York – materialised in the first rap hit, the Sugarhill Gang's 'Rappers Delight' (1979), which repro-duces the bassline from Chic's disco hit 'Good Times' – hip hop has been conventionally read as an alternative to and critique of disco, perceived as too commercial, too white, too gay. The distance between hip hop's spatial imaginary – the hood, the street, the cypher – and the black and Hispanic dancefloors that nurtured disco, house and techno has been reproduced in debates around the music. The sometimes extreme hetero-normative masculinity of hip hop – which draws on what Henry Louis Gates has called the 'virulent form of homophobia that is associated with Black Power and Black aesthetic movements' (Gates 1993: 233[22]) – has militated against a proper analysis of the relationship between hip hop and house, and an understanding of how race plays within house music culture and its various generic offshoots, including acid house.

Indeed, for some scholars of black music, disco – the precursor of house – is conceived as merely another example of black-originated genres that have suffered dilution by white appropriation and commercial exploitation, the anti-alchemy that turns 'black roots' into 'white fruits' (Garafalo 2002: 112). Radical and bourgeois ideologies join forces in their condemnation of disco's commercialism and triviality, its inherent, and problematic, femininity (James 2018). Here, disco is read as an appropriation of soul and jazz funk comparable to the gentrification of jazz in the 1930s, rock and roll's neutering of rhythm and blues in the 1950s and the 'assassination' of living black musical tradition by the 'British invasion' of the 1960s (Baraka 1967c: 18). This line of thinking can be read in the work of black nationalist critics, like Nelson George's arguments that disco contributed to 'the death of Rhythm and Blues' (George 1988; see also Lawrence 2003: 380) and Houston Baker's celebration of hip hop's 'reassertion of black manhood rights (rites)' against the racial and sexual instability disco represented (Baker cited in Lawrence 2003: 383). Tim Lawrence notes Baker's (perhaps unwitting) echoing of the homophobic 'disco sucks' discourse and provides convincing evidence of influence and crossover between genres which suggests that the rap–disco divide is a 'purely mythological' simplification of a far more complex interdependent relationship (Lawrence 2003: 384; Lawrence 2016: 15).

House music, in its form and forms of consumption and its challenge to the securities of racial and sexual identity, confounds simple racial or gender readings. Dispensing with the conventional sonic symbolism of black music – the black voice, jazz instrumentation, the ingredients of the 'blues aesthetic' (Baraka 1991), which have been argued to define blackness in musical expression – and professing reverence for European forms of pop and electronic avant gardism, house, despite the fact that it was, at least initially, the creation of black Americans in the cities of the north-eastern United States, has been considered to lie outside the canon, 'strange and problematic ... almost incomprehensible and indigestible' (Iton 2008: 281–2) within the frame of African-American music.

Locating itself in a less obviously black space-time and, on occasion, projecting images of community that are wilfully non-racial or pan-racial and poly-sexual (like the image of the 'house nation') and drawing on musical traditions from outside the diaspora that are coded as white, house music challenges a simple division of music into black or white, straight or gay, masculine or feminine. As such, it poses a particular challenge to those absolutists who seek to read black vernacular culture as the ethnic property of a stable racial community embodied by the patriarchal heterosexual family (Gilroy 2000: 179).

How, then, might we connect acid house and rave to the black Atlantic continuum? The first task is to place acid house in its historical and social context. Though its particular cocktail of music, drugs and 'mental' attitude is distinctive, and arguably distinctively British, acid house emerges out of innovations in electronic music and dance culture from further afield than London or Ibiza. These innovations, happening within relatively autonomous black, Latinx and gay dance music scenes, from disco to house, in Chicago, Detroit and New York, bear the traces of the race-space politics I have been arguing partly define all diasporic black music, and though house and techno take a different attitude to space and place than hip hop, they can still be understood as embodying a particular response to the racialisation of space.

Secondly, we need to trace the pathways by which house had come to London, long before the acid house outburst of 1987. Through import record shops, pirate radio shows and the cultural work of a group of dedicated but, during rare groove, somewhat marginalised DJs and sound systems, house music and its practices had been seeding the ground for the rave explosion for several years. The club scene innovated by the Ibiza four – at Shoom, Spectrum and the Trip – was undoubtedly transformative and influential on the rave scene that followed. But there were other spaces, closer to the circuits of sound system and the warehouse parties, where acid house was being played, mixed, conjured with and deformed – spaces like Clink Street, Brixton squat parties and Rage at Heaven – which opened up a new set of possibilities in the years to come.

Beforehand, it bears repeating that any such recontextualisation needs to practise a 'skilful dance', being aware of the difficulties of discussing the political and cultural work of those designated as the racial other while remaining alert to 'the pernicious effects of race and raciological thinking' (Walcott 2005: 3–4). Pertinent here is Gilroy's strategy for addressing the question of the relationship between race and music through an 'anti-anti-essentialism' which concedes no ground to absolutist definitions of culture (though it recognises that these definitions are reworked and conjured with within black music) and focuses attention on the hybrid nature of black music cultures, bearing in mind that specific traditions and practices reappear in black cultural practice as tactical responses to immediate political and social circumstances, 'in the intimate interactions' of performative space (Gilroy 1991: 128; Gilroy 1993). So here I want to focus on how black music traditions and the work of black cultural producers, which are obscured by the Ibiza myth and the idea of rave as absolutely novel and which remain unexamined in so much discussion of club culture, fed into (and out of) rave.

From disco to house

House music is derived from disco, an uptempo danceable fusion of soul, Latin, gospel and jazz which emerged in the early 1970s. With the development of digital production technology in the mid-1970s – sequencers and samplers – the disco cuts being played in New York and Chicago clubs from the late 1970s took on a harder, more mechanised edge influenced by European synth pop and Euro-disco, which were mixed by the DJs into seamless all-night blends. The most significant DJs in the transition from disco to house in the early 1980s were: Larry Levan, resident at the black gay members-only club Paradise Garage at 84 King Street in Lower Manhattan, which opened in 1977; Tony Humphries, who worked the decks at Zanzibar in New Jersey from 1982; and, above all, Frankie 'Knuckles' Nicholls, who presided over the three-storey former industrial building on South Jefferson in Chicago's West Loop, opened as the members-only black gay club the Warehouse in 1977.

The disco club culture within which house was incubated, as Tim Lawrence argues in his history of New York nightlife *Love Saves the Day* (2003), was built through multiracial collaboration, involving gay and straight New Yorkers, white, black and Hispanic, working in clubs, gay, straight and mixed, which promoted a powerful sense of community based on the model pioneered by David Mancuso at his members-only, alcohol-free Loft Parties established in 1970 which actively promoted a non-conformist multiracial ethos (Lawrence 2003). House gets its name from the music Frankie Knuckles played at the Warehouse – a mix of disco, electro and synth pop with a percussive edge drawn from Latin music, often pitched up, mixed and re-edited using tape reels – and the new music his mixing inspired. The defining feature of house is a pulsing four/four kick drum; the more highly syncopated gospel-drenched variant (where the rhythm is split between thudding kick drum and hissing hi hats, bmm-tsiss) is known as garage, after Levan's Paradise Garage club. Techno is a first cousin of house, and emerged from Detroit in the early 1980s; it employs house's four-four rhythm in a stripped-down spacey futuristic soundscape which moves even further from disco's soul and gospel roots into the territory of 'post-soul' (see Albeiz 2011).

These pioneers, building on the mixing and editing skills of a previous generation of New York DJs like Nicky Siano, Francis Grasso and Michael Capello[23] and studio producers like Tom Moulton, Shep Pettibone and Walter Gibbons, who innovated the intense dancefloor-oriented extended mixes which isolated and emphasised the most rhythmic aspects of the disco songs, built an all-night dance scene in collaboration with their loyal, mostly black and Latinx gay clientele.

In 1983 Knuckles bought a drum machine (from Chicago producer Jeff Mills), which he used to enhance his live mixing, a move which influenced the production in Chicago of a new form of electronic dance music by young producers like DJ Pierre, Chip E and Jesse Saunders, who strove to emulate Knuckles. House producers drew on black music genres like disco, funk and hip hop production techniques, but they also incorporated the electronic experiments of pioneers in rock, synth pop and Euro-disco like Giorgio Moroder (whose fifteen-minute epic 'I Feel Love' with Donna Summer from 1977 had a huge impact), Yellow Magic Orchestra, Depeche Mode and Kraftwerk (music which, it should be noted, was also influencing other black music producers in New York hip hop – with works such as 'Planet Rock' by Afrika Bambaataa and the Soul Sonic Force – and in go-go from Washington, DC – like the Kraftwerk-inspired 'Trouble Funk Express' by Trouble Funk).

In the late 1970s, disco had offered a lifeline to the ailing American music industry, providing a new source of revenue and energy with the slumping of rock sales during a global recession. In 1979 legendary Atlantic producer Jerry Wexler invited the readers of the music industry trade journal *Billboard* to 'imagine how bad business would be if we didn't have disco' (Wexler cited in Lawrence 2003: 367), and labels like West End, Atlantic, Casablanca and Salsoul were reaping the financial benefits of disco, inspiring major labels to fall over themselves to adapt the disco sound for the rock market. But the economics of disco was 'tricky' (Lawrence 2003), relying as it did on the continually moving tastes of a multicultural gay club scene that record labels did not under-stand, or appreciate, and that cared little for the albums, band careers or stadium performances which lay at the heart of the conventional rock industry business model. The sense that disco might redeem the fortunes of the industry – especially after the huge commercial success of *Saturday Night Fever* in 1977 (the first tie-in soundtrack and movie block-buster, delivering a hit movie, a number 1 album and four chart-topping singles), which seemed to offer the possibility of a disco super-group which could make the genre palatable to America's straight white rock consumers – led to the 'disco-tising' of everything and the proliferation of inferior disco versions, which didn't even make a mark on the disco dancefloors, let alone on the charts or the labels' balance sheets.

When the Bee Gees' follow-up to *Saturday Night Fever*, the soundtrack to a misconceived rock opera movie based on the Beatles' *Sergeant Pepper*, bombed in 1978 it seemed the disco bubble had burst and a backlash was gathering. The late 1970s saw the rise of the 'disco sucks' movement, which denounced disco as commercial and degenerate, a movement laced with a barely veiled racism and homophobia (Frank 2007). This reached its climax at the infamous 'Disco Demolition' at the Chicago White Sox stadium Comiskey Park in 1979, when rock radio DJ Steve Dahl exhorted a crowd of 70,000 to chant 'disco sucks' as he detonated a huge pile of disco records which had been collected at the gate from more than 10,000 fans (the pyre included, it would later emerge, not just disco but many soul and funk records[24]). Sales of disco records slumped and the industry moved on to the new pastures of electro-pop and new wave, leaving the warehouse and other black underground clubs free to push their funky mix of classic disco, electronic experimentalism and Latin rhythms, and the pan-sexual multicultural politics they implied, in new directions.

A period of intense experimentation ensued, orchestrated by black Chicago DJs, like Knuckles and Ron Hardy, analogous to the evolution of hip hop in New York: 'I was combining all of these great genres together that I loved – new wave, reggae, funk, disco, and classic rock into a sound that could bring everyone together', producer Jesse Saunders told journalist Jack Needham (Needham 2017). Here the apparent death of disco can be understood as its triumph, as house emerged from the DJ booth and home studios enabled by cheap digital production technology. Reflecting on this period, Frankie Knuckles commented that the rise of house should be understood as 'disco's revenge' (see Lynsky 2011).

House as black music

House music has a complex and ambivalent relationship to the politics of race. Because of its facelessness and lack of identifiable stars and the absence of obvious forms of black sonic symbolism, it is not necessarily received or understood as black music, and its origins in disco complicate the picture. Certainly the producer/DJ pioneers of house music, acid and techno – Knuckles, Levan, Humphries, Ron Hardy, Jesse Saunders, DJ Pierre, Loletta Holloway, Steve 'Silk' Hurley, Farley 'Jackmaster' Funk, Darryl Pandy, Alexi Shelby, Juan Atkins, Kevin Saunderson, Larry Heard, Kym Mazelle – are all black, as was a large part of the audience. But because of its form, based around dancing to records in clubs, not live performance or videos, played on records by a DJ who might not even be visible to the crowd, and focused around an aural rather than visual experience, the 'race' of the music is considerably less obvious, especially once it is abstracted from black spaces in which it is gestated, than that of, say, soul or hip hop. The twelve-inch singles which since the mid-1970s had been the prime commodity within club culture (the first commercially released twelve-inch was Walter Gibbon's extended mix of Double Exposure's 'Ten Percent' on the Salsoul label in 1976) were generally released without cover art or liner notes, and producer identities were hidden behind a dizzying array of ambiguous pseudonyms – Phuture, Bam Bam, Mr Fingers, The Nightwriters, JM Silk, Rhythim is Rhythim, Model 500 – which defeated attempts to categorise them in place or racial pigeonhole, just as the music refused to fit easily into the lineage of black popular music.

Though previous strongly black-coded genres continued to reverberate in house – soul and gospel-inspired 'diva' vocals, funk basslines, conga drums – the unashamed application of digital sequencing technology and sonic references to European forms of rock and pop further complicated any simple equation between house and blackness. This is especially the case with the techno starting to emerge from Detroit in the mid-1980s, where producers like Juan Atkins, Kevin Saunderson and Derrick May (who had been travelling to Chicago to study at the feet of Frankie Knuckles) struck out on a new path, one which dispensed with traditional instrumentation and vocals altogether in favour of a stripped down, sped-up electronic pulse, fusing P-funk influences with the affectless machine futurism of German synth pioneers like Kraftwerk, which retained only the most tenuous link to black music tradition through the presence of the heavy 'space bassline'. This was deliberate. Techno amounted not only to a rejection of 'soulfulness' and the constricting racial identity it connoted but, according to Kodwo Eshun, a rejection of the compromised category of the human itself (Eshun 1998). For Eshun this does not necessarily mean that techno is not black music but that it fits into an alternative tradition of black avant gardism – somewhere between space jazz Afronaut Sun RA, P-funk trickster George Clinton and Kingston dub savant Lee 'Scratch' Perry – which Eshun terms Afro-futurism.

House music deterritorialises black music, displacing it from the spacio-temporal cartography of black music, the musical map that links New Orleans and the Mississippi Delta to 42nd Street and the South Bronx. Absent from house music is the imagery of racialised space that links articulations of blackness in place, such as the invocations of 'the ghetto' by artists including Donny Hathaway, Marlena Shaw and the Philadelphia International All Stars[25] or hip hop's articulation of the black 'hoods' of Brooklyn, 'Strong Island' or the 'Boogie Down Bronx'.[26] The primary spatial imaginary of house is the dancefloor itself, and the body-in-motion to be found there, which might, under certain conditions, serve as a site of alternative community, where 'everybody is free to feel good'. The spatial imaginary of techno is the future world beyond neighbourhood, race and perhaps the human itself, which draws on the Afro-futurist narratives of escape from the earth and its failed promises, an escape from power geometry into the pure mathematics of sound (Eshun 1998; Albiez 2011). In doing so, house, acid house and techno undermine the stability of racial and other social categorisations bound up with notions of place.

Yet, not coincidently, house and techno emerge precisely from the American urban space that is strongly marked by racial segregation; its rejection of the politics of place and race is a refusal of the very power geometry within which it is born. The idea of the 'house nation' developed at the Warehouse, for example, can be read as a conscious rebuttal not only of American national identity, which continually failed to offer all American citizens the rights it promises (Iton 2008), but also of the racialised local politics of the cities where house and techno were born.[27] Reflecting on the Detroit in which he grew up and where techno developed out of the black gay after-hours scene where funk met disco (Zlatopolsky 2014), producer Juan Atkins recalls that 'we were brought up with this racial conflict thing, instilled in us since babies … if you're a [black] kid in Detroit, [you might] never see a white person, unless they're on TV' (cited in Reynolds 1999: 58). The New York clubs and loft parties where disco was nurtured and garage emerged and the Warehouse in Chicago, which actively sought to bring together black, white and Hispanic, gay and straight, were potent precisely because they sought such a mix against the backdrop of American apartheid (Bourgois 1995). As David Theo Goldberg has argued:

> At a macro level American urban space is shared; New York, Chicago, Detroit and Los Angeles are racially mixed. But at a micro level, segregation – enforced through unequal access to capital – is profound, and far more marked than in equivalent European cities […] whites and blacks still tend to inhabit separate spatial worlds. (Goldberg 2004)

In the context of this spatial segregation, overlaid with everyday homophobia and gendered spatial forms of power geometry, mixed/gay clubs like the Paradise Garage and the Warehouse couldn't but take on a political edge. Here's Saunders on early-1980s Detroit:

> The landscape was that of the Black Panthers, Angela Davis, the Civil Rights Movement, and there was a hope that things would get better. But at the same time, there were streets you couldn't walk down if you were black; people with Confederate flags and shotguns just waiting to see a black face infiltrate their neighborhood. So when Robert Williams opened The Warehouse in 1977, it brought an outlook with it that people were coming together. Our total goal was to move asses on the dance-floor, and whatever high energy, funky, rhythmic sounds we came up with is what we put in our music. (Saunders cited in Needham 2017)

In this way house music can be read as embodying a distinct spatio-political response by African-American music makers and their collaborators to the restrictions of racialised space.

Here a restless form of musical experimentation, a form of bricolage or tinkering, an orientation towards technology and rhythm that Tricia Rose identifies as distinctive of black cultural production (1994) and Rietveld defines as 'black secret technology' (2014), drives both the dancefloor and the genre forwards. The way that acid house itself came about, through what DJ Pierre has described as a happy accident in the programming of his TR-303 bass synthesiser, which produced the distinctive squelchy bassline that defines the acid sound,[28] can be read as an example of black Atlantic aesthetic practice. Toni Morrison and James Snead both describe black aesthetics as that which works with what is at hand (DJ Pierre's TR-303 was second-hand – production had ceased in 1984 – and he had no manual or training in how to use it), where notions of correctness are subordinate to chance and accident is folded back into a larger sense of order (see Snead 1984; Gilroy 1993; Rose 1994). For the filmmaker and artist Arthur Jafa, techno should be understood as a product of 'black people's relationship to technology', an imaginative reworking of the human–machine interface by those who have been treated only as productive machines: 'We are the technology that drove the American industrial engine' (Jafa cited in Brown 2018).

Rhythmically, house troubles simplistic notions of blackness. Unlike funk and the hip hop that derives from it, house and its offshoots take a different rhythmic course, foregrounding a steady and implacable 'four to the floor' pulse. This rhythmic regularity at a relatively high tempo (usually 110–130 beats per minute) led to resistance from soul, funk and reggae fans more used to slower, heavily syncopated rhythms played by human drummers. House was disparaged as simplistic and soulless; it sounded, as the die-hard soul boy and radio DJ Robert Elms told the makers of the *Soul Patrol* documentary, like 'music made by metronomes'. But this rhythmic regularity achieved through the use of quantised digital drum machines and sequencers is given a high value by house, rave and techno audiences, who consider the repetitive nature of house rhythm an aid to achieving transcendent trance-like states on the dancefloor.

From Ibiza to London: Brixton acid and rave

Disco critic Walter Hughes has suggested this rhythmic discipline can have a socio-psychological payoff, subverting both race and sexual normativity. Submission to the 'insistent, disciplinary beat' of disco and house, Hughes argues, has been instrumental in deconstructing the conventional ego of straight society 'in order to refashion it, much in the manner of military … or sado-masochistic discipline' into a new type of gay identity: 'By allowing the synthesized disco beat to move you, you surrender yourself to becoming an extension of the machine that generates the beat' (Hughes 1994: 151). Here, voluntarily becoming a 'slave to the rhythm', submitting to the 'empire of the beat', which is a sonic analogue of desire, offers new forms of non-essentialist freedom:

> The identity that disco offers is sustained by the beat and its twin, desire: it could conceivably go on for ever, like our dancing, if the music is right, but it will never be permanent, fixed or naturalized. Therein lies the freedom that disco constructs through our subordination to it. (Hughes 1994: 154)

House rhythm, which derives from disco, thus carries this strain of black popular music back towards the rigid militarised regularity so comprehensively usurped in New Orleans with the birth of jazz syncopation. Following Hughes we can see it as an alternative strategy for remixing identity in the dance. Emerging from the context of American racial segregation, combining Afro-futurist imaginaries with new technology enabling the projection of new forms of black gay identities, house presents a set of new sonic and social possibilities which, though they were largely ignored in the United States beyond the tight circuits of underground club culture found a receptive home across the Atlantic, where relations of race, sexuality and gender were already being remixed on the dancefloor.

House comes to London

Acid house mythology obscures the way in which New York and Chicago clubs and the house music they were incubating had been exerting an influence on London since long before Ibiza '87. DJs with family connections in the United States, like Norman Jay, visited New York regularly and got to hear what Larry Levan was doing downtown at the Paradise Garage. New York exerted a centripetal pull on London club DJs and promoters, especially after Freddie Laker launched his cut-price Skytrain service between London and New York in 1977, dramatically reducing the cost of air travel. London-based DJs copied the model of New York, like promoter Steve Swindells, whose mixed/gay club the Lift at the Gargoyle in Dean Street, and later the Lyceum, were inspired by his trip to the Paradise Garage (Swindells 2014).

But clubs were only one way to circulate the music, and with the rising influence of rare groove in the mid-1980s, nightclubs playing house music in London were relatively rare (unlike in cities in the north of England where rare groove never found a foothold – see Wilson 2013). More important than the clubs were the import record market and pirate radio. Uptempo disco and the more electronic house which came from it were circulated through the import shops in the West End and the suburbs – like Bluebird, Groove Records, Black Market, Rhythm, Record Shack and Contempo – and curious staff and forward-thinking DJs began to take notice from the moment proto-house started to appear on record in 1983/4 (though there is controversy over which was the very first Chicago house track to be released on vinyl, a strong candidate is Jesse Saunders' 'On and On', from 1983).

One example among many was the record store and DJ equipment shop Spin-Offs, on Fulham Palace Road, owned by black New York DJ Greg James, who had come to London in the 1970s to play at Jeremy Norman's Embassy Club (styled after Manhattan's Studio 54) and was one of the first DJs in the UK to beat-mix. Michael Schiniou from suburban Edmonton in north London, an ardent soul, jazz and funk fan and aspirant DJ, worked in the store and got the pick of the new music that started to arrive from Chicago labels like Trax and DJ International. Under the DJ name Jazzy M, he landed a radio show on LWR, the pirate station launched in 1983, which he dedicated to house and named 'the Jacking Zone', referencing the dance style developed in Chicago to match the new music. Jazzy M's Jacking Zone was a primary conduit through which house music flowed into London, though, as he told dance music historian Greg Wilson, his brand of music met resistance:

> Most of London was still caught up in that Rare Groove and Hip Hop thing. A lot of people were saying to me 'why are you playing this Hi-NRG' and it was hard work. (Jazzy M cited in Wilson 2013)

Among the group of DJs who joined Kiss FM in 1985 were two other influential house evangelists: Colin Faver and Colin Dale. East-Ender Faver had ditched a career in advertising to work in the Small Wonder record shop in Walthamstow in 1977, just as punk was breaking, and had a hand in the early careers of post-punk bands like the Cure and Bauhaus. Starting as a DJ in hospital radio – a job from which he was fired for playing the Sex Pistols – Faver moved on to warming up at live shows at the Marquee club in Wardour Street, gradually extending his taste beyond post-punk and industrial into the new sounds of electro and house. He was regular at the Camden Palace from 1983, where he played alongside 'Evil' Eddie Richards, another house pioneer, and the wild gay club Pyramid at Heaven. A few years older than his peers, Faver became something of a godfather of the nascent house and techno scene, DJing at early acid house clubs like Hedonism and Shoom and orbital raves once acid house broke.

The other Colin – Dale – grew up in Brixton surrounded by reggae – his father's records, the lively reggae sound system scene – but he found himself drawn to the rock and pop he heard on Radio Luxembourg, and the soul and disco he discovered when he started going out:

> For me it was it was definitely soul music and disco: reggae was just out the window. My cousins were different; they stayed with reggae and used to curse me out, call me a 'batty boy' for the way I dressed, the tight jeans…. I didn't know the link [between disco and] gay culture at all; it was just the music. (Colin Dale interview, 30 July 2017)

As a teenager, Dale was a regular at Cracker's Friday lunchtime sessions and formed a dance crew, Base 3, with some of his friends (including

Fitzroy Heslop), who performed at soul and funk nights like Tim West-wood's night at Gossips in Dean Street. He worked his way up from handing out flyers for Westwood to a warm-up slot on the decks, where he learnt the DJ trade. Dale got a slot on the local Brixton pirate station Phase One, above Mendozas, a Brixton shubeen, alongside other Brixton DJs Grooverider (Raymond Bingham), Fabio (Fitzroy Heslop) and Dave Angel (David Angelico Gooden). In 1985 Dale joined Colin Faver at Kiss FM, where his 'Abstract Dance' show provided a showcase for the more beat-heavy experimental end of funk and rare groove. Because he, like many DJs, also worked at a record shop – Swag Records in Croydon – he had access to the latest imports from New York and Chicago.

In 1986 Dale switched his Abstract Dance show entirely to playing house, despite some resistance from the rare groove faithful. House at this point was fracturing the dance audience. Dale recalls that around this time he was booked to play a night at Munkbery's in Jermyn Street with 'soulful' house DJs Bobbi & Steve and Paul 'Trouble' Anderson. The night was billed as a 'boogie' night, a London term for electronic post-disco music (which was known as 'electro-funk' in the north of England – see Wilson 2013) with electronic beats but which stayed closer to the polyrhythms and soulfulness of funk rather than the technological four-four pulse of house. 'They sacked me after a week', he recalls; they said his music was 'too hard, too experimental. Two years later they were championing the same music they had sacked me for playing' (Colin Dale interview). Faver and Dale at Kiss FM and Jazzy M at LWR proved critical in circulating the nascent sounds of house through the London airwaves, even as rare groove dominated in the clubs, laying the ground for the subsequent explosion of acid house.

By 1986, Chicago, under the influence of DJs like Frankie Knuckles and Ron Hardy, had begun producing increasingly mesmeric house records that were starting to be integrated into London club playlists. The compilation *The House Sound of Chicago Volume 1*, featuring releases from the Chicago label DJ International, was released in the UK on London Records. This project was overseen by the DJ Pete Tong. 'Love Can't Turn Around' by Farley 'Jackmaster' Funk, released in 1986,

featuring the histrionic gospel vocals of Darryl Pandy, and Steve 'Silk'
Hurley's 'Jack Your Body', from the following year, were widely played
in clubs across the capital, by jazz funk and rare groove DJs like Norman
Jay and Paul 'Trouble' Anderson as well as by Faver at his residency at the
Camden Palace and he Pyramid. 'Love Can't Turn Around'[29] reached
number 10 in the national chart in August 1986; Farley Jackmaster Funk
and Pandy appeared on *Top of the Pops* and did a promotional tour
of London club nights, where the flamboyant Pandy performed for
crowds at the Limelight on Shaftesbury Avenue, the gay club the Jungle
at Busbys and at Soul II Soul's Sunday night at the Africa Centre. This is
not as unlikely as it might sound. Though Soul II Soul were associated
with rare groove, heavy funk and electro with a reggae bounce, they
were also open to the new sounds: Soul II Soul affiliates like DJs Jazzy
Q and Lawrence 'Kid' Batchelor were early house adopters. The idea
of an unbreachable border between the too-cool retro black sounds of
rare groove and the exciting new electronic music of acid house is an
artefact of rave ideology. Also on the Jackmaster Funk tour was the
producer Joe Smooth, who, on his return to Chicago in late 1986, wrote
'Promised Land', a Motown-influenced gospel-house track inspired
by his visit to London, whose soulful vocals promised 'brothers and
sisters' of all races that 'one day we will be free'. The following year the
song became the quintessential acid house anthem at Shoom.

House music was arriving through the import record market, being
disseminated via pirate radio and gestating in the clubs, often juxtaposed with other forms of contemporary black music. A key site of
this was the Delirium night at the Astoria on Tottenham Court Road,
promoted by Robin King and Nick Trulove, which started in September 1986, with the Watson brothers, Noel and Maurice, as resident DJs.
As it was a theatre, the Astoria was licensed to stay open to 6 a.m., far
later than most venues (Bainbridge 2013: 35). At Delirium, the Watsons
folded house music into a wider mix of African-American dance music,
including funk, electro and hip hop. Prominent hip hop acts of the time
like the Beastie Boys and Run DMC visited the club when they were in
town. While Noel would play breaks and hip hop, Maurice, who had

recently returned from New York and was determined to recreate something of the Paradise Garage vibe, would play disco and proto-house, often much to the displeasure of the hip hop crowd. Soon the promoters had to install a cage to protect the DJ booth from flying bottles when Maurice played house. But despite the hostility, frequently expressed in homophobic terms – 'Guys would come up to us and say "Don't play that gay music or we'll come and beat you up"' (Noel Watson cited in Bainbridge 2013: 36) – they stuck to their guns, and in the summer of 1987 invited Frankie Knuckles over to do a residency when the Music Box closed in Chicago. Though few beyond the cognoscenti knew who Knuckles was, many who saw him play began to understand the specific appeal of his brand of spiritual, uplifting house.[30]

Hedonism, RIP and Brixton acid

Delirium was in some ways a continuation of the West End club scene, dating back to the late 1970s punk and the glam gay-friendly Blitz scenes, pulling in a trendy mixed crowd partly through exposure in the style press (Dan Benedict interview, 12 August 1998). But there were other significant, less well-publicised routes of house. Black soul sound systems, which had been so important in establishing soul and rare groove among the multicultural audience in London, were also instrumental in incorporating house music into the circuits of black London subculture. North London's Mastermind Roadshow – a collective of Herbie Laidley, Dave VJ and Max LX, who had originated a unique six-deck mixing style – began to incorporate house music into their electro and hip hop sets around 1986, and while some of the audience at this point were ambivalent about the newer, faster sounds, Mastermind made sense of the new form for its black crowds by mixing it with more familiar electro and hip hop. Similarly, the London-based Shock sound system, run by brothers Stan and Dean Zepherin, with their friends Cecil Peters, Paul Denton and Ashley Beadle, which formed as a reggae/soul sound in 1983, was open to the new music. Shock travelled frequently to play in Nottingham, Derby and Birmingham, where black crowds who were not under the spell of rare groove welcomed house music as an extension of electrofunk (Wilson 2003). In 1987 Shock returned to playing primarily in London, where they started mixing house and acid house into their bass-heavy hip hop and electro sets (Stan Shock interview, in Melville 1995: 20).

In February 1988, away from the Ibiza-reunions, came a key moment in the transition from rare groove to house. At a series of 'Hedonism' parties in a print works in Alperton Lane, in unprepossessing Brent, west London, run by Simon Gordon with his brother Alun and a group of friends, inspired by a visit to New York where they had visited both the Paradise Garage and the intense gay club Tracks, the balance shifted towards house music. Simon Gordon, who derided rare groove as 'stale and backward looking' (Cheeseman 2016), had visited Shoom and been turned on to the acid formula. He booked John Dean's heavyweight sound system and DJs who were pioneering house – Colin Faver, Kid Batchelor and Justin Berkman (who opened the Ministry of Sound in 1991). Hedonism had two rooms, one for funk and rare groove, and the other a larger space, for house, with the heavyweight John Dean sound system, symbolising the shift in status for this previously reviled music. The parties also featured a live jam session, where members of the north London band Push played, and when Colin Faver DJed he played alongside musicians – including trumpeter Gordon Barrowman and rapper Mr C – who together formed an early prototype of the Shamen (an indie-dance band Mr C would shortly join), anticipating the fusion of house and jazz that would come with acid jazz a few years later.

Another innovation was the wide availability of ecstasy. The four Hedonism parties, between February and May 1988, brought together a wide range of London clubbers, including many of the rare groove and soul DJs like Roy the Roach (Roy Marsh), Martin Madhatter (Martin Wilson) and Soul II Soul (whose sound system was used for one of the parties) and much of the Warehouse crowd. Roy the Roach, a renowned funk DJ and proprietor of the specialist Quaff Records shop (see figure 3.3), recalls being surprised that rare groove had the small room at Hedonism: 'Why wasn't the music of the day in the main room? And

Figure 3.3 Counter at Quaff Records, Soho, 1988/9, capturing the moment when rare groove was giving way to house, with store owner and DJ Roy the Roach (left). Courtesy Roy Marsh

what was all the smoke about?' But his objections waned, as he saw the energy of the ecstasy-fuelled crowd orchestrated by Kid Batchelor: 'I couldn't wait to finish my set so I could get into that main room and get down with the happy people' (Roach cited in Cheeseman 2016).

The last Hedonism party was in May 1988. That same month, north Londoners Paul Stone and Lu Vukovic, avid followers of Jazzy M's LWR show, opened RIP (Revolution in Progress) – the party described at the start of this chapter –initially at a venue in Eversholt Street in Camden, but moving to a former prison in Clink Street by the Thames in Bankside in June that year. Though this area is now a well lit and gentrified tourist area, a short walk from Shakespeare's Globe and the Tate Modern, at the time it was 'a desolate dystopia' (Brewster 2016). RIP fused the sonic aesthetics of the sound system and the mixed crowd of the warehouse parties with the new model of acid house, presenting house in the context of bass culture. Deliberating eschewing the luvved-up fluffiness of the Balearic clubs and the members-only elitism of Shoom,[31] RIP attracted 'a real cross-section of different sorts of people, colours and classes' and a much more racially diverse crowd than the Balearic clubs (Mr C cited in Bainbridge 2013). The promoters signed up the most progressive of London's new house DJs – Faver, Eddie Richards, Kid Batchelor, Mr C, alongside the Shock sound system with DJ Ashley Beadle. The music at RIP was hard, uncompromising and relentless, focusing heavily on the output of the Chicago black avant garde. RIP provided a bridge between the uptown gay club scenes where Faver and Richards had been defining a new house sound for London and the sound system-derived sonic experiments in London's black music communities away from the centre, in places like Hackney and Brixton.

Among the crowds at the earliest RIPs were the DJs from the Phase One pirate radio in Brixton – Colin Dale, Fabio,[32] Dave Angel, Nigel 'Jumping Jack Frost' Thompson and Bryan Gee. They had all started out in reggae sound systems and moved though the soul and jazz funk scenes at Crackers and the Electric Ballroom, the warehouse parties and Soul II Soul at the Africa Centre and Oakenfold's Balearic nights at Ziggys. All of them had built their names as soul, funk and rare groove DJs on Brixton pirates and at local clubs like Mendozas, the 414 club on Coldharbour Lane and Carwash on Clapham Road and on sound systems like Kleer (also run by Bryan Gee and Frost). Frost, an avid 'shuffler' at roots reggae sound system Jah Shaka in the early 1980s, had been inspired by the open-minded mix of Soul II Soul, describing himself as a 'graduate of the Africa Centre' (Jumping Jack Frost interview, 27 March 2017). Did these bass culture veterans view acid as a break with or a continuation of the practices of the black dance? It varied. Though Frost could see evident continuity between the warehouse parties and sound systems, what he saw at RIP 'was a different thing altogether. I was taken in by the unity and the love between people, because obviously the people were on ecstasy, d'ya know what I mean?' He welcomed the break with what came before and acid's sonics, which took it away from the rootsy reggae–funk lineage. But for Colin Dale, the sonic connections between disco and soul and even the most avant acid were still evident: 'I could hear the blackness in it straight away, I could hear it. What it was for me, it was really stripped down [but] if you played it on a good system, and I won't deny that drugs had a big part to play in what was happening, it was magical' (Colin Dale interview, 30 July 2017). For all of them 'it was a turning point' (Bryan Gee interview, 2 March 1999).

The DJs returned to their Brixton scene and set about introducing acid and house to their Brixton funk and reggae audience: 'We all changed', says Bryan Gee. 'We started buying the music and introducing it onto our radio show, then all of a sudden our whole radio show was like that and we started getting stick for it.' Frost recalls similar antagonism: 'The Brixton crowd said we were playing "Devil music"'. For Bryan, the issue was access to acid clubs; this was not something that could be fully appreciated just by hearing the music – it needed to be experienced:

> If someone had just played the music to me I probably would have said 'take that fucking shit out of my face, that's just noise'; that's how people perceived it in Brixton. Don't forget that you've got to go to this kind of thing, to feel it, you can't just hear it on the radio and say 'yeah I'm into this thing'. It was the whole vibe, the lights, the people, everything that made it happen ... people just thought we were on drugs in Brixton. (Bryan Gee interview)

But Bryan, Fabio, Frost, Dale, Grooverider and Dave Angel were hooked on acid and to 'raving' as much as possible, both in the West End (see plate 6) and at the orbital raves beyond the city. They established a small acid house scene in Brixton itself, despite the reservations of their soul and reggae crowd. They instigated a series of nights that presented rave in the context of black club culture. Carwash, which had been a rare groove club, started playing acid house around the same time as Shoom and Spectrum were taking off, and these cultural producers exploited the relative tolerance of late-night music in Brixton, hard-won by the reggae sound systems, to establish an after-hours Brixton scene for those ravers who wanted to continue the party when those uptown clubs shut.

'Because Brixton had these lax laws', recalls Colin Dale, 'the after-hours clubs boomed. We took over a house on Brixton Hill, a squat; we would open at four. You knew if you went down to Brixton there would be something happening.' Brixton could be dangerous at night but the DJs and promoters knew how to manage it:

> It's Brixton, so you're going to get people coming down trying to take advantage. But it was our manor so we could look after our own. It took the Brixton crowd a little bit of time, especially people on the reggae scene, but soon they were coming up to me begging for the tunes. (Colin Dale interview)

Such pockets of black rave culture sprang up across London. In east London the reggae soul sound system Shut Up and Dance (SUAD) run by Phillip Johnson (PJ) and Carl Hymen (Smiley), who had been remixing American hip hop in an east London reggae context for years, scored an unintentional rave hit with their 1989 satire of rave's musical simplicity '5678'. Sonically the music fit well into rave culture, yet SUAD were critical outsiders making ironic commentaries on the supposed collectivism, unscrupulous promoters and the gullibility of the drug-addled audience with their subsequent releases '£10 To Get In' (and the remix '£20 To Get In') from 1991 and '(Raving) I'm Raving' in 1992. Though ravers, unaware of or untroubled by the irony, embraced the tunes enthusiastically, Smiley remained sceptical of the claims made for rave togetherness:

> People always argue that raves have successfully united blacks and whites, but in reality that argument's bollocks. Everyone at raves is on a fucking E [ecstasy]. If you took the drugs out of the raves and everyone was just on spliff and drink, you know what would happen? There'd be fights. In fact if you take E's out of the rave scene it wouldn't even exist in the first place. (Interviewed in *i-D* magazine, July 1992, cited in Collin 1997: 243)

Other sound systems, like the inter-racial Top Buzz crew[33] from Tottenham, formed in 1988, took a similarly irreverent attitude to raves, refusing to accept their claims to novelty, yet enjoying the 'mental' part of raving and featuring the reggae-inspired toasting of Mad P over the acid rhythms: 'I never saw it as that different from reggae or hip hop', says DJ Mikee B (Michael Bennett). 'We just mixed everything up together' (cited in Melville 1998).

By 1989, the Brixton DJs were established as the most in-demand DJs for the big out-of-London raves like Sunrise and Biology. Fabio was able to quit his job as an insurance agent, Grooverider his day job as an accounts clerk and Colin Dale gratefully left his job in a bank. In an ironic twist, opportunities arose because the Balearic DJs and their hip associates, like the mod-inspired Boy's Own collective, were increasingly scornful of the proletarianisation and commercialism of the orbital rave scene, which was sucking in suburban audiences. Boy's Own coined the motto 'better dead than acid ted' to distinguish the 'original' elite model of rave from the lumpen ravers flocking to orbitals (Thornton 1995; Reynolds 1999), and often refused offers to play at the big raves out of London.[34] This left the way open for veteran black DJs like Paul 'Trouble' Anderson, Carl Cox and the Brixton acid mob to step into the breach. By 1989, Fabio and Grooverider were 'rave heroes' (Collin 1997), appearing at bigger and bigger raves as they spread from London across the south-east and north as far as Scotland.

As out-of-town raves grew, London clubs were also transforming. In 1989, Fabio and Grooverider were booked by promoter Kevin Millins to play the upstairs bar at Heaven, for a new night called Rage. Downstairs, Colin Faver, Trevor Fung and a range of US guests like Frankie Knuckles and Jeff Mills played four-to-the-floor house and techno, while upstairs Fabio and Grooverider experimented by manipulating rhythm, playing dub versions and using mixing and sonic trickery to emphasise the breakbeats hidden within the synchronised four-square house rhythms. By pitching techno tracks up or down and playing the beat loops on B-sides they roughed up the smooth surface of house so beloved of the hippie aesthetes of rave, and instead accentuated the rough, raw, energy of acid, which structurally linked it to the lineage of Afro-futurism, psychedelic jazz, P-funk and hip hop (Eshun 1998). When hip-house arrived around 1989, a short-lived mash-up of house and hip hop from Chicago by acts like Doug lazy, Tyree and Fast Eddie Smith, they incorporated its breakbeats into their sets, mixing them into the house, deforming the 'straight time' of house's four-four in much the same way as drummer Earl Palmer had signified on military rhythm in the New Orleans development of funk. The sonic manipulations of the Rage DJs brought the syncopations of funk and jazz drumming back onto the rave dancefloor (Fintoni 2015). Fabio recalls that this experimentation did not always go well – 'Don't get me wrong, the proper house purists weren't happy about it', he told Gilles Peterson in a radio interview – but promoter Millins backed them. Downstairs at Rage, Faver and Fung had been heading in the opposite direction, towards a 'purer', rhythmically even, techno sound, a stark contrast to the unruly beats upstairs. One night, Faver was unwell so Fabio and Grooverider took the main room; they never let it go. Rage was where new fusions of house, techno, hip hop and funk emerged, and a new form of music, initially called hardcore and then jungle, was gestated (see the next chapter).

Conclusion

Invited in 2017 by the Radio London DJ and journalist Robert Elms to reflect on acid house, Norman Jay, whose rare groove scene was rudely elbowed aside by the arrival of acid and who you might imagine had every reason to despise it, was generous in his praise:

> I absolutely loved it. It was a punk ethic, it was chaos, it was free. We were living in oppressive times under a Thatcher government. It united all the kids. Driving round the M25, you didn't have to like the music to recognise that it was special. Our [warehouse] parties were essentially artistic, creative, stylish, very in-house London. The London snobbery, 'your name's not down you're not coming in' … the rave thing was a reaction against that…. For a short while there was a clubbing utopia, black, white, Asian, straight, gay, upper class, working class. That had never happened before. (Norman Jay interviewed by Robert Elms on Radio London, 7 August 2017)

Acid house certainly disrupted London club culture, opening space for younger promoters and space on the dancefloor for generations of white youth who had never ventured there before. For black Londoners, acid represented a challenge to the supremacy of reggae, soul and funk and was greeted by some as an alien invader – too fast, too white, too gay. Yet through the work of promoters and DJs black and white, acid house took root in the city, and for ravers of all races, genders and classes, raves and acid clubs offered the possibility of new forms of sociality not based on restrictive notions of belonging – race, gender, class, sexuality or any other. There was huge promise in the rave moment for every young person who encountered it. All of my informants were affected by it to some degree.

'Rave' was the first dance music subculture in the city that was not predicated on models of black culture, either from America or from the Caribbean. Acid house's faceless post-human technology and transcendence-through-drugs aesthetics replaced the embodied black voice of soul, the 'dread' aesthetics of reggae and the Africanised drum breaks and black power symbolism of rare groove, facilitating its recuperation as an essentially British, and therefore essentially white, phenomenon. Ironically, this was achieved partly through the way rave capitalised on the Afro-futurist work of black cultural producers in Chicago and Detroit, who were exploring the possibilities of transcending racialised space and the restrictions of racialised identity through technology.

Rave certainly succeeded in getting a large number of a generation of white men to ditch their heteronormative aversion to dancing, in an atmosphere 'where everyone was kissy-kissy' (Reynolds 1999: 44), but we should be sceptical of the claims for the universality or the long-term effects of this. The social disinhibiting effects of ecstasy may indeed have been 'a miracle cure for the English disease of emotional constipation, reserve and inhibition' (Barry Ashworth cited in Reynolds 1999: 47) but the claim that this is universal can be made only if we ignore those communities who were immune from this disease (and excluded from the category of Englishness), for whom music and dance already 'nurtured forms of self-consciousness, historicity and sociality [and] orchestrated the relationship between the individual and the group' (Gilroy 1997: 22).

For journalist Simon Reynolds, raving was about 'losing it, losing your cool, losing your self-consciousness' (1999: 39) in the rush of drug-induced euphoria. But for those black Londoners for whom dance had always been at the centre of their cultural lives, ecstasy-trance dance, through many gave it a go, was just one among many ways in which to lose yourself, and find yourself, in music. Reynolds' claim that rave was totally different to previous dance cultures in the UK because 'this was totally sweaty, abandoned, Dionysius dancing'[35] reveals a historical blindness to the kinds of intense dancing, without ecstasy, that characterised the dancefloors at Jah Shaka, Crackers, the Electric Ballroom or the warehouse parties.

The way rave has been celebrated has been partly a function of the fact that, for many, rave was the first dance culture they were part of, one that fulfilled their desire for a rapprochement between black music, punk and the electronic avant garde.[36] In moving away from the conventional symbolism of black music, house offered white ravers the prospect of laying claim to a dance music that was not obviously the ethnic property of the black community. For those, like Reynolds, with a well documented antipathy to 'soul humanism' and the 'naff' sounds of jazz funk and Brit-soul (Banerjea and Banerjea 1996: 122–3) acid offered an escape from the human into 'pure intensity' which seemed to leave the political complexities of black music and racial politics behind.

But rave's utopian moment was short. By the end of the 1980s, with huge profits on offer from the staging of illegal raves and supplying the drugs, competition between promoters became fierce and criminal gangs – some associated with the football crews who had got luvved up at Spectrum and Shoom – infiltrated rave promotion (taking over Colston-Hayter's Sunrise operation, for example). The popularity of raves stimulated the production of new forms of 'rave' music, initially from the UK, and then from other northern European countries, including Germany, the Netherlands and most significantly Belgium, where the R&S label was based, which distilled the parameters of rave music down to the base elements of abrasive, punishing machine rhythms (dubbed 'Belgian hardbeat'), and progressively severed the links to

Afro-diasporic musical forms like disco and soul which underpinned American house (Reynolds 1999: 56).

At the same time, the newly expanded market for ecstasy drew competitors into the business, who increasingly cut what had been relatively pure ecstasy in the early days with all kinds of additives. As the music got harder and faster, the drugs got speedier and the atmosphere more intense and threatening (Collin 1997: 270). By the early 1990s, getting 'on one', which had been a new experience for many of the 1987–9 ravers, had become, for some, an almost a daily ritual (there were raves and rave clubs every night somewhere). For some, one pill was no longer enough, with predictable consequences. Rip-offs, drug deals gone bad and fakes proliferated: at the giant Fantazia rave at Castle Donnington near Leicester in 1992, attended by 25,000, police seized hundreds of 'ecstasy' tablets, 97 per cent of which turned out to be hay fever capsules, vitamins or paracetamol (Collin 1997: 273). Infamous 'snowballs' appeared on the scene in 1992, delivering a huge dose of MDA, which rendered many dancers unable to dance or move, and instead collapsed in heaps in corners (Collin 1997: 275).

The scepticism of those like SUAD's Smiley who doubted rave's claim to cross-racial togetherness seemed to be confirmed by the return of restrictive door policies.[37] Despite the rhetoric that raves were characterised by trans-racial, cross-class unity, some black clubbers, like the Bristol DJ Roni Size, maintained that they were not welcoming to a black audience (see Melville 1997). For all the initial promise of new forms of 'mind/body/technology assemblage' (Pini 1997: 124), its new sounds and new freedoms, rave failed to deliver its audience to the promised land. What had felt to participants as adventurous started to look like a new form of conformism, a retreat from rather than an extension of cultural self-determination: 'You paid your twenty quid to get in, your twenty quid for a pill, and there you were', says Femi Williams, 'with everyone else, feeling the same thing, doing the same thing, making someone else rich' (Femi Fem interview, 8 July 1999).

The argument in this chapter has been that house entered London via multiple routes, and through the cultural work of a wide range of producers, club and radio DJs, and sound systems operators, all well versed in the music and dance traditions of the black public sphere, something that is obscured by the Ibiza myth. Though acid house and the rave scenes it spawned introduced new sonic and psychoactive practices into London dance culture, there were nonetheless significant continuities with the dance cultures around reggae, soul, jazz funk and disco, and many black Londoners perceived rave as merely part of the continual evolution of black dance genres, rather than a fundamental break. What might have looked entirely novel for those with no experience of the reggae dance or the rare groove warehouse party was received by many black clubbers as a logical progression, 'the obvious next step' (DJ Dodge interview, 4 August 1998). Ecstasy certainly added something new to the mix – and briefly enabled a lessening of tension among groups like the football firms who turned up at Shoom, Spectrum and the Trip, temporarily suspending their turf wars and the rigid boundaries of male heteronormativity under the influence of the socially disinhibiting effects of ecstasy.

Rave encapsulated a complex politics that allowed both appropriation of black gay music in an entirely new context by white working-class Brits involved in thinking through their own relation to nation, others and themselves (analogous to mod and soul, both northern and southern) and the work of black Londoners loosening ties to the strong cultural affiliations of diaspora – reggae, or those offered through hip hop – a 'fluxing up' (Reynolds 2009) of culture orchestrated by a new drug technology which lowered social inhibitions and provided, temporarily, sources of affiliation across boundaries of race, class and gender. Just like all drug highs, though, there was a steep come-down, which opened up new sonic possibilities, and these are explored in the next chapter.

Notes

1 The relationship between acid house and rave is tricky to pin down. In this book I use 'acid house' to describe the music (initially from Chicago, on labels like Trax and DJ International), defined primarily by the 'wobbly'

basslines of the TR-303 bass synth, but also the club scene of 1987–89, where what became known as 'acieed' was incubated. I use the word 'rave' to define the large, often outdoor, parties which took inspiration from the early acid house clubs in the city, and also for the music which was being made, increasingly by European producers taking inspiration from Chicago and Detroit, but giving it a distinctly British twist. As it spread, and the early days of acid house subsided, the 'rave scene' came to define the wider phenomena, especially as it spread. Acid house itself can be regarded as a small subset of house music.

2 This is the title of a Channel 4 documentary on rave by Derek Jones and Craig McDougall, first screened in 1994.

3 Byrd is credited with discovering James Brown, and Brown joined Byrd's band the Flames in 1955 (the Flames became 'the Famous Flames' that same year, and Brown emerged as its presiding genius). Byrd served as Brown's musical director and co-wrote many of Brown's hits, including 'Get Up (I Feel Like Being A) Sex Machine' (though it was credited only to Brown). He co-formed the label People Records with Brown in 1970. He finally quit the James Brown band for good in 1973 following disputes over songwriting credits and pay.

4 A poor-quality recording of the concert was released as a live album, under the name Bobby Byrd and the J. B. Allstars, by the German label Rhythm Attack Productions, in 1988.

5 See the *Independent*, 22 February 1998. Within a few years Carleen was joined in London by her cousins Jhelisa and Pamela, both of whom recorded and released records with London-based bands and producers: Pamela as vocalist for the band D*Note and Jhelisa releasing a series of solo albums for the Dorado label.

6 Proctor was an early pioneer of electronic and alternative dance music, who began DJing at a 'Roxy/Bowie' night in Liverpool and promoted gigs by the emergent New Romantic bands like Spandau Ballet, Ultravox and Blue Rondo à la Turk. Following his stint at Polydor, he was one of the early adopters of the Balearic sound, and DJed at many of the early acid clubs and raves. like Shoom and Sunrise.

7 'Jouissance was to be understood as access to a dimension of experience which is outside of or unconditioned by ordinary patterns of gendered behaviour' (Gilbert 2006: 186).

8 *The Agony and the Ecstasy: The History of Rave*, first broadcast in the UK on 13 August 2017, narrated by Norman Jay himself.

9 According to *The Economist* (27 July 2000), of the two million visitors to the island in 2000, some 711,000 were British, attracted by the burgeoning twenty-four-hour club culture that was kick-started by acid house and its Ibiza mythology.

10 This is a point made by DJ and dance historian Greg Wilson: 'with the Ibiza

From Ibiza to London: Brixton acid and rave

story overriding everything that had gone before, I couldn't help but regard it as a whitewashing of black culture in this country…. My hope was that someone would come along to set the record straight – but it didn't happen. Article after article, then book after book began to appear, but there was always this great glaring omission with regards to how things had originally flourished via the black scene. Although it often felt as though the sinister undertones of cultural racism were at play, I came to realise that the writers simply weren't aware of what had happened because they were never a part of the black scene – most had only got into dance music with the advent of Acid House and Ecstasy, so had no personal knowledge of the black clubs that had led the way. Instead of making the proper connection to what had gone before, they generally took the easy, more romantic option, making Ibiza '87 their starting point, and thus creating a mythology that persists to this day' (Wilson 2013).

11 The jazz dance DJ Gilles Peterson was also on the trip but did not participate in the drug taking so missed out on the acid house revelation.

12 Hardy, who was given the track by DJ Pierre of Phuture, reportedly played the track four times in one night. The first time it cleared the floor, but by the fourth the crowd were going crazy.

13 Carl Thomas, aka MC Flux, who became an ecstasy dealer in the late 1980s, collaborating with the Crystal Palace football 'firm' he was part of, explained how he got into it to Nick Chester: 'Some people who attended the raves would see five black geezers and think these lot look the type to get pills from'. Thomas started directing buyers to a dealer he knew, and eventually began dealing himself (Chester 2016).

14 Manchester had for at least a year been developing an acid house scene of its own through the work of DJs Mike Pickering and, later, Graeme Park, at The Hacienda. See Bainbridge, 2013 for the debate between the Manchester DJs and the 'cockney's' over who first originated acid house.

15 The etymology of the word 'rave' draws an interesting and appropriate connection between ancient signs of madness ('raving mad'), early-twentieth-century notions of fad, and 1950s and 1960s ideas about wild parties (examples of such usage include 'Rave On' recorded by Buddy Holly in 1958 and *Rave Magazine* from 1964). Popular with the mod subcultures, the term fell into disuse, though it survived as a common term within Jamaican music cultures (Bob Marley released a song called 'Midnight Ravers' in 1973) until it was revived in the late 1980s.

16 Tony Colston-Hayter, an ambitious blagger entrepreneur and sometime professional gambler from Staines, started out promoting the Gatecrasher Balls, which were raucous parties for rich kids, and went on to promote Sunrise events, some of the biggest raves in the UK, earning him the nickname 'Tony Cost-Inflator' for the high ticket prices he charged (Mr C cited in Bainbridge 2013).

185

17 Staines was a libertarian conservative activist brought in by Colston-Hayter to do PR for Sunrise. Following the decline of rave, Staines returned to his previous role as a right-wing political activist, becoming infamous as the scurrilous right-wing blogger Guido Fawkes.
18 'The moral panic appears to us to be one of the principal forms of ideological consciousness by means of which a "silent majority" is won over to the support of increasingly coercive measures on the part of the state' (Hall et al. 1978).
19 This dossier (available at https://discovery.nationalarchives.gov.uk/details/r/C16328940), titled 'Acid House Parties: Home Affairs, Sept 1989', contains a fascinating range of internal government communications discussing, in sometimes hysterical and largely mystified terms, what to do about acid house – including contributions from senior ministers Malcolm Rifkind, Geoffrey Howe and Virginia Bottomley, as well as Margaret Thatcher herself.
20 A letter from Andrew Turnbull MP concerning Coke's original letter carries a scribbled note from Margaret Thatcher herself: 'Yes, if this is a new "fashion" we must be prepared for it and preferably prevent such things from happening. MT.'
21 Though the issue of race is glanced at in work by Hildegonda Rietveld and Tim Lawrence, it is a notable absence from the otherwise comprehensive discussion of dance music theory *Discographies* (Gilbert and Pearson 1999), something which one of the authors, Jeremy Gilbert, acknowledged ten years after publication: 'The one great absence from the book in my view is any serious discussion of the politics of "race"' (Gilbert 2007: 7).
22 Gates goes on to state that of course this is not to say 'that the ideologues of black nationalism in the United States have any unique claim on homophobia' (Gates 1993: 233).
23 Tim Lawrence's research reveals the predominance of Italian-Americans in the first phase of New York disco culture (from the late 1960s to the late 1970s), a fact he puts down, in part, to the influence of the Mafia over New York nightlife (Lawrence 2003, 2016), as well as generally pervasive racism. Gradually, space opened up for Hispanic DJs, like David Morales, Armando Galvez and David Rodrigues, and subsequently the black DJs Levan, Humphries and Knuckles, who emerged as the leaders in the early 1980s (Lawrence 2003).
24 House producer Jesse Saunders described the 'Disco Demolition' in these terms: 'It was a bold statement to basically say "We don't like blacks, the gay community, or anybody who sympathises with them and their music"' (Saunders cited in Needham 2017).
25 Donny Hathaway, 'The Ghetto' and 'Little Ghetto Boy' (1970/2, Atlantic); Marlena Shaw, 'Woman of the Ghetto' (1969, Bluenote); Philadelphia International All Stars, 'Let's Clean up the Ghetto' (1977, Philadelphia International Records).

26 Cut Master DC, 'Brooklyn's in the House' (1985, Zakia Records); J.V.C. F.O.R.C.E., 'Strong Island' (1988, Be Boy Records); Man Parrish, 'Boogie Down Bronx' (1985, Sugarscope Records).

27 According to a comment posted on the YouTube page of the Housemaster Boyz track 'House Nation' (1993, Trax Records), the term 'house nation' should be read as a specific rejection of local Chicago gang affiliation. The dominant street gangs of the time were called the Folks Nation and the People's Nation. Expressing affiliation to the house nation was a way of indicating that you weren't affiliated with either gang, that you weren't a gangbanger. Comment by Jasin Carpio, 2015, at https://www.youtube.com/watch?v=MKxX-yWEpv8 (accessed 1 July 2019).

28 'I started twisting the knobs, seeing what they do, because that's what I do: twist knobs. So I was doing that and we fell in love with the sounds it was making. We fell in love with how I was twisting the knobs with the beat. And then I started twisting them a certain way, and putting emotion and feeling behind it and Spanky was like, 'Yo Pierre, keep doing that, I like that.' I was like, 'Yeah, this is something!' (DJ Pierre interviewed by Ruth Saxelby for *Fader* magazine, autumn 2017).

29 A reworking of Isaac Hayes' 1975 disco track 'I Can't Turn Around'.

30 Knuckles often spoke about his practice in religious terms, describing himself as 'priest' of the dancefloor and the Warehouse as a 'church'. Partly this was because many of his black gay audience, estranged from the black churches in which they grew up because of their sexuality, were seeking alternative forms of spiritual transcendence on the dancefloor (see Petrides 2014).

31 Boy George, Patsy Kensit and members of Frankie Goes To Hollywood, ABC, and journalists Robert Elms and Gary Crowley all attended Shoom (Collin 1997: 66, 73).

32 Though many people have assumed that Fabio is Italian, Fitzroy Heslop in fact chose his DJ pseudonym almost at random, when, just before his first pirate radio set, someone told him Fitzroy wasn't a cool enough name. See Fabio interview with Gilles Peterson, 30 May 2017, at https://www.mixcloud.com/worldwidefm/gilles-peterson-with-fabio-30-05-17 (accessed 1 July 2019).

33 Top Buzz consisted of the black DJ Mikee B (Michael Bennett), MC Mad P (Patrick McPhee) and DJ Jason Kaye, of Greek-Cypriot descent, who often referred to themselves as 'Two Blacks and a Bubble' (bubble, derived from the Cockney slang term 'bubble and squeak' – Greek).

34 Promoter Nicky Holloway recalls that the Boy's Own DJs Terry Farley and Andrew Weatherall refused a request to play at a rave because Fabio and Grooverider's names were on the flyer (Holloway cited in Bainbridge 2013: 158).

35 See 'Fraternization Machine: Simon Reynolds on U.K. Dance History', 28 June 2016, at https://www.afropop.org/articles/first-draft-simon-reynolds-interview (accessed 1 July 2019).

36 'Acid house, you know, comes from black Americans. It comes from guys in Chicago taking a piece of music technology and using it in ways that the manufacturers didn't intend. And initially when you hear it, you don't necessarily think of black music. When I first heard it in the late '80s, it reminded me of things from Germany, groups like D.A.F., these sort of hard, electronic, almost industrial dance records. In a way what was so exciting about it was just this sort of alien lack of reference to previous music. It didn't remind you of anything, these strange bass patterns. It was just futuristic and alien. You could imagine that it was the sound of the emotions that might be felt by black holes or asteroids or something like that.' Simon Reynolds in 'Fraternization Machine' (see note 35).

37 Kenny Ken in Jo Wiser's 1994 film *A London Some'ting Dis* (Sharper Image Productions), first broadcast on Channel 4 on 4 June 1993.

Chapter 4

'A London Sum'ting Dis':[1] diaspora remixed in the urban jungle

June 1997. Sunday. Metalheadz at the Blue Note, Hoxton Square

The club is just one room, a low-ceiling rectangular box, decks at one end, the same level as the dancefloor, and the big Eskimo sound system dominating. It's like being inside a bass bin. I've been to this club before; it used to be the Bass Clef jazz club, where Norman Jay had his Musiquarium night, but it's changed now – dark-blue walls, stripped down, dank. You can smell the Caribbean food they serve upstairs. It's packed and the walls are sweating – someone has rigged up a makeshift sleeve over the pipe right above the turntables to stop condensation dripping on the records as they play.

Style is urban combat – sportswear, camo jackets, funki dreads and chains. There's a man with a mic, not chatting but singing, snatches of jazz, soul, and making comments, almost like a sermon. But it's the music which holds the crowd, suspending them between passages of serenity and drops of the biggest deepest bass, shuddering through our collective body. New Orleans break-beats, sped up to impossible tempos, horn stabs, vocal samples – a montage of B-movies, 'bad bwoy' styling, diva vocals – everything from jazz to rave, lovers rock to techno is folded into the music and subordinated to the bass, which is delayed, suspended teasingly, then, when it drops, the crowd jump up as one. It sounds totally familiar and totally new, simultaneously, like music made just yesterday or a hundred years in the future.

The early 1990s saw an unprecedented explosion in dance music production in the UK. Raves across the country had enculturated new generations of white British youth in the practices of all-night dancing to loudly amplified bass-heavy music and white youth taste was undergoing a major shift away from indie rock, pop and post-punk towards dance music. For this audience, rave recoded dance music, stripping it of its associations with disco, thought to be trivial, feminine and conformist by the rock audience (Dyer 1979), and replacing it with connotations of pharmacological rebellion, nocturnal adventure and utopian promise. This rock–dance rapprochement crystallised in the 'Madchester' moment at the end of the 1980s with the emergence of a hybrid club culture in Manchester around the Hacienda club, owned by Factory Records impresario Tony Wilson, where the guitar rock and house that had circled each other warily through the mid-1980s necked a pill and fused in a sweaty embrace. Long-serving indie bands like Primal Scream and the Shamen from Scotland, and Manchester's own Happy Mondays and the Stone Roses,[2] who had been turned on to acid house and ecstasy by Hacienda DJs Mike Pickering, Dave Haslam, Graeme Park, Colin Curtis and John Da Silva, began integrating electronic effects, house-y rhythms and raving references into their music and were scoring chart hits and front pages in the indie press by the end of the 1980s.

In March 1990 there were violent disturbances on the streets of London. These were not the racialised uprisings of previous years but protests against the poll tax (community charge) introduced by Margaret Thatcher's Conservative government in 1989. A crowd of 200,000 protesters marched on Westminster and were met by poorly prepared police, who sought to contain them and panicked in the face of the enraged crowd, sparking what became known as 'the battle of Trafalgar Square'.[3] What resulted was the worst violence seen in central London for a century, with 113 injuries and 340 arrests. Rave music – primarily techno – served as the musical accompaniment to the march, blasted from speakers mounted on the back of lorries. The march, which was peaceful for most of the day, with drummers, jugglers and children in the crowd, had the unmistakable feel of a rave (and served as a precursor to the 'Teknival' free rave circuit which sprung up across Europe in the 1990s – see Wolton 2008). Dance music had, briefly, become the soundtrack of militant protest, fusing with the punk and indie aesthetics that were touchstones for white youth rebellion.

In May 1990 the Stone Roses played to a crowd of 30,000 at Spike Island in a field outside Widnes, near Liverpool. Billed as a 'gathering of the clans', the much-mythologised concert had Hacienda DJ Dave Haslam and Ibiza veteran Paul Oakenfold on the bill, cementing the new fusion between psychedelic rock, indie and acid house. After Spike Island, even the most dyed-in-the-wool indie kid was, in the words of the 1995 hit by the arch Sheffield guitar band Pulp which commemorates the concert, 'sorted for Es and Wizz'. A hot summer coincided with the England football team's unexpected advance to the semi-finals of the Italia '90 World Cup – remembered for Paul Gascoigne's tears and (West) Germany's predictable triumph in the penalty shoot-out – which lent that summer an air of 'mass hysteria'. Journalist George Chesterton, watching England's 'plucky' semi-final defeat in the pub, saw how this mood was underpinned by the now mass experience of rave: 'So many of that crowd had had their lives changed by rave culture and this was a rave without the pills (well, not many)' (Chesterton 2018).

The annexation of rave by football fans and guitar bands was only the most conspicuous sign of the influence acid house and rave were having on UK culture and music. Following the long summer of love at the end of the 1980s, UK dance music production entered a new phase of 'incredible creative intensity' and 'sonic innovation' (Gilbert 2009). Taking inspiration from Chicago and Detroit imports and the late 1980s influx of European variants like Italo-house and Belgian new beat, and rapidly assimilating the production techniques of house, techno and hip hop (Hesmondhalgh and Melville 2002), British producers started to use the newly available digital production tools – Roland drum machines like the TR-808 and TR-909, and especially the TR-303 bass synth that produced the wobbly acid basslines – to put their own stamp on dance music. The introduction of the Steinberg Cubase program in 1989, with its easy-to-read graphic interface allowing even untrained musicians to construct their tracks by eye, meant that 'bedroom' producers could now make complete tracks for next to nothing on inexpensive and rudi-mentary computers like the Atari or Commodore Amiga.

The first fruits of the acid influence on electronic dance music in the UK, on tracks like 'Pump Up The Volume' by M/A/R/R/S (1987) and DJ Mark Moore's S-Express's 'Theme From S-Express' (1988), which both topped the chart, were in truth little more than radio-friendly funky pop records with acid garnish, but with the release of Guy Called Gerald's 'Voodoo Ray' and 808 State's 'Dream State' (both from Man-chester) in 1989, and many others, British producers started innovating club-oriented dance music at a furious rate. Up north, indie electronic labels like Poverty and WARP from Sheffield – which self-consciously identified themselves as 'hardcore' (Reynolds 2009) – were putting out English acid known as 'bleep', often mixed with hip-house, as in Nightmares on Wax's 'Let It Roll' from 1989. But bleep retained a strictly northern flavour, like chips and curry sauce.

In London the luvved up optimism of the Balearic and early rave scene was evolving into new hyper-intense variants, accelerated by chemical shifts. In 1992 Simon Reynolds, an eloquent ethnographer of this nascent scene, writing in *The Wire* magazine, noted the connection between changes in the pharmacological and rhythmic technologies which fed into what he called 'ardkore:

> The vibe has changed (from trance-dance to mental-manic) as Ecstasy has become adulterated with amphetamine, or replaced by pseudo-E concoctions of speed, LSD and God knows what. Chemicals have directly altered the subculture's metabolism, with the beats per minute (last count: 140–150 bpm) soaring in sync with pulse rates and blood pressure levels. (Reynolds 1992)

As Ibiza revivalists and techno purists, appalled by the massification of rave, retreated into a various forms of elite clubbing in the centre of London and denounced emergent 'ardkore as juvenile noise, 'ardkore took hold in the more proletarian night spots of east London, in venues like the Labyrinth at the Four Aces in Dalston (a renowned reggae venue) and the Dungeons on Lee Bridge Road, Hackney, which were notoriously lax about age limits. Tempos increased alongside drug intake. Crowds were incited by the MCs to 'get on one' and 'go radio rental' (mental). Reynolds describes 'ardkore as 'the most brazenly druggy subculture in eons' (1992), reading East End 'ardkore as a continuation of the traditions of white working-class leisure: 'the latest variant on the sulphate-fuelled 60-Hour Weekend of mod and Northern Soul lore' where 'speed-freak' kids were running away from their problems into a drug-fuelled glimpse of 'fugitive bliss'. Hardcore, for Reynolds, was senseless, nihilistic, an 'aesthetic of disappearance', all of which he approved in music (1992).

In 2009 Reynolds retrospectively developed the idea of 'the hardcore continuum', which starts with acid and 'ardkore and proceeds 'through jungle and UK garage to grime, dubstep and bassline' (Reynolds 2009; see also Gilbert 2014). His claim was based on what he identified as key continuities: of infrastructure (clubs, pirate radio); of personnel (those rave DJs who had developed 'ardkore and jungle had gone on to innovate UK garage and dubstep); of audience, rituals and attitude; and of sound, with the dark sonorities of bass at the core (Reynolds 2009). Reynolds's idea (which he first floated at a FACT symposium in Liverpool in 2009) was much discussed and debated among theory-smart music writers (Fisher 2009; Gilbert 2009; Williams 2009), especially for his claim that the ''nuum' (i.e. continuum) was running out of steam in the late noughties (Gilbert 2014). Here I'm more concerned with the other end of the timeline, and the claim that 'ardkore represents the moment of genesis. After all, a bass culture had been alive and well in British sound system culture for decades.

If, as Reynolds does, you ground this continuity on personnel, infrastructure, ritual and bass, why start there? Many DJs of the 'ardkore period, as has been discussed throughout this book, were bass culture veterans of reggae, funk, soul and disco; the new pirate radio stations of the early 1990s (of which more below) were modelled on and continuous with the practices of mid-1980s pirates like Kiss FM; the attitude of 'ardkore and especially jungle drew equally on the rituals and norms of suburban soul and the reggae dancehall as much as it did rave, and drew audiences from these scenes. And the 'sound', new juxtapositions of drum, bass and technology, can also be traced back through rave to disco, funk, hip hop and dub reggae.

As Nabeel Zuberi argues, the notion of the hardcore continuum is 'historically shortsighted' and sets up a troublingly gendered and classed division between ''ardkore' and its presumed to be feminine, tacky and conservative opposite: 'softcore', perhaps? Zuberi notes that this is of a piece with Reynolds' hostility to 'naff' jazz-funk and 'soul humanism' (Zuberi 2014: 190; Reynolds 1999). In effect the 'hardcore continuum' idea allows the extraction of those elements of urban black music that seem to echo punk, experimental rock and the European avant garde – dub, hip hop, hardcore, jungle – and leave behind the debased 'soft' traditions of soul, lovers rock and R&B, whose 'faux sophistication', sweetness and associations with feminine working-class leisure, 'intelligent' critics, for whom this music was the opposite of the everything they looked for in music, found unpalatable. The hardcore continuum idea also has the effect of severing the dance music history of the 1990s onwards from the complex racial politics I have been describing, packaging it for a white avant-gardist audience who would rather not think about race. This view seems most excited by 'ardkore's punk spirit, its 'intensity' and 'will to chaos', which Reynolds reads through the work of (then) fashionable philosophers like Paul Virillo and Felix Deleuze (Reynolds 2009). Predictably, therefore, such 'modernist' sociological categories as race, class and the human subject are largely missing from these accounts.

But there are novel features in 'ardkore. The normalisation of synthetic drugs in the music scenes of the 'ardkore continuum – 'class As', as they were known after the official classification of the Misuse of Drugs Act 1971 – *do* make a difference, as we will see. Reynolds is right, I think, that 'ardkore was a working-class twist on house and techno, 'another classic example of British youth … remotivating a black American music' (Reynolds 2009), with the centre of gravity shifting definitively from the aspirational West End to the unfashionable and under-resourced areas of east and north London: Tottenham, Dalston and Forest Gate. In this way, hardcore is continuous with mod and northern soul and with acid house, which was enthusiastically taken up by many white soul boys and girls, from London and the eastern suburban crescent, before spreading across the country. But unlike mod and soul, 'arkcore emerges from estates and areas where white and black working-class youth had been collaborating in creating 'richly syncretic cultures' based on the model of the reggae sound system for at least a decade (Back 1996). These in-fluences were to come to the fore in the music that starts to emerge from what Reynolds (1992) calls the 'cultural engine' of London, within which black cultural producers and sound system veterans were central.

An aside in Reynolds' 1992 article on 'ardkore gives a hint of what was to come. He notes the arrival of 'Jungle music', which constituted, he notes, one of 'ardkore's 'interesting subgenres' in 1992. The term 'jungle' (which Reynolds says is 'racist') identifies the arrival within hardcore of the unmistakable influence of black musical forms increasingly expunged from the rave dancefloor: hip hop, soul, jazz and reggae. Early musical hints of jungle include 'We Are I.E.' by Lenny De Ice of the Alms House Crew from Forest Gate in east London, released through the record shop De Underground in 1989, which combines electric acid washes with a sampled breakbeat (an early use of the 'Amen' break), a digital 'ragga' bassline and a sampled vocal line from 'N'Sel Fik', a Rai song by Chaba Fedala and Cheb Saraiouh. Another is 'Wickedest Sound' by Rebel MC (the pseudonym of Islington hip hop DJ Mike West, also known as Beat Freak and, later, Congo Natty), also from 1989. 'Wickedest Sound' has the collage texture of hip hop, with samples from Herbie Hancock, James Brown and reggae singer Barrington Levy, a fast breakbeat, hip-house rapping and a vocal from the dancehall singer Tenor Saw. It was fresh and rough enough to be played on rave dance-floors but it brought with it hip hop cut-and-mix aesthetics and sound system bass. For some, this return of black music to the rave dancefloor, which attracted new generations of black dancers into rave space, was received as an unwanted intrusion; for others, it was a much longed-for reconnection of house with its bass culture cousins.

This chapter is about jungle and the reorganisation of racial space it precipitated in London. It investigates the relationship between jungle's putatively 'new forms' and the black Atlantic bass culture I have been concerned with throughout this book. Though it does explore the club spaces where jungle cohered, it moves into different spaces, the space of the 'studio', where producers applied diaspora aesthetic practices to new technologies, and the imagined community of the nation (Anderson 1983). If jungle is indeed 'the first truly British black music' (Collin 1997: 260), what is its relation to national identity? Can we read the emergence of jungle as evidence of a generation of black-British Londoners creatively resolving the tension between the two sides of their hyphenated identities? How does this square with jungle's claim to be 'a multicultural inter-racial dance thing' (as the jungle MC Conrad would frequently declare on the mic)? This period of intense creativity is marked by discursive struggles over musical 'darkness', legitimate rhythm and who can claim to 'run jungle', struggles that replay the racialised debates about black music I have been highlighting throughout this book.

Whitening of rave

Jungle (we'll get to the racial politics of the name shortly) as musical genre and club scene emerges in the 'ardkore clubs and pirate radio stations of Dalston, Forest Gate, Hackney, Bow, Tottenham and Brixton before claiming the centre by occupying clubs on the Tottenham Court Road and in Hoxton Square in the mid-1990s. It was inter-racial in its production and consumption, but it was black London producers and DJs who first developed the sound. Many of the producers and DJs who originated jungle had made their name as rave DJs and had a deep knowledge of techno, acid and other house styles, including those from Europe (this was, after all, their job). But jungle DJs like Fabio and Grooverider, Jumping Jack Frost, Bryan Gee, Colin Dale, Jason Kaye, Kenny Ken, Rebel MC, Brockie, Smiley, PJ and DJ Hype[4] and MCs like Moose, GC, Stevie Hyper-D and 5ive-o and their many collaborators did not learn about basslines and breaks, DJing and dancing from acid house but from the reggae, soul, jazz, rare groove and hip hop, in which they were equally steeped. If you can't tell the story of jungle without reference to rave and 'ardkore, neither can you understand it only within that narrow frame.

In its sounds and styles, jungle self-consciously reconnected rave culture to its black Atlantic antecedents and contemporaries. As such, it can be read as a response to the whitening of rave, a shifting of the rhythmic and racial parameters, a reclaiming of the space of the dance-floor. As I argued in the previous chapter, acid house in London was racially mixed from the outset. Though led initially by white soul boys, it drew many black and brown Londoners in through the Balearic clubs like Shoom, warehouse parties like Hedonism, the Clink Street parties in SE1 and the 'orbital' rave scene. Raves, usually illegal and consciously hidden from surveillance, were not widely recorded on film, but there is some footage of a few of the earliest open-air raves, Biology, Sunrise and Energy (all from 1989) on YouTube,[5] and these videos attest to the fact that early raves were not entirely white and were more musically diverse than rave became, drawing from a wide range of house styles, including hip-house and breakbeats, alongside the pulsing four-four techno and wobbly acid basslines.

But, as Bryan Gee and Colin Dale testify, acid house was a hard sell to their black reggae and funk audience in Brixton, and those who slipped off to the rave often had to do so without their reggae and soul mates who condemned it as 'devil music' (Belle-Fortune 2004: 10). For some, like Joy White, who danced on the reggae and funk scene, acid house was a noisy, sometimes comic, curiosity. Coming back from Count Suckle's Q-Club in Paddington one Saturday night, she saw loads of luvved-up ravers in Trafalgar Square: 'Why are all those white people in the fountains?' she remembers wondering. Later she went to raves, 'to see what it was like', but their appeal was limited to a black Londoner like her with no taste for synthetic drugs and with other musical options (Joy White in private conversation).

The Brixton acid scene fought hard to convert a portion of its local audience to acid house, and succeeded. Early raves and the impromptu outdoor weekend after-party on Clapham Common – and others like it all over London – were disorganised sites of 'everyday mixity' (Amin

2010), reflecting the ethnic diversity of the area. But as suburban and rural rave circuits grew, black DJs like Frost, Carl Cox, Colin Dale and Grooverider, who were widely booked for big raves, came to accept that they would be playing to predominantly white crowds (reflecting the relatively monoracial populations outside the city). This was not necessarily perceived as a problem. When I asked him if he minded playing to mainly white crowds, Jumping Jack Frost replied, 'Nah, I didn't care about that, I didn't mind at all. I thought it was great to be honest, d'ya know what I mean?' (Jumping Jack Frost interview, 27 March 2017). But with the rise of stripped-down rhythmically brutal forms of Euro-techno, from Belgium and Holland, in the late 1980s, which moved rave further and further from the norms of black music, black ravers drifted away.

Drugs played a significant role. Despite what racial 'common sense' assumes,[6] drug-taking is not prevalent in black clubbing; socially conservative, often religious West Indian households, concerns about the dangers of being out of control in public space, patterned by racial antagonism, the requirement for grace and control on the black dance-floor, all militated against the wide use of drugs in black club culture (Colin Dale interview, 30 July 2017; on ethnic differences in drug use, see Wallace and Bachman 1991). Drugs were not hard to come by, and many black ravers experimented with ecstasy, like Colin Dale: 'I won't deny that drugs were a big part of it … I dived in'. But this was not wild abandon. 'I never wanted to look like I was out of control. If I had taken drugs I didn't want it to be known. Ecstasy did not start me dancing but it made me dance more. If I was feeling it, I would bring out my jazz funk moves' (Colin Dale interview). Other black Londoners, like Brian Belle-Fortune, went to raves for years but didn't take ecstasy, but instead 'perhaps a little weed' (Brian Belle-Fortune interview, 6 March 2017). For black audiences drugs were available, but not required.

Choreographer and dance historian H Patten suggests that the fundamental difference between the dance crowds at sound systems, blues and nightclubs and those at raves is that 'They needed the drugs. We never needed them' (H Patten interview, 18 May 2018). The heavy all-night dance sessions at the sound systems, six hours or more of skanking, wining, bogling and gully creeping (all reggae dance styles), which Patten demonstrated to me in our interview, necessitated a handy change of clothes and an ever-present small towel to wipe off sweat (dangling from the back pocket, just so), but the dancers were driven by the 'natural highs' of endorphins, pheromones and the kudos of dropping the best foot, not synthetic chemicals. White ravers, especially white men, used ecstasy to overcome their social inhibitions and hetero-normative social programming which coded dance as unmanly. Most black dancers needed no such crutch.

Although some raves, especially mega-raves, could operate re-strictive door policies and bouncers could be intimidating (by the early 1990s, most big promoters used well organised, seasoned door staff – some of whom were from football firms or ex-SAS – to protect their considerable takings: see Anthony 2002), we should look for an explanation of the whitening of rave not in rave regulation but in what was happening in other parts of the black music ecosystem. Black Londoners in this period had a wealth of other options. Established 'big men' roots reggae sound systems like Coxsone and Jah Shaka, as well as younger sets featuring DJs developing the British 'fast chat' style, such as Saxon, played consistently in London and throughout the UK during this period. The documentary film *Bass Culture* shows how the development of dancehall and ragga, with its faster digital basslines and exuberantly slack lyrics, was reinvigorating the dances with a younger attendance, and how by the early 1990s there were new waves of younger sound systems across the city which blended ragga, house and hip hop: Poison, Lady Force, Black Mafia, Glamourguard, Wisdom Hardcore and Younger Kilawatt.[7]

More established sound systems, like the Mastermind Roadshow (formed in the late 1970s), Rappattack (1984) and Rampage (1992), played consistently at Notting Hill Carnival and in clubs throughout the city, mixing dancehall reggae, hip hop and electro for black crowds. There were 'soulful' and gospel-influenced house clubs, like Norman Jay's High on Hope and Paul Anderson's HQ Club (both of which started in 1988 in Camden), and all manner of funky soul, hip hop and boogie clubs run by dozens of promoter/DJs. Though the reggae sounds remained primarily arenas of black leisure, many of these were racially mixed and there was also the emergence in the late 1980s of 'acid jazz', reviving jazz dancing and jazz-inflected bass music at Gilles Peterson's Sunday club at Dingwalls in Camden, and hip hop breakbeat-driven options, leading to the development of trip hop (Portishead appeared in 1991) and, in the mid-1990s, broken beat.

The period within which 'ardkore was incubated was also a time of innovation in black American music, as the new jack swing and swingbeat of producers like Aaron Hall and Teddy Riley entered their pomp just as the hip hop golden period began: Public Enemy's 'Fight the Power' was released in 1989 and A Tribe Called Quest's album *People's Instinctive Travels and the Paths of Rhythm* in 1990. Hip hop and swingbeat would merge in the early 1990s in the new genre of R&B (post hip-hop soul, which is not the same as rhythm and blues, but not entirely distinct either), which was led by producers and singers like Rodney Jerkins, Timbaland, Missy Elliott, Mary J. Blige, Jermaine Dupri, Jill Scott and, a little later, Lauryn Hill and Erykah Badu. For all but the die-hard black ravers, there were many other options for a night out. Those die-hards who 'knew the score' and stayed with 'ardkore transformed rave from the inside.

Hello darkness

Rave dance culture began splitting at a furious amphetamine-fuelled rate. On the one hand, much of the early 1990s hardcore was getting faster (140–160 beats per minute) and sillier. To go with the increasingly infantile dancefloor styles of baggy androgynous clothing, combined with the popularity of dummies, whistles, Vicks inhalers and other child-hood paraphernalia, the music increasingly featured theme tunes from children's TV programmes, sped up and distorted, or jokey soundbites ('Maggie's Last Party' by VIM, from 1991, famously sampled Margaret Thatcher, edited so as to be heard recommending the joys of 'E'). In 1992 the Prodigy (with 'Charley', a street name for cocaine) and the Shamen (with 'Ebenezer Good' – geddit?) had chart hits with novelty rock-rave records. Smart E's 'Sesame's Treet', also from 1992, sampled the Sesame Street theme tune. This so-called 'happy hardcore', with its major key piano riffs, heart-racing tempos, sped-up 'chipmunk' vocal samples and its kiddies-gone-wild performance codes, embodied a refusal to grow up, a desire to return to the comforting womb of that first ecstasy rush and the early optimism of raves.

Techno, one of the musical elements of the 'ardkore mix, was evolving too. With the notable exception of acts like Underground Resistance (Juan Atkins, Kevin Saunderson, Mike Banks), techno from Detroit by figures like Jeff Mills and Derrick May was a somewhat austere affair, articulating what Kodwo Eshun calls 'cyborg fantasies', in which humans aim to free themselves from 'sonic identity and to feel at home in alienation' (Eshun 2003: 296). But in the early 1990s, new kinds of European techno like 'gabber' emerged, harder and faster, hyper-masculine, as alienated but more aggressive than anything Detroit produced.[8] Increasingly music was being made in the UK that began to take on a darkness of its own. This is exemplified in 4hero's overdose-death record 'Mr Kirk's Nightmare' from 1991, with its repeated refrain (sampled from a 1970 anti-drugs song 'Once You Understand' by Think) 'Mr Kirk, come down to the station house, your son is dead'. This was conscious disobedience of the rave injunction to be 'uplifting', and introduced instead an ominous tone guaranteed to spoil a raver's high. This tone was welcomed on the 1992 release by Bay-B-Kane (Mel Jalal Tanur) 'Hello Darkness', where a sped-up Simon and Garfunkel vocal sample met breakbeats and sub-bass punctuated with sinister laughter. On the flipside was the equally ominous 'Quarter to Doom'.

A pioneer of this new, darker sound was Clifford Price, aka Goldie, from Walsall in the West Midlands. A hip hop fan and renowned graffiti artist, Goldie had been converted to rave and hardcore through watching Fabio and Grooverider cut black Atlantic breakbeats out of techno and acid at their Rage night at Heaven. Recording for the Moving Shadow and Reinforced record labels as Metalheadz, Rufige Kru and one half of

2 Bad Mice, Goldie helped develop this dark sound on tracks like 'Terminator' and 'Killer Muffin', which were as hard, heavy and menacing as Belgian techno but drew on the polyrhythmic traditions of jazz, funk and hip hop. The emergence of this kind of hardcore, with its scary dystopian textures, suited the state of rave culture at the time, which was rapidly retreating from the Ibiza dream of spiritual togetherness.

The music mix which had been championed by the black rave sounds like Shut Up and Dance and Top Buzz, and the mixing of Fabio, Grooverider and Jumping Jack Frost was materialised in the sounds of what started to be called jungle. Bryan Gee suggests that jungle was a response by black DJs and producers to happy hardcore's turn to the past as a source for new ideas. While white producers were turning back to music from 1970s TV like the theme tunes to Grange Hill and Sesame Street, 'black people started making music from the things that had influenced them, reaching back to what they knew' (Bryan Gee interview, 2 March 1999). Black British rave producers, DJs and the MCs who had begun to find a space on the mic drew on the resources of the black Atlantic to remake London dance music with a new cultural agenda.

In his comprehensive oral history of jungle, *All Crews* (2004),[9] journalist Brian Belle-Fortune provides a detailed picture of the dense web of affiliations of DJs, MCs, promoters, pirate radio stations, clubs and ravers who innovated the new sounds of jungle. His research shows how new sounds started entering the rave and hardcore dancefloor in the early 1990s. In east London, Shut Up and Dance hooked up with the Ragga Twins from Hackney (brothers Damon and Trevor Destouche, aka Deman Rocker and Flinty Badman), veterans of the UNITY reggae sound system, to make music for the local hardcore clubs of east London like the Dungeons, blending breakbeats and reggae chat into the rave formula (Belle-Fortune 2004: 14; Collin 1997: 130–1). On 'Lamborghini', from 1990, over an uncleared sample of the Eurhythmics' 'Sweet Dreams' and an electro beat, the Ragga Twins addressed this rave audience directly in terms that were both avuncular and gently mocking: 'request to all the little acid people dem, when you take your little pill and go mad inna the dance, this is for you.'

For some, this was a conscious effort to shift music away from the European sound that predominated in the early 1990s. 'Being a Londoner, I'd had enough of that sound', the rave promoter Paul Chambers, aka Paul Ibiza,[10] told Belle-Fortune. Chambers, who grew up in Tottenham in a household saturated with reggae since his father was in a sound system, started promoting club nights at the Rocket on Holloway Road and illegal raves in 1989. When he found his King's Cross rave parties getting closed down by police he set up Ibiza Records and started putting out releases which disturbed the even rave template with breaks and reggae-derived basslines. In place of the rigid four-four early Ibiza releases 'Set Me Free' and 'Jungle Techno' featured a tense off-beat patina of sped-up vocals, synth stabs, breaks and the sonic hints of reggae bass.

Meanwhile, within the rave there was a turn towards the practices of the reggae dance hall. London rave promoters Kenny Delsol (aka Kenny Ken) and Bret (who ran the Telepathy and Freedom branded events in Hackney, Stoke Newington and Haringey and staged a mega-rave at the Sobell Sports Centre in Islington in 1989 to which 13,000 turned up) started incorporating elements taken from the reggae culture they both grew up in, including the use of MCs[11] toasting over the music, and rewinds, where the crowd exhorts the DJ to wheel a favoured track back to the start, characteristic of the antiphonal form of the reggae dance (Gilroy 1987; Belle-Fortune 2004: 108–9).

The change became obvious at the Sunday Roast club, which started in 1991 at the huge purpose-built nightclub Turnmills in Clerkenwell (opened in 1990 with the first ever twenty-four-hour licence, a beneficiary of the government's attempts to draw the sting of the illegal rave scene). Sunday Roast started as a house-and-rave all-dayer, but by 1992, when it moved to Linford Studios in Battersea, south-west London, the DJs Ron, Grooverider and Mickey Finn were playing more breakbeats and samples from Studio One reggae classics, providing the instrumental bed for the reggae-derived chatting of MCs Moose, 5ive-o, Det and Stevie Hyper-D. The racial composition of the dancefloor was shifting too, as more young black people began turning up (Belle-Fortune 2004: 109).

'As the music progressed in Jungle, the scene changed', Roast promoter Paul Roast told the makers of a Channel 4 documentary on the jungle scene in 1994. 'Everyone who was on the house scene moved away from Roast. They left us. They said "you're just promoting darkness"' (Paul Roast from *All Junglists*, Channel 4, 1994, cited in Belle-Fortune 2004: 16). Jumping Jack Frost describes this period as 'the slow introduction of the reggae sound', a gradual shift driven by black London DJs; 'you just sneaked, sneaked, sneaked it in, d'ya know what I mean?' (Jumping Jack Frost interview).

The rave explosion had created a new economic ecosystem. Many DJs, like Frost, Colin Dale and Fabio and Grooverider, who had started off taking any gig they were offered, sometimes for a little as £20 (Colin Dale interview), had become aware of how much promoters were making, charging sometimes £25 for a ticket. Staging raves was financially risky: one of the promoters behind the popular World Dance events described putting on raves as 'the best way to lose £15,000' (Belle-Fortune 2004: 112), but the rewards were potentially huge. By 1989 the DJs needed help to manage their bookings and make sure they got paid, and, with the threat of dodgy promoters and hoax raves, where punters paid upfront only to find no rave on the day, booking agents like Groove Connection, founded by Sarah Sandy, emerged to manage DJ bookings.

Changes in the music in the early 1990s were reflected in the shifts in representation. Colin Dale recalls the moment when, as 'the whole techno thing went down the harder faster route', jungle was emerging. 'I played jungle, early '91, '92; everyone was playing jungle then.' But Dale had always favoured a more industrial techno sound, which, as ragga jungle surfaced, was being pushed out: 'it started to split, especially in London clubs. There were London clubs where you couldn't go and start playing techno. They wouldn't have it; they were only jungle' (Colin Dale interview). At this point Dale and his partner from Brixton, Dave Angel, made a conscious decision to take the techno route away from jungle. They split from Groove Connection to join the new techno agency Knowledge, and established their own London-based techno scene with Colin Faver, at the club night Knowledge at the SW1 club in Victoria, where they played primarily European and Detroit techno, with a new 'stripped down minimalist' philosophy which set itself against both rave and jungle: 'none of that fluffy hippy rave stuff. We never played vocals, no rapping, no saxophone solos, no MCs … [music] stripped down its abstract principles' (Colin Dale interview).

With techno 'purists'[12] retreating from hardcore, the way was open for the jungle takeover. In 1993 a new home for jungle emerged at the AWOL (A Way Of Life) night at the Paradise club in Islington. Starting with a variety of house genres – one early resident was Ibiza veteran Trevor Fung – the sounds of breakbeat and reggae-inspired jungle began to elbow four-four aside as DJs Kenny Ken, Mickey Finn, Dr S Gachet and Randall and resident MC GC refined the London jungle model to a crowd which often included other DJs and producers like Goldie, Andy C, Fabio and Grooverider. The feel of AWOL, with whistles and air-horns, breakbeats and bass drops and frequent shifts in rhythm, stops and rewinds, back-and-forth between crowd and MC left behind the seamless contours and orchestrated climaxes of rave for an antiphonal atmosphere much more like Notting Hill Carnival and the reggae dance hall. Dancers rode the half-pace bass or articulated the double-time breaks. The musical spacings of jungle folded rave and reggae, hip hop and fast chat, New Orleans breaks and deep reggae basslines into a cele-bration of 'immanence' (Gilbert 2014: 174), reflected in the common MC invocation of the hallowed space of the dancefloor, 'inside the place'.

Pirates return

Clubs were where the live element of jungle happened, but jungle was not confined to club space. In the late 1980s there was an(other) explosion of pirate radio activity. Kiss FM, which had gone off air in 1988, returned with a legal licence following the 1990 Broadcasting Act and BBC Radio 1 had started playing significantly more dance music, recognising its growing importance to its target demographic, by hiring ex-pirate DJs like Pete Tong, Danny Rampling and Judge Jules (who had left his roots in rare groove far behind and switched to playing epic house). Yet licensed broadcasters continued to lag behind the taste of the club audience. With the invention of the 'micro-link' system, which meant that signals could be relayed to distant transmitters, making pirate stations harder to trace and close down, pirate stations proliferated in 1989/90, with more than 600 in the UK and at least sixty in London (Reynolds 1999; Wolton 2010). New pirates dedicated to rave like Sunrise, Dance FM, Fantasy and Centreforce, broadcasting from tower blocks in east and north London, drove the expansion of raves, showcasing the music, building the scene, giving details of raves, and pushing the development of the music from acid house to rave and hardcore. Dan Hancox writes:

> It's hard to overstate how vital the pirates have been to the incubation and growth of eighties and nineties dance genres, a meeting point; a testing and rehearsal ground for new and established talent live on the mic and on the decks; a place where hits and stars are made; a communication channel and a binding agent, for the community contained within the earshot. (Hancox 2018: 82)

In March 1991, *Touch* magazine, a London-based 'street culture and music monthly', trailed an upcoming feature, on the music policy and bandwidth details of forty-three London-based pirate stations. The Department of Trade and Industry (DTI), whose staff evidently read the magazine, issued a writ to prevent publication of the feature, warning it was a criminal offence to publish details of illegal broadcasters. Instead, journalist Bill Tuckey used his next column on radio in the magazine to predict a massive increase in pirate activity, because 'while there are listeners that are not being catered for by legal stations, pirates will always find a way of operating' (Tuckey 1991). The official warning signalled a concerted effort on the part of the authorities to close illegal radio stations. In the period between 1991 and 2002, DTI raids on pirate radio stations more than doubled (Hancox 2018: 82), yet the best efforts of the enforcement officers (some of whom were on first-name terms with station operators, as they knew them well from previous raids) and the many raids they launched on the transmitters of pirates, while they did hit individual stations like Centreforce (which closed in June 1990) and Fantasy (closed in 1991), could not prevent dozens emerging to fill the space on the FM dial. Rush, Eruption, Kool FM, Girls FM, Don FM, Star Radio, Rave FM, Touchdown, Defection, Index, Format, Pulse, Impact, Don, Chillin', Destiny, Function and many others crammed the FM bandwidth with a dense web of dance music and insider club slang, nurturing the emergence of first hardcore and then jungle.

Pirate radio reached out beyond the club networks and pulled new recruits into the emerging jungle nexus. Former sound system DJ and jazz singer Cleveland Watkiss, for example, first heard jungle in 1994 on the Hackney pirate station that his teenage daughter was listening to. Having no interest in rave, he had not heard the way that reggae and funk influences were permeating 'ardkore. Jungle's mix came both as revelation and as recognition: 'I welcomed jungle as an old friend'. Within a year, Watkiss was the sole MC at Goldie's Sunday night Metalheadz at the Blue Note club in Hoxton Square, singing and chatting on the mic to a crowd peppered with a new generation of jungle producers and MCs, including Grooverider and Fabio, Peshay, Dillinja, Doc Scott and Photek alongside the occasional celebrity (both Bjork, then Goldie's girlfriend, and David Bowie attended). Watkiss told stories, jokes and improvised around the beat. Lyrics were improvised around what were, for him, familiar patterns: 'If you knew reggae then you knew when the tunes would change, when the beats would start and stop' (Cleveland Watkiss interview, 7 July 1996).

Jungle's multi-networks

Jungle, for Brian Belle-Fortune, was pre-eminently a product of 'a musically open multicultural society' (2004: 15). In its aesthetic form and the composition of its audience, it put to the test the race and space coding of the city, operating at the border of the city and the suburb, of white area and black areas, and of the music which was supposed to express the communities who lived there (Noys 1995). Jungle, through the pirate stations, was strongly associated with London council estates, especially in economically deprived east London – Leyton's Oliver Close Estate alone boasted three pirate stations in the early 1990s (Belle-Fortune 2004: 61). Jeremy Gilbert called jungle an 'essentially local music scene' (2009: 120) because it drew on a dense filigree of local, family and friendship connections. This is confirmed in Belle-Fortune's mapping of jungle producers: 'Lemon D and Dillinga are neighbours. As were DJ Ron, MC 5ive-o and GQ. GQ and Det were in the same class at school. MC Det and DJ Brockie lived across the road from each other' (Belle-Fortune 2004: 30). As we saw in the previous chapter, the Brixton acid crew, Fabio and Grooverider, Frost and Bryan Gee, Colin Dale and Dave Angel, had been friends since they were young and ran together for a decade or more.

Because of its association with the estates of east London, jungle has sometimes been understood as the musical record of a new class-based form of allegiance across racial boundaries, a 'new underclass'. In its rough tones, street lingo and ominous soundscape it can be read as a record of, and escape valve for, 'inner-city pressure',[13] articulating a distinctly working-class urban voice. So what can we make of the fact that one of the key hardcore labels which helped develop jungle was called Suburban Base and based in Romford in Essex? Jungle also flourished in Croydon and in Reading. Rob Playford based his Moving Shadow label in his hometown of Stevenage; Origin Unknown (Andy C and Ant Miles) are from Essex; Source Direct (James Baker and Phillip Aslett) and the producer Photek from St Albans, in Hertfordshire. The most obvious explanation for this is that rave had collapsed the space between the urban inner city, the suburbs and the shires, as white youth from outside the city who had little access to sound systems or dance music got a chance to experience bass culture at orbital and rural raves (see chapter 3). But it goes further back than that, connecting to sound systems, which, when they weren't doing their own dances, were providing the hardware for raves[14] and in some ways travelling the same pathways as suburban soul and jazz funk, the genres which, as one of the main DJs describes, had since the early 1970s been 'East London black fused with white Essex boy' (Chris Hill cited in Cotgrove 2009: 170).

Rob Playford, for example, who started the Moving Shadow label and engineered Goldie's early tunes, hails from Stevenage in Hertfordshire. His first exposure to dance music was via the powerful transmitters of London soul stations LWR and Kiss FM, on which he could listen to soul and rare groove and the house shows of Jazzy M and Colin Faver. He started DJing electro on the local Charisma sound system and with the rave explosion it was off to M25 raves, and then on to the all-night raves of north-east London, where he met Paul Chambers of Ibiza Records, who took him under his wing and integrated him into the nascent jungle scene, which was emerging from the Tottenham sound systems (Rob Playford interview, 18 August 1998; Chambers cited in McQuaid n.d.). As well as white suburbanites, London's centripetal force pulled in black cultural producers with reggae and funk sound system links from outside the metropolis: Bryan Gee is from Gloucester, DJ SS (Leroy Small) was a breakdancer in his native Leicester; DJ producers Ray Keith and Digital (Steve Carr) are from East Anglia. Many prominent junglists come from the sound system-saturated and racially mixed Bristol club scenes: Roni Size, DJ Krust, DJ Die, Suv, Flynn and Flora (Johnson 1996: 185).

The class form of jungle is not homogenous. Affiliations with hip hop, which was popular among middle-class white youth but which was often dismissed by working-class soul fans as insufficiently soulful and by the reggae audience as too American (Rodney P interview), drew many members of London's metropolitan middle class towards jungle. White Londoners like Gavin King (DJ Aphrodite) (who had a university education), Matt 'MJ' Cole, Matt Quinn (Optical) and John B were drawn into jungle production, and the No U-Turn label (Nico Sykes and Ben Settle, aka Ed Rush) emerged in the leafy south-west London suburb of Barnes.

Jungle took the threads of the reggae sound systems, the suburban soul scene and the rave scene, integrated them with the networks of record stores, pirate radio stations, recording studios and dubplate mastering offices, and knit them into 'a series of unstable cultural and musical hybrids' (Noys 1995: 331).

Isms and schisms

Jungle has been given many names in an effort to describe its distinct hybridisation of reggae, rave, hip hop, house and funk: from 'techno-hip hop' (Noys 1995) to 'cyber-Jazz', 'digi-dub', 'gangsta-rave' (Reynolds 1999) and 'raggamuffin-techno' (Collin 1997). But the name 'jungle' has stuck. There is, as is usual with music genres, no consensus on the origin of that name. Paul Chambers from Ibiza Records, who released the track 'Jungle Techno' in 1992, says that he got the name from the James Brown compilation *In the Jungle Groove* released in 1986. Others have argued that it is taken from the name, the jungle (or 'dungle'), used to refer to the Tivoli Gardens ghetto of Kingston, references to which were carried from Jamaica on 'yard tapes' (tapes of sound system performances) and sampled on British productions by producers like Rebel MC. In a straw poll of DJs, producers and promoters, Belle-Fortune gets as many answers as he has respondents: it was named after a raver called 'Danny Jungle' (Sarah Sandy); it was from a cassette recorded at a Dreamscape rave where the Top Buzz MC Mad P described the music as 'Hardcore-Jungle-Techno' (Rob Playford); it was MC Moose chatting about 'jungle, the new phenomenon' at Roast (Kingsley Roast); it was 'the people dem that named it jungle' (Rebel MC/Congo Natty) (Belle-Fortune 2004: 16).

As we have seen, Simon Reynolds, in 1992, felt the term was racially disparaging, the return of the negative associations of unruly rhythm, coined by ravers concerned that the darkness connoted by break-beats, reggae basslines and the return of the black voice was spoiling their high. Smiley from Shut Up and Dance argued that the term had primitivist connotations and was racist, and refused to use it, but it rapidly got taken up within the emergent subculture. Paul Chambers started putting the word 'jungle' on his Ibiza Records releases, the Roast club printed a banner proclaiming 'Roast Jungle' and by 1993 events using the name, like the 'Jungle Fever' series of raves, were ubiquitous. Members of the network began to identify themselves as 'junglists'. The term 'jungle' encapsulates a racial instability, connoting both notions of the untamed 'African jungle' and the cluster of stereotypes attached

to this idea, and the resignification of these ideas within black music –
from Duke Ellington's self-conscious integration of high swing and low
rhythm that he himself termed 'jungle' (Middleton 2000: 70–5)[15] to
depictions of the city as a 'concrete jungle' mythologised in music from
Sly Stone and Bob Marley to Grandmaster Flash.

Anxieties about jungle were mapped onto the class-based discourse
that had accompanied the spread of rave and early hardcore, where the
influx of young working-class east Londoners into the utopian dancefloors of early rave had been greeted with the denunciation, promulgated
in particular by the Boy's Own collective, which produced a rave fanzine
(largely written by indie-rave DJ Andrew Weatherall), of 'acid teds' and
'love thugs' – a proposition that rave was being invaded by ravers who
were not sufficiently committed to the utopian-bohemian vision of acid
house (Collin 1997: 123). As Sarah Thornton argues in *Club Cultures*, this
was a process of distinction-making where, in pursuit of (sub)cultural
capital, a mythical 'mainstream' is cast as 'a disparaged other' ('Sharon
and Tracey dancing round their handbags'), which contributes to a
sense of community and shared identity for those within groups who
imagine themselves to be 'original' or truly 'underground' (Thornton
1995: 111). But, though Thornton's argument is a useful corrective to the
overblown claims for rave utopianism, she is insufficiently attentive to
the politics of racialised space that forced black clubbing underground
when the mainstream was denied them, or the desire to create an alternative musical and cultural space outside the norms of the Saturday
night piss-up, which could so often devolve into racial violence. Notions
of the underground are more than merely the discursive jockeying for
status Thornton imagines them to be.

For many ravers, jungle and its audience represented an even greater
threat than had the 'acid teds', laying bare the limits of their rave dream
of pan-racial harmony. 'A lot of people couldn't understand the reggae
and hip hop references', says Bryan Gee. 'A lot of house DJs couldn't
understand what the fuck was going on. All of a sudden you started
to get a split in the hardcore scene. The brothers started to come into
the scene, and many ravers left' (Bryan Gee interview). Not only was

the new music ominous, fractured and 'dark' – records with titles like 'Darksides', 'The Psycho' and 'Doomsday' made by artists calling themselves Phuture Assassins and Kaotic Kemistry – but also many of the new jungle crowd consciously avoided ecstasy, the precondition of membership in rave's 'neo-tribal communitas' (Gore 1997: 55). The first wave of 'dark' hardcore soon gave way to even more explicit references to reggae, as dancehall MCs like Supercat, Tenor Saw and Top Cat were sampled or recorded live by producers like Shy FX and A Guy Called Gerald. The split was explicitly racialised. The perceived 'darkness' of jungle, in terms of both form and content – the return of the breakbeat, dystopian samples from horror films, the cockney-Caribbean patois of the MC, the return of black dancers to the rave – triggered conventional readings of blackness as threat.

The rave establishment galvanised against jungle and suggested that it was a betrayal of their rave ethos. In 1994 the fanzine *Ravescene*, for example, posed a series of questions: 'Has jungle devoured the final remnants of the good vibes? Does it even aspire to the originality of punk? Is it bleak, negative and retrogressive?' The answers were 'yes', 'no', 'yes', the conclusion 'Rave is dead. Jungle killed it' (*Ravescene* no. 51, 1994). In April 1994 the dance music magazine *Mixmag* posed a rhetorical question of its own, 'Is Jungle Too Ruff?', and detailed the violence and drug-taking – including of crack cocaine – which had become associated with jungle clubs in the year the genre broke big. It is the case, as the *Mixmag* article details, that there were violent incidents at jungle raves that year. As jungle grew in popularity, large crowds descended on often poorly planned raves with tickets oversold and inexperienced door staff. But similar events had happened throughout the history of dance music and rave, and many familiar with the racial politics of club culture detected behind ravers' anxieties about darkness an unspoken fear of the black dancefloor: 'Jungle, so the racist myth goes, is what turned every raver's little Woodstock into an Altamont with bass bins' (Eshun in *iD* magazine, May 1994, cited in Collin 1997: 259).

A racialised panic swept post-rave dance cultures as the make-up of the audience and the tenor of the music brought the sound system connections latent in rave to the fore. This letter, published by *Touch* magazine in 1994, makes the case for the defence:

> Jungle-Dark? See how all the happy housers stay. It contrasts greatly with happy hardcore, but dark sounds don't necessarily mean bad vibes. It's only recently that the rest of the rave scene has acknowledged its existence: the Jungle – heavy bouncing basslines, synchronized rhythmic drumbeats combining to give the natural buzz. As with any underground music, Jungle will have its critics – and the inevitable 'link with drugs'. But to those who know this is the normal criticism of black music. The critics do not – and cannot – understand.[16]

From its name and argot to its sonic references and codes of embodiment, jungle articulated race in ways drawn from familiar sources – reggae, hip hop – but with a distinctly new rhythm. The reaction it provoked, however, drew largely on the all-too-familiar architecture of racial stereotype. This was not only an aesthetic reaction to jungle's abrasive textures and jagged breakbeats, so disruptive of the smooth peaks and troughs of 'happy' house, but a response to the changing ethno-socio-spatio-economics of the jungle moment: 'The panic about Jungle commenced when black people ceased to be a minority and were visibly in control of the scene' (Collin 1997: 259).

But control was a relative term in such a fast-moving and unstable subculture. In 1993/4 jungle grew rapidly and took a distinct turn towards dancehall with 'jump-up' basslines and reggae samples and the voices of MCs, some with a more hip hop flow and others chatting a cockney/patois hybrid that owed much to the legacy of the Saxon sound system from Lewisham and their fast-style innovators (some of whom, like Tippa Irie, translated easily into the jungle milieu). Collectively, jungle MCs evolved a distinctive jungle vocal practice that combined patois, London street slang, popular culture, football references and American rap in a scattershot verbal fusillade of 'code switching' (Back 1996) that pointed the way to the development of grime at the end of the decade (Hancox 2018).

In 1994 the producer M-Beat had a major hit with 'Incredible', featuring the reggae toaster Paul 'General' Levy from north-west London, which was an anthem at that year's Notting Hill Carnival and reached number 8 in the national chart. Featured in *The Face* magazine, Levy was quoted as claiming that 'I run jungle at the moment' (Whitehurst 2015) and he purportedly described himself to autograph hunters as 'De Oriogional [*sic*] junglist', much to the fury of those who considered themselves the founders of the scene.

In late 1994 a group of London promoters and DJs convened a convention to 'attempt to tighten the control of jungle by its family' (Belle-Fortune 2004: 19). They agreed not to play 'Incredible 'and to shun General Levy (which had a serious impact on his career – see Whitehurst 2015). Later that year, at Manchester's first jungle event, at Sankey's Soap, where veteran dancehall chatters like Tippa Irie toasted over jungle beats as if jungle were just the latest rhythmic development in dancehall reggae, Jumping Jack Frost grabbed the mic and stated 'Jungle ain't about this' before stalking off. The jungle fraternity feared, in Belle-Fortune's words, that jungle was becoming 'a poor ragga hybrid, run by Jamaicans' (Belle-Fortune 2004: 19). But the following year another ragga-jungle hit, 'Original Nuttah', by Shy FX, featuring the MC UK Apache (Abdul Wahab from Tooting, south London, who performed with the reggae sound system Lord Gelly), suggested that the bad-boy lyrics of ragamuffin reggae had taken over jungle.

A fracture opened up within jungle. Some, like Paul Chambers, tried to hold on to the DJs-plus-MCs formula by founding the Jungle Splash series of events (a very deliberate reference to Reggae Sunsplash in Jamaica), with many of the original jungle DJs and MCs, the first of which, at Bagley's in King's Cross, pulled a crowd of 7,500 and was filmed for French TV. Chambers' aim, as he explained to online magazine *Ransom Note*, was to give black youth in the city access to rave culture: 'Clubs and raves were stopping the black kids from experiencing the rave culture. So I made up my mind to start Jungle Splash for the black community' (McQuaid n.d.). Meanwhile, new strains of the music emerged which moved away from Jamaican-inspired MC vocals entirely and towards complex instrumental dissections of breakbeats and basslines, on labels like Rob Playford's Moving Shadow, Goldie's Metalheadz, No-U Turn, run by Ed Rush and Nico, and the Good Looking/Looking Good label run by LTJ Bukem (Danny Williamson). This music drew more on the sonic resources of hip hop production, jazz funk sophistication and ambient atmospherics than dancehall lyricism. The term 'tech-step' was coined for the colder, more Euro-techno end of the spectrum, 'intelligent' for the more jazz funk and ambient music end; both wished to distance themselves from the ragga end of the jungle spectrum. Ed Rush, Optical and J Majik made the futuristic big bassline and breaks tunes; LTJ Bukem's 'Horizons' (1995), with its sample of the American poet and novelist Maya Angelou, was indicative of the self-consciously high-brow 'intelligent jungle'.

Soon the term 'drum and bass' emerged as an alternative to 'jungle'. This rebranding, which began appearing on club flyers, in record shops' descriptions and the way the music was discussed in the media, seemed to be an attempt to dissociate jungle from its rude-boy reputation, coinciding with the mainstreaming of the music at West End clubs like Speed and Metalheadz, which attracted a mixed media-friendly crowd, and the release of Goldie's debut album *Timeless* (which blended soul, jazz funk and jungle breakbeats) on FFRR/London Records to glowing notices and respectable sales (it reached number 7 in the UK album chart). For some, the development of jungle into drum and bass was a 'logical progression'. But for others, it connoted a withdrawal from the unstable mix that made the scene so exciting.

Reynolds, for example, considered the term 'drum and bass' an act of 'unwise self-gentrification' and for some black junglists it felt like racism: 'I think there was a subtext with Drum and Bass meaning white friendly, middle-class. Jungle meaning "A bad boy ting"' (Bret from Telepathy cited in Belle-Fortune 2004: 21). Paul Chambers points out the irony of the term:

> The name drum n bass is of black origin anyway, it said on my dad's old [reggae] records 'drum n bass or version' – but what we think of as drum & bass now … jungle is black and drum n bass is white, is that what you're telling me? (Paul Chambers cited in McQuaid n.d.)

Chambers suggests that the excision of the link to ragga and this attempt to clean up jungle by those producers with access to expensive new digital production technologies like Pro-Tools (which cost in the region of £10,000), as opposed to the basic Ataris with which the scene had started, is what pushed many black jungle producers and DJs into the adjacent subgenre of UK garage, a slinky skippy-beat version of house which brought the soul-vocal aspects of US house music back into London clubs, a sound which had been bubbling away since the mid-1990s, often played in the second room at jungle events like AWOL (McQuaid n.d.).

Fussing and fighting

That jungle in this period was associated with violence cannot be put down just to residual discursive racism. Unlike self-consciously upwardly mobile rare groove, or the mobile circuits of rave, jungle was local, nurtured in the tough neighbourhoods of north and east London, where poverty, exclusion and violence were endemic. Since the rise of mega-raves, where the profits from staging raves and selling ecstasy were considerable, criminal gangs had muscled their way into promotions and dealing. Jungle raves in the inner city attracted their element of local rude boys and professional criminals, just as had reggae dances, raves, high-street discos and Soho nightspots. Belle-Fortune argues that tension is an inevitable consequence of multiracial sociality and 'violence is a distressing part of everyday social interaction. The Jungle/Drum and Bass scene', he admits, 'does suffer from it' (2004: 120). Many junglists had themselves had hard-knock lives: Paul Chambers, Bret from Telepathy, Kenny Ken, MC Flux and Jumping Jack Frost (as he details in his autobiography *Big Bad and Heavy* – Thompson 2017) had all served jail sentences. For many, jungle promotion, production, DJing and MCing provided one of the few viable economic alternatives for those 'destined for nothing in life' (DJ Hype quoted in Belle-Fortune 2004: 31).

The ubiquity of drugs on the dance scene since rave ensured that dealers were ever present, rip-offs were common and turf wars could always break out. The nature of the unstable jungle mix, which brought together groups from different London neighbourhoods who might otherwise never have socialised together, without the balm of ecstasy that had held the antagonisms between football fans and local affiliations briefly in check at the raves, meant conflict was always possible. Did the ragga-infused 'bad bwoy' jungle – which one journalist visiting AWOL described as obsessed with 'gangster and gun culture, the more sexist, the more violent, the better' (Styles 1994) – incite violence, as some argued?

I was at a New Year's jungle rave in 1995 when, during a particularly intense ragga-jungle tune, the five young black boys dancing next to me all pulled out their Stanley knives and waved them around. This performative violence was both jokey and intimidating; it seemed to confirm both the argument that violent imagery was playful braggadocio and should not be taken literally and that jungle created an atmosphere of extreme intensity where anything might kick off at any time. Nothing happened, but it felt that anything could. As Jeremy Gilbert notes, both jungle, and the UK garage scene which came after, 'were notorious as sites of aggressive, exclusively heteronormative masculinity' (Gilbert 2014: 172). Talking to a film crew in 2018 for the film *Bass Culture*, Paul Chambers suggests that by 1995 things had got out of hand and he stopped promoting because he felt he had 'created a monster'.

In an informed discussion of jungle's 'worries in the dance', Belle-Fortune does not sidestep the issue of violence at jungle raves, and points out that many jungle producers and DJs felt the same as Chambers and were concerned about rising violence in London jungle raves. He highlights the micro-tensions that are inherent in multiculturalism in the context of the continuation of racial power:

> On the whole white people get the upper hand, but the dance is ruled by predominantly black music. In raves, on their home turf, black people, usually black males, are the only ones free to be the bad bwoys. White guys come in peace to dance, especially if they are in the minority. The majority of black guys also come in peace to rave, but if some have got the front they can exploit the bad-bwoy-in-the-dance niche…. Problems

that affect thousands of people, can be set off by a tiny minority. (Belle-Fortune 2004: 120)

But Eastman, a white working-class veteran of sound systems and founder of the jungle pirate Kool FM, puts the worries over jungle violence in the historical context of turf wars between white youth in the 1970s and 1980s:

> if you think you've seen trouble at [jungle club] Club UN, you should have been at the Tottenham Royal every Sunday night ... you used to get little crews from Hackney fighting Tottenham. Tottenham fighting Enfield. If anyone dared come down from Broxbourne or Cheshunt they'd get bashed. When I was younger in the sound system days ... everyone walked with a knife. (Cited in Belle-Fortune 2004: 120).

It is important to remember that jungle gestated in some of the most socially deprived regions of the UK (Christodoulou 2011: 47), which had been subject to the economic and social violence that comes from de-industrialisation, under-investment and a sense of futility. In this context we can understand both the aural violence that the sonic intensity of jungle music foregrounds and the stressed environment in which actual violence is always a possibility. Jungle raves, like football terraces in previous times, became the venue for violence of which they were not the cause.

Jungle, according to Paul Chambers, was short-lived, lasting for only a year or so (1994–5) before it flew apart into subgenres. New generations of DJs and producers – like the Pay As You Go crew – had tried to break into jungle but felt locked out by the already established promoters and producers, and so moved on to the UK garage scene, where a different relation to black music history and a different balance between drum and bass was being established. Built on a speeded up and bass-heavy version of American garage, especially the work of New Jersey producer Todd Edwards and Armand Van Helden from Boston, UK producers like Grant Nelson and the Dreem Team (which included Mikee B from Top Buzz) developed a new dance scene that brought gospel/soul vocals, 'skippy beats', female dancers and a certain kind of post-disco sophistication back to the club dancefloor.

As ragga jungle waned – a victim of its own success – intelligent, tech-step and drum and bass moved jungle sonically and physically up-town. At the Metalheadz night in Hoxton Square with which I began this chapter, Goldie and his collaborators, including the female DJs Kemistry (Valerie Olukemi Olusanya) and Storm (Jayne Conneely), showcased a new, more clinical, technological sound that eschewed ragga vocals – the only MC was jazz singer Cleveland Watkiss. Attracting a diverse and media-savvy crowd, Metalheadz symbolised the mainstreaming of the jungle scene. In 1997 Roni Size (Ryan Williams), the Bristol sound system veteran who had been developing a 'jazz-step' sound with DJ Krust and his Reprazent crew, the vanguard of a Bristol invasion that included DJ Die, Dj Suv and Flynn and Flora, won the Mercury Prize for his drum and bass album *New Forms*, released by Gilles Peterson's Talkin' Loud label. In his 1998 book *Creative Britain* Chris Smith, Minister for Culture, Media and Sport in the New Labour government of Tony Blair which had swept to power in 1997 (ending eighteen years of Tory rule), noted that music was now more significant to the British economy than steel, and singled out Jazzie B of Soul II Soul and Roni Size as beacons of this exciting new British creativity (Smith 1998: 7).[17] An almost decade-long journey from marginal illegality to the centre of government attempts to rebrand the nation was complete.

Jungle's strange patriotism

Just how British is jungle? Jungle producers frequently evoke its sense of place, especially as a way to emphasise that it is the first black musical genre that is not merely a version of American or Jamaican music. For Terry Tee, producer of many early jungle tunes on Ibiza Records, including the anthemic 'I Bring You The Future', it is 'the first genre with an English stamp on it'.[18] If it is English or British,[19] then it is a new idea of Britishness. If it is patriotic, then it is a 'strange patriotism' (Reynolds 1999). The space of the nation is not understood by reference to timeless history and warm beer but as a crossroads of musical and cultural traditions – reggae and punk, hip hop and techno – that jungle mixes and extends. Jungle collapses the time-space of club music in London. Take, for example, one track from 1994: 'Burial' by Jumping Jack Frost recording as Leviticus for the V Recordings/Philly Blunt label he runs with Bryan Gee. 'Burial' combines synth washes reminiscent of acid house with a sped-up funk breakbeat, a bassline and vocal melody from the 1976 album track 'Mademoiselle' (a big hit on the rare groove dancefloors of the mid-1980s) by Florida funk band Foxy, and a 'big, bad and heavy' vocal sample from rough-voiced Jamaican ragga toaster Jigsy King from his 'My Sound a Murder' (with singer Tony Curtis) from 1996 (a song based on the classic 'real rock' riddim). The 'lovers rock' remix features a sweet reggae-style vocal from Frost's sister Yolanda. Thus lovers rock, roots reggae, dancehall, soul funk, hip hop and acid house coexist within one sound text. It is this musical recombination which leads MC Navigator (Raymond Crawford) to identify jungle as a mixture that could not have happened elsewhere: 'We've taken from reggae, rave, rare groove, hardcore, Belgian techno ... so it's a UK sound, born here.'[20]

Jungle's brand of patriotism forces the nation to imagine itself in terms of its post-colonial cities, and London in particular, and to acknowledge the racial hybridity that is there. But this is not a vapid celebration. Jungle does not aspire to dissolve difference either sonically or socially, as rave did. Instead, it foregrounds the anxiety of difference: it is tense, coiled, foreboding, it makes conflict and paranoia explicit formal themes. It does not retreat into trance and utopianism predicated on the ingestion of pacifying ecstasy. If jungle encapsulates Britishness it is not a national character of unalloyed good fellowship and phlegmatic tolerance, it is of 'inner-city pressure', a unifying experience of urban crisis, unemployment, racialised strife. For Jumping Jack Frost, London, 'an eclectic cosmopolitan city', is far more easy to identify with than any form of national identity: he rejects the still imperial connotations of national identity, even the nascent black British or 'UK Blak' identity posited by Jazzie B's Soul II Soul project – 'When it suits the British for us to be British, then we're British. When it doesn't we're black. So I just keep it black' (Jumping Jack Frost interview).

Jungle, as Nabeel Zuberi argues, is emphatically diasporic music, taking elements of Afro-American and Afro-Caribbean form and sending them back along the routes of the black Atlantic – this time *from* Britain:

> the diasporic subject's return to Africa is impossible, [but] the black artist has pieced together, juxtaposed and digitally mixed up the fragments from the past – rummaged through the rubble of the past, the documents of barbarism, in Benjaminian fashion – to create something that bears the traces of a history of ruptures. (Zuberi 2001: 174)

As such, it is an expression of the 'sustained confrontations between same and different, black and white, native and interloper [that] have been staged for the benefit of the national community as a whole in urban environments, usually […] those that London has supplied' (Gilroy 1997: 3–4).

From the outside, the racial identity of jungle might have looked straightforward. Writing about the emergence of jungle in 1996, the American hip hop writer Greg Tate suggests that it was 'the first original form of music to emerge from the black experience in the United Kingdom, a sound and a movement that UK blacks can un-equivocally call their own' (Tate 1996). But for jungle producers, DJs, MCs and crowd, while the black experience and black music styles are central to the musical subculture, jungle is pre-eminently the music of multiculture, a hybrid form which is produced and performed in mixed space by a diverse group of producers. Though producers like Paul Chambers might decry the 'white element' that he felt was gentrifying jungle, the evident importance within the circuits of jungle production of white producers/DJs like Jason Kaye (a Top Buzz alumnus), Nicholas Andersson-Gylden (aka Nicky Blackmarket, DJ and co-owner of the Black Market record shop which championed jungle), Matt Quinn (aka Optical, DJ engineer and producer) and Kevin Ford (aka DJ Hype), and many others, meant that jungle was not something that black Londoners 'called their own': instead, it was always promoted and discussed as a product of London's multiculture and its distinct musical history. 'It's not about black and white', declares MC Conrad, 'it's a multicultural, inter-racial dance thing'.[21]

If anything, jungle projects, and places a value on, a kind of mongrel identity. In an interview with the *Guardian* in 1998, Goldie suggested that jungle provides the musical correlative to his experience of growing up mixed race in 1980s Britain: 'I would look at the colour of my skin and think: I'm not black, I'm not white, I'm not anybody, who am I?' (see Aikenhead 1998).

Jungle rhythms and sonics

I now turn to jungle rhythm and production. Here I want to connect the threads of the discussion of jungle as a site of reconvening, rupture and confrontation by examining the sound text and production strategies of jungle and to think about what is happening in the space of 'the studio' (which is often at home) where jungle is made. Defined by its distinctive rhythmic form, jungle is different from techno and house because it deliberately eschews the pulsing four-four kick that is the defining rhythmic feature of these genres, instead using breakbeats usually sampled from funk records (the most famous of which is the six-minute break from an obscure 1969 B-side by the Winstons called 'Amen, Brother' – Gilbert 2014: 173). But though it shares breakbeats with hip hop, jungle deploys them in very different ways. Rather than providing a secure and consistent bed for the rapper, jungle producers use multiple breaks, sometimes six or more in a single tune, which typically change tempo frequently within each 'sound text'. Unlike hip hop or house, it is not easy to categorise jungle in terms of beats per minute (bpms) because of these rapid-tempo fluctuations. As opposed to the 80–100 bpms typical of hip hop and soul or the 120 bpms of house, jungle breakbeats will often clatter along at 160 bpms. But jungle is not simply 'fast' or 'hyper' music. It exhibits a rhythmic pluralism because the basslines move nearly always at about half the speed of the breaks (approximately 80 bpms). Jungle foregrounds poly-rhythm and poly-meter; it uses 'rhythmic contrast' or 'rhythmic clash' in a way that links it to the general form of black music identified by the composer/ musicologist Olly Wilson (1983: 4).

This has the effect of offering two possible dance tempos, two temporal spaces inside the music, for the dancer to enter. Plural rhythm could be jungle's most obvious and defining feature; it dramatically alters the feel of the dancefloor and the forms of movement licensed there. Producer Pete Haigh, who releases records as Omni Trio, describes this in his discussion of the rhythmic pattern he calls a 'soul step':

> When the tune is rolling at 160 bpms the first and third beats are empha-sised [as in funk] ... which gives the illusion that the tune is running at 160 and 80 bpms at the same time. It gives the music room to breathe and is much easier to dance to. Like the half speed Reggae bassline, the soul-step has made Jungle smooth-grooving, wind-your-waist music; sexy even. (Haigh cited in Reynolds 1994)

This rhythmic doubleness played a significant role in the cross-generational appeal to black crowds; older crowds more used to soul and reggae (like Cleveland Watkiss), the same crowds alienated by fast uni-rhythmic rave, could dance to the basslines while the youth more attuned to ragga could 'jump up' to the fast breaks. The jungle dance floor accommodated different age groups in a way that materialised its debt to reggae and soul cultures – the spheres of black expressive (more than youth) cultures – rather than its more frequently touted rave antecedents.

Diaspora science

Like the sound system operators of the 1970s and 1980s, few jungle pro-ducers had formal musical or engineering training. Getting their hands on whatever technology they could afford, or blag, they made it up as they went along. Using rudimentary samplers and drum machines and cheap digital production tools they improvised, exploring the capacities and pushing against the technical limits of digital equipment like the Yamaha TG-77 synthesiser workstation, the Mini Moog and the Waldorf Pulse (which enabled the manual oscillation of frequencies) combined with the TR-808 and TR-909 drum machines for the kick, organised using digital production suites like Cubase and Pro-Tools. Jungle and drum and bass producers particularly valued the distortion that comes with overdriving the bass frequencies, because, once clubs and raves had installed speakers adequate to the task, they could reproduce the sub-bass frequencies below 60 Hz, which, rather than heard, are felt in the body (Henriques 2011). This echoed the experiments with bass that had always defined the vernacular sonic science of the sound systems and the production practices of dub. 'As someone who came up in the sound system era in the '70s', says Cleveland Watkiss, 'when it was all about the science of sound, [jungle] was the closest I had ever heard to that' (cited in Burns 2013).

Reggae producer Dennis Bovell describes how in the studio he often pushed bass frequencies above the limits dictated by studio gauges, much to the horror of the trained studio engineers, for whom distortion was a mistake (Dennis Bovell interview, 24 February 2017). Junglist producers, in a way similar to Public Enemy's Bomb Squad producers discussed by Tricia Rose in *Black Noise*, 'play in the red', pushing technology beyond its usual capabilities, where it distorts, buzzes and creates a disruptive dissonance. In Rose's argument, this rupture questions the ideological division between music and noise, and by extension the whole series of binary distinctions by which racialised power holds ideological sway (Rose 1994).

Like DJ Pierre's acid bassline, or the pop and crackle of the original vinyl on the Quincy Jones sample that underlies the Pharcyde's 'Passin' Me By' (1992), mistakes and discrepancies which would be expunged in 'correct' mixing practices are reincorporated, folded back into a larger sense of unity, almost as a way to assert control over the painful happen-stances of racialised life (Snead 1984). 'Some of the best things are mistakes', says Bristol producer DJ Krust, 'you hit a button accidentally and a sound comes out that you like. The attitude we have about music is to be spontaneous, you don't make something and bash it into shape, you do it and it feels right and there it is' (cited in Melville 1997).

This 'deliberate experimentalism' is often described through the trope of science (Gilbert 2014: 171), especially in the more 'techie' strand of drum and bass that emerged from 1995. While we should be a little cautious of taking at face value subcultural claims to rebellion, and drum and bass producers could be particularly fetishistic about technology; nevertheless, the intense experimentation of this period betrays an attitude – one that Goldie described to *Guardian* journalist Decca Aikenhead (1998) as 'joy-riding technology' – that links it directly to Afro-diasporic aesthetic practices. Despite the many hours devoted to producing and exploring the capacities of technical equipment, this attitude involves a disavowal of technical expertise and of hard work. Describing his compositional practice, Roni Size calls it 'headtop' (a term for improvisation, derived from reggae sound system culture – see Jones and Pinnock 2017: 64):

'We don't go into the studio with a list of things, yeah we'll have the bass drum there and the bassline there and we'll have X dbs, nah man, you switch on and hit those buttons. I don't know kilohertz but I know killer beats.' But surely you use the digital technology, I asked him. 'Yeah, I use Cubase but I also use pots and pans, I use wooden leg.' (Melville 1997)

Size connects his sonic practice directly to the bass culture sound system traditions he grew up in in Bristol, where economic marginalisation and technological failure offer new aesthetic possibilities: 'We didn't have a proper system. We were always blowing the amps and the bass bins. I like it when the speakers blow. I like the sounds harsh. What's too toppy for you might be lashing for me' (Melville 1997). We can read this through novelist Toni Morrison's definition of the practices of diasporic art which foregrounds 'the ability to use found objects, the appearance of using found things' and which 'must be effortless, you must not look like you're sweating' (Morrison cited in Gilroy 1993: 78). This recalls Houston Baker's concept of 'deformations of mastery': the use of objects, products, technologies in ways not sanctioned or anticipated by the institutional forces that produced them (Baker 1987). Both Tricia Rose (1994) and Charles Mudede (2013) discuss this tendency in hip hop: the high value placed on noise, disturbance and mistake ('rupture'), a 'wild-style' approach to recording conventions (Mudede 2013) and an antipathy to the too-clean, the too-planned. Jungle foregrounds just this ambivalence about technological rationality.

The feature of 'time-stretching', for example, was inbuilt in samplers in the late 1980s as an 'invisible' production aid to allow the tempo of recordings to be altered without changing the pitch, to fix mistakes in vocals and allow the seamless stitching together of different parts of a recording. The high-pitched 'chipmunk' vocals on many early hardcore records were a result of producers sampling vocals without using time-stretching (something that became for a while a valued part of the 'mental' hardcore aesthetic). Time-stretching opened up new aesthetic opportunities to jungle producers undreamt of by the sampler design-ers. They used it to rip the breakbeats apart or compress them in such a way as to emphasise technological mediation and the presence of the producer. Roni Size's minimalist 1994 release 'Time Stretch' (V Record-ings) demonstrates the woozy sonic possibilities of time-stretching. As Andrew Goodwin argues in relation to new digital production technol-ogies, these practices eschew 'illusionism': they are not trying to create the impression of a 'real human community' and as such they serve as a riposte to 'rationalisation in the recording process' (Goodwin 1988: 48). As Christodoulou puts it, in drum and bass production, 'technology itself as the medium of power in the post-industrial city has become "renegade" in the sense that it has been appropriated by those who are routinely oppressed, exploited and rendered surplus to requirements' (Christodoulou 2011: 52).

Digital music and the post-human

Jungle draws attention to itself as technologically, digitally produced[22] and because of this it has been placed by Kodwo Eshun in the lineage of Afro-futurism, which attempts to generate the escape velocity necessary to transcend the 'pointless and treacherous category' of the human itself (Eshun 1998: 5). Certainly there are cyborgian strains like the 'neurofunk' subgenre of the late 1990s championed by Grooverider and Orbital that suggests in its iconography and sounds new syntheses of man and machine. The 'sonic futurism' of drum and bass can be read against the 'nourishing, soul-warming' pleas for inclusion in the human family that characterise the humanist soul tradition, as Eshun does so brilliantly. But is it really post-human? This argument stands up only if you treat the genre as pure sound and ignore the space within which it comes to be.

Because it is a dance music, even the most technological drum and bass is mediated by the dancing body – 'our live element', says producer Rob Haigh, 'happens on the dancefloor' (cited in Reynolds 1994) – in the face-to-face relationship between music, dancing crowd and DJ. 'The only way you can perform dance music is DJing', says producer Matt 'MJ' Cole:

> it's the performance element of the music. It seems to be such a simple thing, but the more I do it the more I recognise my responsibility to the crowd, it is an interaction with the crowd … of course it can be a total shambles. (MJ Cole interview, 10 September 1998)

Thus, I think, jungle resists both post-humanist theorists and humanist technological determinists who suggest that digital production is corroding the soul of music.

Jungle embodies neither a complete rejection of the compromised human body, fatally marked by identity and its attendant plea for realness voiced by the notion of 'soul', as Eshun (1998) believes, nor is it a fatal retreat from the complexity of fragile humanity embodied in the soul and reggae tradition, as Paul Gilroy has argued. In the essay 'Analogues of Mourning, Mourning the Analog', Gilroy argues that there is a loss embodied by digital music production: 'digital audio, stagnation and what we could politely call recycling have intervened to make live music less pleasurable.… This loss involves grieving for a certain fragile, precious relationship between black music and black politics' (Gilroy

1999: 262). He laments the squeezing out of 'feeble, fragile humanity' by 'deskilling, dehumanizing technologies' and the 'imprisonment of rhythm' within a quantised digital matrix in 'house and its dismal off-shoots' (Gilroy 1999: 267–9).

Though it is not clear if he includes jungle as one of these 'dismal offshoots' (he told me in 2017 that he 'loves jungle') his argument establishes an unsustainable binary between 'real' music made using analogue technology that supported the 'performance-centred' cultures of diasporic dance music and a debased digital simulacrum. This somewhat fogeyish technological determinism[23] seems to contradict his own case for what made black music cultures significant in the first place. He has always argued that there are political meanings in the 'performance' elements and spatial practice of black music cultures, irreducible to their mode of production, which reside in the unfinished nature of black music recordings and the way they are put to use in remote, often partially hidden sites of intercultural collectivity. He once considered the role of dance, of cut and mix, of dubbing and DJing and the fact that these took place in partially hidden spheres to be part of the political charge of this culture. Without providing empirical evidence for the disappearance of this culture, you are left with the impression that what has actually changed is the relationship between Gilroy himself and the music cultures he discusses. Nor does he attempt, in this admittedly polemical piece, to distinguish between different cases. Of course, a lot of crap music is made digitally, but was that not also the case with electric guitars (which are also technology, greeted in their own time with technophobic dismissal for example with Bob Dylan as Judas!)? Producer Matt Quinn agrees with Gilroy that 'computers have been very detrimental to [music] because they have a grid on it and everything is very rigid'. In his production practice, just like that of the hip hop producer JDilla, he turns off the 'grids' which quantise the music (arranging it into a pre-set even pattern) and 'just goes by ear and feel' (DJ Optical (interview, 2 March 2017). And although since the turn of the millennium digital dance music has been widely circulated online and experienced on headphones and in the digital space, jungle and drum and bass is still a music made to be experienced in social space, on the dancefloor, in real time, via speakers with paper cones and analogue eardrums. Jungle 'is not a question of giving up "humanness" to accept the machine and a cyborgian future' writes Zuberi, 'but the integration of technology into existing discourse of musical creativity' (2001:169).

Conclusion

By the end of the 1990s, London black music culture had moved well beyond drum and bass. UK garage achieved hegemony over black clubbing for a few short years, subgenres like dubstep, wonky and bassline emerged and subsided, and a new rap-based genre, grime, emerged, developed by a younger generation in the same east London breeding grounds that produced jungle (Hancox 2018). But jungle/drum and bass was not dead: it had just gone outernational. As the internet facilitated the rapid globalisation of music cultures, drum and bass – the London contribution to black Atlantic bass culture – started influencing music production in America; Goldie recorded with KRS-One; hip hop legend Afrika Bambaata added jungle into his DJ sets; R&B producers like Rodney Jerkins and Timbaland started adding junglish rhythms to their productions; drum and bass producer Rupert Parke (Photek) moved to LA to make movie soundtracks. Meanwhile, following the routes of internationalised club culture in which London was the strongest brand, jungle DJs started to travel widely to cities across Europe, America and Australasia, where proto-drum and bass scenes emerged. Jumping Jack Frost claims to have DJed in all the major cities of the world; drum and bass clubs and festivals sprang up in Croatia, Sardinia ('Sun and Bass'), the Netherlands, Japan, Singapore and Dubai. Jungle/drum and bass is, twenty-five years later, in rude economic health, providing viable careers for a wide range of London music producers and DJs, though its rebellious energy has been tamped down through its institutionalisation.

Though this has been a great boon for careers and bank balances of DJs and producers, others have mourned the decline in the UK of the last pre-digital 'local' and future-oriented music, which was not reliant, as both EDM and grime are, on YouTube or social media. For the music theorist Mark Fisher, for example, jungle represented the last gasp of musical modernity's 'future shock': 'Play a jungle record from 1993 to someone in 1989', he wrote in 2013, 'and it would have sounded like something so new that it challenged them to rethink what music was, or could be', whereas 'the 21st Century is oppressed by a crushing sense of finitude and exhaustion. It doesn't feel like the future' (Fisher 2013). Instead, we have been delivered into a world of endless recycling, defined by 'retro-mania' (Reynolds 2010). A world where the future has been cancelled.

For the cultural theorist Jeremy Gilbert, the problem is that jungle and drum and bass never delivered the political solidarities, institutions or transformations its sonic radicalism implied, serving instead to dissipate into political impotency, unable to establish the new subjectivities which might be able to resist 'its own ongoing exploitation' (Gilbert 2014: 184). For these thinkers, the idea of a drum and bass festival in the air-conditioned ex-pat enclaves of authoritarian Dubai or Singapore in 2018 would precisely symbolise the problem, their very definition of 'post-future' hell, of jungle failing to fulfil our desires for art to fix reality. But this is to burden the music with a weight it cannot bear. But what jungle/drum and bass has become does not exhaust its significance.

If, as I have done in this book, you place jungle in the context of the racialised divisions of London, the emergence of reggae sound systems in the 1960s and 1970s, the warehouse parties of the 1980s, rave and hardcore in the 1990s and the musical subcultures of UK garage, dubstep and grime which followed, jungle can be read as the sonic articulation of a racially mixed city. It is not segregated by necessity, as is reggae, nor hidden away like the warehouse parties; it does not resolve the tensions of multicultural heterogeneity through a premature pharmacological utopianism, like rave. In fact, it makes these tensions part of its aesthetic practice, refusing to resolve itself into any simple equation of black or white, British or diasporic, body or intellect. As such, it marks the moment when London finally puts something back into the circulating flows of black Atlantic culture from which it has taken so much, when

'A London Sum'ting Dis': diaspora remixed in the urban jungle

London multiculture finds – in the cockney patois of its MCs, the digital codes of its production software, the clashing rhythms of its breakbeat – the resources for the construction of a language of its own.

Notes

1 The title of a jungle track by Code 071 (1992).
2 Ironically perhaps, the Stone Roses were a key influence on both Oasis and Blur, the bands that would launch the indie fightback against dance, in the guise of Britpop, in the mid-1990s. Jeremy Gilbert, for example, reads the Britpop–New Labour alliance as an explicit ideological attempt to push back against the influence of 'black' dance music (see Gilbert 2014).
3 The *Guardian* on 31 March 2015 suggested a police van deliberately drove into the crowd.
4 Kevin Ford, aka DJ Hype, is a white Londoner from Hackney who had grown up with both black and white friends. They knew each other but would not socialise together, he says, until rave. See Belle-Fortune (2004: 23).
5 See for example https://www.youtube.com/watch?v=xQbfN3EGgTE and https://www.youtube.com/watch?v=pU4F706VsMA (accessed 1 July 2019).
6 I had a conversation with a white public-school-educated financial advisor in 2017 who, though he had no personal knowledge, refused to accept that ecstasy and cocaine use was far more common among the white middle classes than in the black club scenes of Brixton.
7 *Bass Culture* is a documentary made by the London-based youth production company Fully Focused in 2018 as part of the Bass Culture research project funded the Arts and Humanities Research Council. It premièred on 9 May 2019 at Regents Street Cinema, London, but at the time of writing the film had yet to be broadcast or receive a commercial release. The film explores the links between reggae sound system culture and post-rave genres like jungle, UK garage and grime, through interviews with four generations of black British artists, including Wretch 23, Giggs, Jammer and MC Navigator.
8 'Gabber' is Amsterdam slang for 'mate'. Gabber institutionalised a strong heteronormative masculinity, used a strong over-driven bass pulse, and cele-brated violence, drugs and profanity on tracks called, for example, 'Cuntface', 'Skull Domination' and 'We Will Dominate'. It attracted large, almost exclu-sively white male crowds. It became popular within the neo-fascist raves scene of northern Europe and the Midwestern United States.
9 Originally published in 1998 as *All Crews Mus Big Up*, it was reissued in 2004 as *All Crews* with new material covering the late 1990s.
10 Paul Chambers admitted in an interview with Ian McQuaid that when he chose the name Ibiza for his label he'd never been to the island, and didn't

even have a passport – 'I was imagining what the whole rave culture was like in Ibiza' – a direct example of the potency of the Ibiza mythology. See McQuaid (n.d.).

11 The terms can be confusing. In post-disco club culture, the DJ is the one who plays the records, whereas in reggae sound system culture the DJ is the vocalist, or toaster, who garnishes the music with lyrics, and the records are chosen by 'the selector'. Both uses of the term 'DJ' derive from the radio 'disc jockey', who both played records and talked into the microphone. For simplicity in this chapter I use DJ to refer to the person playing the records, and MC (which is what vocalist are called in hip hop – derived from 'master of ceremonies') to indicate the vocalists. See Zuberi (2014) and Henry (2006) for expert discussions of the importance of the MC in black music.

12 Purity was a value highly prized in the techno scene: Pure was the name of an influential techno club in Edinburgh, which ran from 1990 to 2000.

13 The title of a track from Goldie's debut album *Timeless* (1995, FFRR). Dan Hancox borrowed the term for his book on the history of grime (2018), a musical genre which, as he makes clear, owes a lot to the innovations of jungle.

14 The story of Ben Jones from Bracknell, a New Town in Berkshire, thirty-four miles from London, is typical. Bracknell offered limited musical opportunities, until rave. Then Ben's friend took him to a rave in the late 1980s. 'I didn't know what to expect. Once I was there I couldn't believe it, I became obsessed.' Rave offered Ben connections to a network of clubs and ravers throughout the south of England. Through this network he found access to others: he found work with the reggae sound system Renegade, which was at that time providing the sound system for raves, and this was the first time he had been in close social contact with black people. Working as a 'soundboy' (a fetching and carrying dogs-body for the sound system) he strove to earn the knowledge and respect that were the currency of these informal networks. This sound system connection brought him into jungle.

15 Musicologist Richard Middleton argues that Ellington's jungle period (1927–32) exhibited a complex 'double consciousness': both a blatant exoticism, attractive to white audiences, and a sophisticated, reflexive commentary on primitivism. The UK's jungle, like that of Ellington, avoids 'ideological closure' (Middleton, 2000: 70–5).

16 Letter from 'A Junglist, N.W. London', *Touch* magazine, 7 June 1994, p. 58.

17 Smith's argument was somewhat undermined by his obvious unfamiliarity with his examples – he called both Roni Size and Jazzie B 'singers'.

18 Terry Tee in the *Bass Culture* documentary.

19 The slippage between the terms is a symptom of the fact that no one – in England – really understands the difference between Britain, England and the United Kingdom.

20 MC Navigator in the *Bass Culture* documentary.

21 MC Conrad in Jo Wiser's 1994 film *A London Some'ting Dis* (Sharper Image Productions), first broadcast on Channel 4 on 4 June 1993.

22 Both Roni Size (New Forms, 1997) and Goldie (featuring KRS 1, 1998) have recorded tracks called 'Digital'. Digital is also the name taken by producer Steve Carr.

23 To be fair, Gilroy acknowledges that his argument might be read as a version of 'things ain't what they used to be': 'I feel obliged to confess that my own critical standpoint has been shaped by a sense of loss that is my demographic, geographical and generational affliction' (Gilroy 1999: 262).

Epilogue: music and the multicultural city

Back in the late 1990s, at the highpoint of drum and bass, it seemed plausible to be optimistic about the prospects of transcending old divisions of race and space in the city, and the role music might play in this process. The emergence of jungle – with its assertion of a confident, pan-racial Brit-*ish* identity (Zuberi 2001), making use of the Afro-diasporic music of the past reconfigured through digital technology and the combinatorial London sensibility – seemed to offer a multi-cultural alternative to stale forms of ethno-nationalism and racialised power geometry. But such optimism now seems much less plausible, even naive. Mark Fisher was perhaps right that, with the arrival of digi-tised plenty – streaming services like Spotify have catalogues of tens of millions of songs across genres and historical periods – the possibilities of music delivering 'future shock' have been cancelled, along with the idea of the future itself (Fisher 2013). Is Jeremy Gilbert correct that, as potent a cultural force as jungle appeared to be, it failed to deliver the kind of political transformation its sonic radicalism implied? Gilbert has argued that though club cultures like rave and jungle offered the possibility of 'the deterritorialisation of certain kinds of subjectivity – and the potentiation of radical new modes of collective desire', these processes are all too easily 'reterritorialised by new figures of sexualised and commodified identity' (Gilbert 2007: 7). In this writing about the possibilities of music cultures to offer new alternatives, melancholy is the pervasive tone. What has happened to London space in the early twenty-first century seems to confirm this view.

The reshaping of cursed London

As early in the new millennium as 2004, Stuart Hall had already noted the trends that were undermining the promise of racially diverse, post-colonial cities like London to offer more equitable multicultural futures. London, he argued, was being 'reshaped' by the forces of globalisation, deindustrialisation and migration that were fragmenting city space, dividing it between the gilded but increasingly empty enclaves of the 'ultra high net worth individuals' for whom property is investment not dwelling, the defensive zones of the 'white flight suburbs and estates' and the 'run down inner urban areas' of social deprivation and economic dislocation (Hall 2004). Against the backdrop of the triumph of market fundamentalism – the low levels of regulation, the shrivelling welfare state and the global capital flows he named as neoliberalism (Hall 2011; see also Davies 2014) – Hall's 'divided city' was seeing 'multiculturalism … stretched to breaking point' (Hall 2004). He saw little reason to be optimistic about its future.

Such gloom has only been deepened more recently by studies like journalist Anne Minton's *Big Capital* (2017), which shows how in-equality in the city has been fuelled by London's property market. That market has been catastrophically distorted by the flagship 'right to buy' and 'buy to let' policies of Conservative governments and by the financialisation of the London property market.[1] Two million council homes have been sold off, 40 per cent of which are now in the hands of private landlords charging unaffordable rents, and the in-flow of global capital invested in housing as a strategic asset is hollowing out formerly diverse neighbourhoods. In 2018 the National Crime Agency estimated that in the region of £90 billion[2] was being laundered through the UK annually (Reuters, 22 March 2018), the majority of which was invested in London, 'the world capital for corruption and money laundering, the proceeds being funnelled straight into the super prime and prime property markets' (Minton 2017: 1). The city 'is a space increasingly made by, and in response to, the raw power of supremely monied individuals', argue the authors of a paper on 'plutocratic' London, creating an 'urbanism of two different speeds and directions: the super-charged rush of capital and bodies to the luxury districts' and an 'exodus of lower paid and marginal groups that are seen as an illegitimate burden on the newly wealthy' (Atkinson et al. 2017: 181, 194). This has consequences for the spaces where 'everyday mixity' can emerge in the city: the warehouses and club spaces of Bankside, Paddington Basin and Kings Cross, where club multiculture was incubated, have been brought within the realm of fixed and dominated space through their transformation into high-end residential, commercial and leisure zones, promising luxury living, innovation and, as the *South China Morning Post* put it in 2017, exceptional returns for Hong Kong investors.[3]

A grim symbol for the failed promise of London is the charred hulk of Grenfell Tower, the twenty-four-storey social housing block in west London that was engulfed in flames on 14 June 2017, leading to the death of seventy-one residents and the displacement of hundreds of others. Though what poet Ben Okri described days after as 'a burnt matchbox in the sky' (Okri in the *Financial Times*, 27 June 2017) was concealed behind white plastic just before the first anniversary of the fire, the traumatic images of that night watched live on TV by millions are not so easily forgotten.[4] That the fire was accelerated by the external cladding fitted by the council to improve the look of the block in one of Europe's wealthiest areas and that the council, despite repeated warnings from residents about the inadequacy of the fire safety provisions, had failed to fit a sprinkler system or fire escapes, have rendered Grenfell a potent image for local authority neglect, corruption and the failure of the city's multicultural promise.[5]

The ethnic diversity of Grenfell made manifest the lived multiculture of London's housing estates, but the fire and its aftermath revealed the growing gulf between city communities and the processes of turbo-gentrification which were conspiring to clear the area of residents of 'ultra low net worth'.[6] Grenfell residents galvanised a dignified and potent political campaign to highlight the inadequacies of local-authority and government planning,[7] within which London musicians have been prominent (see Hancox 2018: 287–91). Grime and hip hop artists AJ Tracey, Akala and Lowkey helped to keep Grenfell in the public eye and the performance by grime MC Stormzy at the Brit Awards in February 2018, broadcast live on terrestrial TV, addressed Prime Minister Theresa May directly, asking 'where is the money for Grenfell' and calling her inaction 'criminal'.[8]

In 2018 the London-based genre drill, a 'dark and nihilistic' (Hancox 2018: 304) adaption of a bleak version of Chicago rap made predominantly by black working-class youth from the housing estates of Brixton Hill, Tulse Hill and Kennington in south London, became subject to a moral panic for its glorification of violent crime and drug dealing (Thapar 2018a). In May 2018 YouTube removed thirty videos by London drill artists, at the urging of the Metropolitan Police, for their 'incitement of gang violence'.[9] Ciaran Thapar, a youth worker and journalist, does not exonerate London drill from playing a part in fermenting turf wars and knife violence – songs distributed via YouTube that fuel 'postcode' feuds, celebrate stabbings using an array of slang synonyms for knifing (chef, ching, wet) and urge retribution are shared widely on social media – but he does make the point that it is a sense of social, economic and physical vulnerability rather than the music which encourages youth to carry knives, and that the music is both a form of 'vicious rebellion' and 'a source of catharsis, legitimate income, digital visibility, and a means of exposing hidden, localised truth to the outside world' (Thapar 2018b).

Before the moral panic around drill, London musicians had been making links between the rise of plutocratic money-laundered London and the rise of desperation and knife violence on the streets in ways politicians had signally failed to do.[10] In 'Hangman', released in February 2018, the Streatham grime/hip hop artist Dave provided a sonic counterpoint to Grenfell,[11] addressing knife crime and postcode wars – 'too many youts are dying and I'm sick of it' – over a heart-breaking piano riff and deep sub-bass. The recent jailing of his brother and the rise in stabbings – 'Snaps in a prison cell, bodies in a coffin' – leads Dave to conclude that 'London is cursed, this city's got a problem'.[12]

Them changes

But there are rays of light in the gloom. Though drill narrates a bleak vision of the London stuck on the wrong side of gentrification and could be read as both a cry for help and a bitter warning of the consequences of exclusion, neglect and the continuing consequences of urban racism, it is simultaneously building an audience far outside the confines of south London estates, through the internet, and its moral economy is expanding as voices emerge from within drill determined to speak against gang violence and push the aesthetic possibilities of the music (Tharpar 2018b).

There is an analogy here with the story of grime, the London-born British rap genre which emerged from the estates of east London at the end of the 1990s, drawing on the sonic models of the reggae sound system, jungle and garage but placing the MC – the rapper – at the centre. As journalist Dan Hancox shows in his definitive grime history, *Inner City Pressure* (2018), the genre's restless inventiveness and adept colonisation of the digital space allowed it to transcend the grim circumstances of its gestation, defeat the limitations imposed on it – like the notorious risk assessment Form 696 which curtailed grime shows in London because of fears of violence and which was scrapped in 2017 – build a global following and become, by 2018, an established pop genre. The Thornton Heath grime artist Stormzy in 2018 established a publishing imprint with Penguin, through his Merky brand; he has endowed scholarships for disadvantaged youth at Cambridge University and headlined at the Glastonbury Festival in 2019. Grime and drill are, in many ways, distinct from the dance multicultures of rare groove, rave and jungle. They are not in a strict sense dance genres, as they are based more on music production and the centrality of the now distinctive form of London rap voice. But, as the testimony from many of the major players in grime attests – including Kano, Giggs and JME, gathered by the producers of the *Bass Culture* film, made by the London youth production company Fully Focused in 2018 – grime draws on deep familial, cultural and aesthetic connections to sound system, funk, rave and garage. And as with reggae, garage and jungle, though a majority of the producers of the music are black (though not all of them), the grime audience, both in London and that built globally through the internet, is decidedly multicultural (there is even a passionate grime scene in Japan).

Alongside the rise of grime has come a renaissance of London jazz. Live performances by an array of new jazz acts – influenced both by a range of American jazz styles, from hard bop to spiritual jazz, and by Nigerian Afrobeat and spurred in part by the reintegration of jazz into American hip hop by LA artists like Flying Lotus, Thundercat, Kendrick Lamaar and Kamasi Washington – have emerged in the city, offering a viable alternative to disc-based club culture. This new jazz scene has emerged in small venues like the Total Refreshment Centre in Stoke Newington,[13] the free jazz jam SteamDown in a small bar in Deptford, the Mau-Mau Bar in Portobello Road and the Church of Sound at St James the Great Church in Clapton and, increasingly, at established venues like the South Bank and the Roundhouse. This scene – which includes Ezra Collective, Sons of Kemet, Kokoroko, Binker and Moses and the Seed Ensemble – has been nurtured through a network of music schools, training programmes like that run by the Tomorrow's Warriors organisation and funding streams provided by the Arts Council and PRS foundation, and has constituted itself as a lively club culture where young multicultural audiences are dancing to jazz inflected with both the traditions of black Atlantic music and the influence of post-rave club culture and grime. This jazz scene – unlike, say the white middle-class acid jazz scene of the early 1990s – is distinguished by the fact that it is driven and supported by young black multicultural Londoners, with a far higher proportion of prominent young women – for instance tenor sax player Nubya Garcia, composer and bandleader Cassie Kinoshi, trumpeter Shelia Maurice-Grey (see figure 5.1) and multi-instrumentalist and producer Emma Jane Thackery – than any of the male-dominated club cultures ever achieved.

Figure 5.1 Cassie Kinoshi (baritone sax) and Sheila Maurice-Grey of Kokoroko, performing the Fela Kuti songbook with the Ezra Collective at the Church of Sound, Clapton, June 2017. Photograph by Mochles Simawi

Both jazz and new forms of rap like drill and Afro-swing reflect the changing composition of multiculture in London. A shift in London's black population since the 1980s, which saw a large influx of migrants from Nigeria, Ghana, Sierra Leone, Congo and Somalia, has meant that black London is no longer majority Caribbean, and this has had an influence on the music being produced in the capital. Numerous jazz, grime and Afro-swing artists – Skepta, Dizzee Rascal, Lethal Bizzle, Donae'o, Sneakbo – hail from West African families and the influence of the West African music they heard at home is placed in juxtaposition with the reggae, hip hop, rave and garage music of the city, producing distinctive new hybrids (Hancox 2018: 43; Adegoke 2018).

As I write these last lines, London, as viewed through its black music multicultures, seems to be looking in both directions at once. Drill is articulating the consequences of the violent economic re-ordering of London space, and the narrowing of the options for black working-class youth whose access to spaces of security and sociality has been dramatically cut (eighty-one youth clubs have closed in the city since 2011, according to BBC News, 20 March 2018); they have often been excluded from school (as part of the neoliberal race to boost rankings), employment and access to the zones of vibrant multiculture. On the other hand, London jazz celebrates this very everyday multi-culture, which the new generation recognises has an economic value in a global market where multiculture sells (Gilroy 2000); as the Ezra Collective drummer Femi Koleoso joked, his band, with two black players, two white players and one of mixed race, 'looks as if they were a box-checking boy band dreamed up in a record exec's boardroom' (Hutchinson 2018). The new jazz draws on the rich resources of the black Atlantic and its 'ethic of antiphony' (we're talking about people moshing to tuba solos) and London's musical past, to tell an affirma-tive history and project a bright future for a city where colonial people and their 'stubbornly post-colonial' children have remade space, both physical and sonic, in the interests of freedom and love. Drill warns that this hard-won multicultural space is not open to all, and even as its innovative packaging of difference becomes articulated to the global ambitions of brand Britain, it might yet shrink away. These are two sides of the black music coin – joy and pain, beauty and alienation – and we need to keep listening carefully to what they are telling us.

Notes

1 The right of council tenants to purchase their council houses ('right to buy') became a core part of the Conservative Party platform under Margaret Thatcher and was enshrined in law in the Housing Act 1980 (see Davies

2013). 'Buy to let', a bundle of polices designed to increase the pool of private landlords by encouraging ordinary people to invest in rental property, took off in the 1990s, enabled by the Housing Act 1988, which placed limits on the rights of sitting tenants. Both policies created 'vast opportunities for asset appreciation' but had a destructive impact on those communities who were 'in the way' (Paccoud 2016: 858).

2 In fact, the report's authors argued that £90 billion was probably an underestimate.

3 'Paddington Regeneration: Affordable Waterfront Living in Central London', *South China Morning Post*, 14 August 2017.

4 Residents argued that the covering was the wrong colour and should have been green, the colour adopted by Grenfell survivors to symbolise their loss and that the tragedy should not be forgotten. See https://metro.co.uk/2018/05/05/grenfell-tower-covering-changed-wrong-colour-7522761 (accessed 1 July 2019).

5 After Grenfell, it was revealed that Robert Davis, the chair of the planning committee on neighbouring Westminster council, had been extravagantly wined and dined more than 150 times by lobbyists for property developers over the previous three years, revealing the extent of collusion between developers and local authorities in London (*Guardian*, 19 February 2018).

6 Local resident Mickey Tracey described the situation in these terms to the *Guardian*: 'We're Muslims, we're Christians, we're Sikhs, we're Hindus, we're Spanish, we're white, we're black, we're Moroccan, we're Algerian, we're everything, and they are just trying to slowly but surely push us out and bring in either the Chelsea set or Russian vacant homeowners'. *Guardian* video, 19 June 2017, at https://www.theguardian.com/uk-news/video/2017/jun/19/grime-aj-tracey-on-grenfell-tower-fire-weve-seen-no-government-response-video-grime-.

7 Including a monthly march which articulated the grief, anger and frustration of the residents through an eloquent silence.

8 See the *Guardian*, 22 February 2018. Stormzy provoked a reaction from the government, which immediately reiterated its commitment to a £52.29 million recovery package, and admitted that initial responses were too slow. Then Prime Minister May publicly admitted her regret for not visiting the site of the tragedy earlier.

9 *Guardian*, 29 May 2018.

10 A good example is Jammz's 2016 grime track 'It's a London Ting': 'corporations move poor people out their homes and they claim they're fixing them / in the endz / apart from pushing up the rental prices Starbucks ain't doing shit for the endz'.

11 Grime follows in the tradition of hip hop depictions of degraded life on London streets. Examples include 'Capsize' by Dels (2011), Roots Manuva's 'Skid Valley' (2011) and Plan B's 'Ill Manors' (2012).

12 'Hangman' is also noteworthy for how Dave addresses directly the furore he caused when, in the light of rising knife crime, he tweeted his support for increased police stop and searches, the controversy over which, concerning the disproportionate targeting of black youth by police, has raged since the era of 'sus' in the 1970s (Hall et al. 1978). Dave was widely criticised, a minor tweet storm broke out, a debate that only deepened when someone filmed Dave himself being subjected to a police street stop only days later. In 'Hangman' he recounts: 'I don't know what I was thinking in the tweets about the searches / But when Harry got murdered man was so emotional / Trying to find solutions / I had some good intentions / but I guess I couldn't word them'.

13 At the time of writing, the Total Refreshment Centre has had to suspend live shows pending an investigation by Hackney council into allegations of unlicensed alcohol sales. This is part of a wider attempt by some local authorities to crack down on music venues, which has led to the closure of some venues and anxiety about how rising rents, property speculation, and the strict application of licensing and noise-abatement laws are shrinking the space for music (see the report by the UK Live Music Consensus at http://uklivemusiccensus.org, accessed 1 July 2019). Sound system operator Lloyd Coxsone confirms that the use of sound-limiting devices (which cut off power once a pre-defined volume has been reached) is preventing reggae sound systems from using the kinds of municipal spaces like town halls which used to provide venues for reggae dances (Lloyd Coxsone interview, 1 November 2017).

Appendix: interviews for the book

This appendix lists the people I have interviewed for this book. Interviewees are listed alphabetically by first name. These interviews are mostly unpublished, with the exception of portions of the interviews with Cleveland Watkiss, Roni Size and DJ Krust, which were published in *Touch* magazine. This list also includes interviews conducted as part of Bass Culture, an academic project funded by the Arts and Humanities Research Council (AHRC) run by Mykaell Riley at the University of Westminster, for which I was a researcher. I have indicated where these were interviews done by me, and where they were done by my Bass Culture colleagues Chris Christodoulo, Jacqueline Springer or Mykaell Riley. Footage of most of the Bass Culture interviews can be found online (https://vimeo.com/basscultureresearch) and the full interviews will be published as an edited collection in due course.

Name (given name)	Profession	Location	Interviewer	Date
Asher Senator (Peter St Aubyn)	MC	University of Westminster, Harrow	Caspar Melville for Bass Culture	13/04/2017
Ben Jolly	Label head	*Barely Breaking Even* offices, Soho	Caspar Melville	05/12/1998

Appendix: interviews for the book

Blacker Dread (Stephen Burnet-Martin)	Selector	University of Westminster, Harrow	Caspar Melville for Bass Culture	12/05/2017
Brian Belle-Fortune	Journalist	His home, London	Chris Christodoulou for Bass Culture	06/03/2017
Bryan Gee	DJ, label head	V Recording Offices, Brixton	Caspar Melville	02/03/1999
Cleveland Watkiss	Jazz singer, MC	Offices of *Dorado Records*, Soho	Caspar Melville	07/07/1996
Colin Dale	DJ, producer	Great North Wood pub, West Norwood	Caspar Melville	30/07/2017
Dan Benedict	Promoter	At his mother-in-law's house, Islington	Caspar Melville	12/08/1998
Dennis Bovell	Sound system operator, producer	University of Westminster, Harrow	Caspar Melville for Bass Culture	24/02/2017
DJ Ade of Nzinga Soundz (Lynda Rosenoir-Patten)	DJ	University of Westminster, Harrow	Caspar Melville for Bass Culture	05/06/2017
DJ Dodge (Roger Drakes)	DJ	His home, Wandsworth, London	Caspar Melville	04/08/1998
DJ Krust (Kit Thompson)	DJ, producer	Back seat of a car, central London	Caspar Melville	04/07/1997
DJ Optical (Matt Quinn)	DJ, producer	His studio, London	Chris Christodoulou for Bass Culture	02/03/2017
Don Letts	DJ, filmmaker, writer	His studio, London	Mykaell Riley for Bass Culture	07/12/2017
Dubplate Pearl (Pearl Boatswain)	DJ	University of Westminster, Harrow	Caspar Melville for Bass Culture	20/08/2017
Femi Fem (Femi Williams)	DJ, promoter	His home, Ealing, west London	Caspar Melville	08/07/1999

Gilles Peterson	DJ, label head, broadcaster	Brownswood basement, north London	Caspar Melville	03/08/2017
Gordon Mac (Gordon McNamee)	DJ, radio head	Mi-Soul Radio studios, south-east London	Caspar Melville for Bass Culture	22/02/2017
H Patten	Choreographer	University of Westminster, Harrow	Caspar Melville for Bass Culture	18/07/2018
Jaimie D'Cruz	Magazine editor	*Touch Magazine* offices, Brixton	Caspar Melville	06/08/1998
Jumping Jack Frost (Nigel Thompson)	DJ, producer	Mi-Soul Radio studios, south-east London	Caspar Melville for Bass Culture	27/03/2017
Junie Rankin of Nzinga Soundz (June Reid)	DJ	University of Westminster, Harrow	Caspar Melville for Bass Culture	05/06/2017
Linton Kwesi Johnson	Dub poet	Book & Record Bar, West Norwood	Caspar Melville for Bass Culture	20/02/2017
Lloyd Coxsone (Lloyd Blackford)	Sound system operator	*Black Cultural Archives*, Brixton	Mykaell Riley and Caspar Melville for Bass Culture	25/07/2017
Marie Loney	Dancer	Her home, Islington, north London	Caspar Melville	06/08/1998
MJ Cole (Matt Cole)	DJ, producer	His studio, south London	Caspar Melville	09/11/1998
Norman Jay	DJ	Radio London studios, central London	Caspar Melville	22/11/1999
Norman Jay	DJ	*Black Cultural Archives*, Brixton	Caspar Melville	15/12/2015
Paul Gilroy	Professor	His home, Finsbury Park, north London	Caspar Melville for Bass Culture	13/01/2017
Paul Gilroy		–	Jacqueline Springer for Bass Culture	21/09/2017

Appendix: interviews for the book

Rachael Bee (Beardshaw)	Promoter	Her home, Brixton	Caspar Melville	10/08/1998
Rob Playford	Producer, label head	Random Café, London	Caspar Melville	18/08/1998
Rodney P (Rodney Panton)	MC	University of Westminster, Harrow	Caspar Melville for Bass Culture	02/10/2017
Roni Size (Ryan Williams)	Producer	Back seat of a car, central London	Caspar Melville	04/07/1997
Sam Kelly	Drummer	University of Westminster, Harrow	Caspar Melville for Bass Culture	12/06/2017
Simon Payne	Producer, clubber	His home, south London	Caspar Melville	04/07/1998
Trevor Nelson	DJ	His home, Finsbury Park, London	Caspar Melville	07/08/1998

Bibliography

Adegoke, Yomi (2018) 'Grime, Afro Bashment, Drill … How Black British Music Became More Fertile Than Ever', *Guardian*, 1 June.

Aikenhead, Decca (1998) 'Interview with Goldie', *Guardian*, 16 May.

Albeiz, Sean (2011) 'Post Soul Futurama: African American Cultural Politics and Early Detroit Techno', in Mark J. Butler ed., *Electronica, Dance and Club Music*, The Library of Essays on Popular Music (Abingdon: Ashgate Publishing).

Alexander, Claire (1996) *The Art of Being Black: The Creation of Black British Youth Identities* (London: Clarendon Press).

Amin, Ash (2010) 'The Remainder of Race', *Theory, Culture and Society*, vol. 27, no. 1, 1–23.

Anderson, Benedict (1983) *Imagined Communities: Reflections on the Origin and Spread of Nationalism* (London: Verso).

Anthony, Wayne (2002) *Class of '88: The True Acid House Experience* (London: Virgin Books).

Atkinson, Rowland, Simon Parker and Roger Burroughs (2017) 'Elite Formation, Power and Space in Contemporary London', *Theory, Culture and Society*, vol. 34, no, 5–6, 179–200.

Avanti, Peter (2013) 'Black Musics, Technology, and Modernity: Exhibit A, the Drum Kit', *Popular Music and Society*, vol. 36, no. 4, 476–504.

Back, Les (1996) *New Ethnicities and Urban Culture: Racism and Multiculture in Young Lives* (London: UCL Press).

— (2000) 'Voices of Hate, Sounds of Hybridity: Black Music and the Complexities of Racism', *Black Music Research Journal*, vol. 20, no. 2, 127–49.

— (2002a) 'The Fact of Hybridity: Youth, Ethnicity and Racism', in David Theo Goldberg and John Solomos, eds, *A Companion to Racial and Ethnic Studies*, 439–54 (Oxford: Blackwell Publishing).

— (2002b) 'Out Of Sight: Southern Music and the Colouring of Sound', in Les Back and Vron Ware, eds, *Out of Whiteness: Color, Politics and Culture*, 227–71 (Chicago, IL: University of Chicago Press).

Bainbridge, Luke (2013) *Acid House: The True Story* (London: Omnibus Press).

Bakare-Yusuf, Bibi (1997) 'Rare Groove and Raregroovers: A Matter of Taste,

Bibliography

Difference and Identity', in Heidi Safia Mirza, ed., *Black British Feminism*, 81–97 (London: Routledge).

Baker, Houston (1987) *Modernism and the Harlem Renaissance* (Chicago, IL: University of Chicago Press).

Banerjea, Koushik (1998) 'Sonic Diaspora and Its Dissident Footfalls', *Postcolonial Studies*, vol. 1, no. 3, 389–400.

— and S. Banerjea (1996) 'Psyche and Soul: A View From The South', in Sharma, Hutnyk and Sharma, eds, *Dis-orienting Rhythms*, 105–27.

Banton, Michael (1977) *The Idea of Race* (London: Tavistock).

Baraka, Amiri [Leroi Jones] (1967a) *Black Music* (New York: Morrow).

Baraka, Amiri [Leroi Jones] (1967b) 'The Changing Same (R&B and New Black Music)' in Amiri Baraka,, *Black Music*, 180–213 [1980 reprint] (Westport, CT: Greenwood Press).

— (1967c) 'Jazz and the White Critic', in Amiri Baraka, *Black Music*, 11–21 [1980 reprint] (Westport, CT: Greenwood Press).

— (1991) *The Leroi Jones/Amiri Baraka Reader* (New York: Thunder's Mouth Press).

Barker, Martin (1981) *The New Racism* (London: Junction Books).

Belle-Fortune, Brian (2014) *All Crews: Journeys Through Jungle/Drum and Bass Culture* (London: Vision Publishing).

Bennett, Andy and Jon Stratton (2010) *Britpop and the English Music Tradition* (Abingdon: Ashgate).

Bewes, Timothy and Jeremy Gilbert (2000) *Cultural Capitalism* (London: Blackwell).

Bey, Hakim (1985) *Taz: The Temporary Autonomous Zone* (New York: Autonmedia).

Bhat, Ashok, Roy Carr-Hill and Sushel Ohri, eds (1988) *Britain's Black Population: A New Perspective* (Aldershot: Gower).

Born, Georgina (2000) 'Introduction: On Difference, Representation and Appropriation in Music', in Born and Hesmondhalgh, eds, *Western Music and Its Others*, 1–59.

— and David Hesmondhalgh, eds (2000) *Western Music and Its Others: Difference, Representation and Appropriation in Music* (Oakland, CA: University of California Press).

Bourdieu, Pierre (1984) *Distinction: A Social Critique of Taste*, trans. Richard Nice (Cambridge, MA: Harvard University Press).

Bourgois, Phillipe (1995) *In Search of Respect: Selling Crack in El Barrio* (Cambridge: Cambridge University Press).

Boyarin, Jonathan, ed. (1994) *Remapping Memory: The Politics of TimeSpace* (Minneapolis, MN: University of Minnesota Press).

Brackett, David (1992) 'James Brown's "Superbad" and the Double-Voiced Utterance', *Popular Music*, vol. 11, no. 3 (October), 309–24.

Bradley, Lloyd (2000) *Bass Culture: When Reggae Was King* (London: Viking).

— (2013) *Sounds Like London: 100 Years of Black Music in the Capital* (London: Serpent's Tail).

Brah, Avtar (1996) *Cartographies of Diaspora: Contesting Identities* (London: Routledge).

Branch, Andrew (2014) 'It's Where You Come From That Makes You Who You Are: Suburban Youth and Social Class', in Subcultures Network, eds, *Subcultures, Popular Music and Social Change*, 65–89 (Cambridge: Cambridge Scholars).

Bibliography

Brand, Anna (2018) 'The Duality of Space: The Built World of Du Bois' Double-Consciousness', *Environment and Planning D: Society and Space*, vol. 36, no. 1, 3–22.

Brewster, Bill (2016) 'Deep Inside: Clink Street Was the Birth of Rave Culture', *Mixmag*, 27 May, accessed at http://mixmag.net/feature/deep-inside on 13 February 2018.

— and Frank Broughton (2018) 'Terry Farley on *Boy's Own* Fanzine and Acid House', *Red Bull Music Academy Daily*, 21 March, accessed at https://daily.redbullmusicacademy.com/2018/03/terry-farley-interview on 14 April 2018.

— and Terry Farley (2017) 'London Warehouse Parties Pre-Acid House: An Oral History', *Red Bull Music Academy Daily*, 13 June, accessed at http://daily.redbullmusicacademy.com/2017/06/london-warehouse-parties-oral-history on 14 June 2017.

Brown, Kate (2018) 'Black People Figured Out How to Make Culture in Freefall: Arthur Jafa on the Creative Power of Melancholy', *ArtNet News*, 21 February, accessed at https://news.artnet.com/art-world/arthur-jafa-julia-stoschek-collection-1227422 on 19 December 2018.

Burns, Todd (2013) 'Nightclubbing: Metalheadz at Blue Note', *Red Bull Music Academy Daily*, 2 April, accessed at http://daily.redbullmusicacademy.com/2013/04/nightclubbing-metalheadz-at-blue-note on 9 December 2018.

Busby, Margaret (2014) 'The Notting Hill Carnival Has an Unsung Hero – Rhaune Laslett', *Guardian*, 24 August.

Bussman, Jane (1998) *Once in a Lifetime: The Crazy Days of Acid House* (London: Virgin Books).

Byron, Margaret (1994) *Post War Caribbean Migration to Britain: The Unfinished Cycle* (Aldershot: Avebury).

— (1998) 'Migration, Work and Gender: The Case of Post-War Labour Migration From the Caribbean to Britain', in Chamberlain, ed., *Caribbean Migration*, 217–32.

Cabut, Richard and Andrew Gallix (2017) *Punk Is Dead: Modernity Killed Every Night* (London: Zero Books).

Carr-Hill, Roy and Drew Davis (1988) 'Blacks, Police and Crime', in Bhat et al., eds, *Britain's Black Population*, 29–60.

Cavanaugh, Dean (2016) 'The UK Roots of Acid House', *Zani* [magazine], 7 June, accessed at http://www.zani.co.uk/zani-music/item/2654-the-uk-roots-of-acid-house-by-dean-cavanagh on 6 January 2017.

Centre for Contemporary Cultural Studies (1982) *The Empire Strikes Back: Race and Racism in 70s Britain* (London: Hutchison).

Chamberlain, Mary, ed. (1998) *Caribbean Migration: Globalised Identities* (London: Routledge).

Cheeseman, Phil (1995) 'The History of Housemusic', n.d., accessed at http://userwww.sfsu.edu/art511_c/tele07/fmmasterf/endproject/history.html on 6 January 2017.

— (2016) 'The Story of Hedonism', 7 June, accessed at http://hedonism1988.co.uk/history/ on 6 January 2017.

Chester, Nick (2016) 'My Life as an Ecstasy Dealer on the 90s Club Circuit', *Vice* [magazine], 24 April, accessed at https://www.vice.com/en_uk/article/dp5nyv/brighton-ecstasy-dealing-network-mc-flux on 2 July 2017.

Chesterton, George (2018) 'Gazza's Tears, Italia '90 and the Madness of Merrie

Bibliography

England', *GQ* [magazine], 18 June, accessed at https://www.gq-magazine.co.uk/article/gazza-italia-90-merrie-england-george-chesterton on 10 October 2018.

Christodoulou, Chris (2011) 'Rumble in the Jungle City: Place and Uncanny Bass', *Dancecult: Journal of Electronic Dance Music Culture*, vol. 3, no. 1, 44–63.

Clarke, John and Tony Jefferson (1973) *The Politics of Popular Culture: Cultures and Sub-cultures*, Occasional Stencilled Paper, Centre for Contemporary Cultural Studies, University of Birmingham.

Cloonan, Martin and John Williamson (2016) *Players' Work Time: A History of the British Musicians' Union 1893–2013* (Manchester: Manchester University Press).

Clout, Hugh, ed. (1978) *Changing London* (Slough: University Tutorial Press).

Coester, Markus (2014) 'Revisiting the "Afro Trend" of the 1960s and 1970s: Musical Journeys, Fusions and African Stereotypes', in Jon Stratton and Nabeel Zuberi, eds, *Black Popular Music in Britain Since 1945*, 47–67 (Farnham: Ashgate).

Cohen, Phillip (1972) *Subcultural Conflict and Working Class Community*, Working Papers in Cultural Studies 2, Centre for Cultural Studies, University of Birmingham.

— and Harwent Bains, eds (1988) *Multi-Racist Britain* (Basingstoke: Macmillan).

Cohen, Stanley (1980) *Folk Devils and Moral Panics: The Creation of the Mods and Rockers* (Oxford: Blackwell).

Collin, Matthew (with contributions by John Godfrey) (1997) *Altered States: The Story of Ecstasy Culture and Acid House* (London: Serpent's Tail).

— (2000) 'Let's Dance', *Guardian*, 24 May.

Connor, Steven (2010) 'Secession', talk given at Sonic Acts XIII: The Poetics of Space, Amsterdam, 27 February, accessed at http://stevenconnor.com/secession.html on 17 July 2017.

Cotgrove, Mark ('Snowboy') (2009) *From Jazz Funk and Fusion to Acid Jazz: The History of the UK Jazz Dance Scene* (London: Chaser Publications).

Cross, Malcom and Michael Keith (1993) *Racism, the City and the State* (London: Routledge).

Davies, A. R. (2013) '"Right to Buy": The Development of a Conservative Housing Policy, 1945–1980', *Contemporary British History*, vol. 27, no. 4, 421–44.

Davies, William (2014) *The Limits of Neoliberalism: Authority, Sovereignty and the Logic of Competition* (London: Sage).

— (2018) 'The Best Books on Moral Economy', accessed at https://fivebooks.com/best-books/moral-economy-will-davies on 15 July 2019.

de Certeau, Michel (1984) *The Practice of Everyday Life* (Berkeley, CA: University of California Press).

Dennis, Ferdinand (1999) 'The Prince & I', in *Granta 65. London: The Lives of the City Granta* 65 (London: Granta).

Dent, Gina and Michelle Wallace, eds (1992) *Black Popular Culture* (Seattle, WA: Bay Press).

Douglas, Mary (1966) *Purity and Danger: An Analysis of Concepts of Pollution and Taboo* (London: Routledge).

Du Bois, W. E. B. (1903) *The Souls of Black Folks* (London: Longman [1965]).

Dumuth, Claire (1978) *Sus: A Report on the Vagrancy Act 1824* (London: Runnymede Trust).

Dyer, Richard (1979) 'In Defence of Disco', *Gay Left*, issue 8.

Bibliography

Eisenberg, Andrew (2015) 'Space', in David Novak and Matt Sakakeeny, eds, *Keywords in Sound*, 193–207 (Durham, NC: Duke University Press).

Elam, Harry and Kennell Jackson, eds (2005) *Black Cultural Traffic: Crossroads in Global Performance and Popular Culture* (Ann Arbor, MI: University of Michigan Press).

Elms, Robert (2008) 'Crackers 1976: Daytime Soul Sessions in London', extract from *The Way We Wore, History Is Made at Night*, 27 June, accessed at http://history-is-made-at-night.blogspot.co.uk/2008/06/crackers-1976.html on 20 April 2017.

Eshun, Kodwo (1998) *More Brilliant Than the Sun: Adventures in Sonic Fiction* (London: Quartet Books).

— (2003) 'Further Considerations on AfroFuturism', *CR: The New Centennial Review*, vol. 3, no. 2, 287–302.

Fared, Grant (1998) 'Wailin' Souls: Reggae's Debt to Black American Music', in Monique Guillory and David Green, eds, *Soul: Black Power, Politics, and Pleasure*, 56–74 (New York: New York University Press).

Farley, Terry (2017) 'The Dancers: A Tribute', *Red Bull Academy Daily*, 17 September, accessed at http://daily.redbullmusicacademy.com/2015/09/a-tribute-to-the-dancers on 5 January 2017.

Farsides, Tony (2018) 'A Tribute to the Legendary Paul "Trouble" Anderson', *Mi-Soul*, December, accessed at https://mi-soul.com/paul-trouble-anderson-tribute-the-pioneering-dj-has-passed-away on 7 December 2018.

Fields, Karen and Barbara Fields (2014) *Racecraft: The Soul of Inequality in American Life* (London: Verso).

Fintoni, Laurent (2015) 'Nightclubbing: Fabio and Grooverider's Rage', *Red Bull Academy Daily*, 21 July, accessed at http://daily.redbullmusicacademy.com/2015/07/nightclubbing-fabio-and-grooverider-rage on 20 February 2017.

Fisher, Mark (2009) 'The "Abstract Reality" of the Hardcore Continuum', *Dancecult: Journal of Electronic Dance Music Culture*, vol. 1, no. 1, 123–6.

— (2013) 'The Slow Cancellation of the Future', *The Quietus*, 28 August, available at https://thequietus.com/articles/13004-mark-fisher-ghosts-of-my-life-extract, accessed on 12 June 2017.

Flintoff, John Paul (1998) *Comp: A Survivor's Tale* (London: Victor Gollancz).

Floyd, Samuel (1991) 'Ring Shout! Literary Studies, Historical Studies, and Black Music Inquiry', *Black Music Research Journal*, vol. 11, no. 2, 265–87.

Foner, Nancy (1978) *Jamaica Farewell: Jamaican Migrants in London* (Berkeley, CA: University of California Press).

Frank, Gillian (2007) 'Anti-gay Prejudice and the 1979 Backlash Against Disco', *Journal of the History of Sexuality*, vol. 16, no. 2, 276–306.

Fryer, Peter (1984) *Staying Power: The History of Black People in Britain* (London: Pluto).

Fusco, Coco (1995) *English Is Broken Here: Notes on Cultural Fusion in the Americas* (New York City: New Press).

Garafalo, Reebee (2002) 'Crossing Over: From Black Rhythm & Blues to White Rock 'n' Roll', in N. Kelly, ed., *Rhythm and Business: The Political Economy of Black Music*, 112–37 (New York: Akashit Books).

Gardiner, Mike (2000) *Critiques of Everyday Life* (London: Routledge).

Gates, Henry Louis (1993) 'The Black Man's Burden', in Michael Warner, ed., *Fear*

Bibliography

of a Queer Planet: Queer Politics and Social Theory, 230–8 (Minneapolis, MN: Minnesota University Press).

Gelder, Ken and Sarah Thornton (1997) *The Subcultures Reader* (London: Routledge).

George, Nelson (1988) *The Death of Rhythm and Blues* (New York: Random House).

German, Lindsey and John Rees (2012) *A People's History of London* (London: Verso).

Gilbert, Jeremy (1997) 'White Noise: New Labour, New Lads, Britpop and Blairism' (first published 1997, reposted in 2014), accessed at https://jeremygilbertwriting.wordpress.com/2014/04/11/white-noise-new-labour-new-lads-britpop-and-blairism/1998 on 10 July 2018.

— (2006) 'More Than a Woman: Becoming-Woman on the Disco Floor', in Rosa Reitsamer and Rupert Weinzier, eds, *Female Consequences: Feminismus, Antirassismus, Popmusik*, 181–93 (Vienna: Löcker).

— (2007) '*Discographies*: Auto-critique and Reflections, 10 Years On', n.d., accessed at https://jeremygilbertwriting.wordpress.com on 10 January 2010.

— (2009) 'The Hardcore Continuum? A Report on the "The Hardcore Continuum?" Symposium Held at the University of East London, April 29th 2009', *Dancecult: Journal of Electronic Dance Music Culture*, vol. 1, no. 1, 118–22.

— (2014) 'Break/Flow/Escape/Capture: The Energy and Impotence of the Hardcore Continuum', in Stratton and Zuberi, eds, *Black Popular Music in Britain Since 1945*, 169–84.

— and Ewan Pearson (1999) *Discographies: Dance, Music, Culture and the Politics of Sound* (London: Routledge).

Gilroy, Paul (1982a) 'Police and Thieves', in Centre for Contemporary Cultural Studies, chapter 4.

— (1982b) 'Steppin' Out in Babylon – Race, Class and Autonomy', in Centre for Contemporary Cultural Studies, chapter 8.

— (1987) *There Ain't No Black in the Union Jack: The Cultural Politics of Race and Nation* (London: Routledge).

— (1991) 'Sounds Authentic: Black Music, Ethnicity, and the Challenge of a "Changing" Same', *Black Music Research Journal*, vol. 11, no. 2 (autumn), 111–36.

— (1993) *The Black Atlantic: Modernity and Double Consciousness* (London: Verso).

— (1994) 'After the Love Has Gone: Bio-Politics and Etho-Poetics in the Black Public Sphere', *Third Text*, vol. 28/29, 25–47.

— (1995) '… To Be Real: The Dissident Forms of Black Expressive Culture', in Catherine Ugwu, ed., *Let's Get It On: The Politics of Black Performance* (London: ICA).

— (1997) 'Exer(or)cising Power: Black Bodies in the Black Public Sphere', in Thomas, ed., *Dance in the City*, 21–33.

— (1998) 'Race Ends Here', *Ethnic and Racial Studies*, vol. 21, no. 5838–47.

— (1999) 'Analogues of Mourning, Mourning the Analog', in Kelly and McDonnell, eds, *Stars Don't Stand Still in the Sky*, 260–72.

— (2000) *Between Camps: Nations, Cultures and the Allure of Race* (London: Penguin).

— (2003) 'Between the Blues and the Blues Dance: Some Soundscapes of the Black Atlantic', in Les Back and Michael Bull, eds, *The Auditory Culture Reader*, 381–95 (Oxford: Berg).

— (2004) 'Melancholia and Multiculture', openDemocracy.net, 2 August, accessed

Bibliography

at https://www.opendemocracy.net/arts-multiculturalism/article_2035.jsp on 3 August 2004.

— (2010) *Darker Than Blue: On the Moral Economies of Black Atlantic Culture* (Cambridge, MA: Harvard University Press).

— and Errol Lawrence (1988) 'Two Tone Britain: White and Black Youth and the Politics of Anti-racism', in Cohen and Bains, eds, *Multi-Racist Britain*, 121–56.

Goldberg, David Theo (1993) *Racist Culture: Philosophy and the Politics of Meaning* (Oxford: Blackwell).

— (2004) 'The Space of Multiculturalism', openDemocracy.net, 15 September, accessed at https://www.opendemocracy.net/arts-multiculturalism/article_2097.jsp on 19 June 2005.

— (2006) 'Racial Europeanization', *Ethnic and Racial Studies*, vol. 29, no. 2, 331–64.

Goodhart, David (2004) 'Too Diverse?', *Prospect*, 20 February.

Goodwin, Andrew (1988) 'Sample and Hold: Pop Music in the Digital Age of Reproduction', *Critical Quarterly*, vol. 30, no. 3, 34–49.

Gore, Georgiana (1997) 'The Beat Goes On: Trance, Dance and Tribalism in Rave Culture', in Thomas, ed., *Dance in the City*, 50–68.

Gutzmore, Cecil (1983) 'Carnival, the State and the Black Masses in the United Kingdom', in James and Harris, eds, *Inside Babylon*, 207–30.

Hall, Stuart (1979) 'The Great Moving Right Show', *Marxism Today*, January, 14–20.

— (1985) 'Signification, Representation, Ideology: Althusser and the Poststructuralist Debates', *Critical Studies in Mass Communication*, vol. 2, 91–114.

— (1989) 'New Ethnicities', in Kobena Mercer, ed., *Black Film, British Cinema*, ICA Documents 7 (London: Institute of Contemporary Arts).

— (1990) 'Cultural Identity and Diaspora', *Identity: Community, Culture, Difference*, vol. 2, 222–37.

— (1992) 'What Is the Black in Black Popular Culture?', in Dent and Wallace, eds, *Black Popular Culture*, 21–37.

— (1994) 'Cultural Identity and Diaspora', in Patrick Williams and Laura Chrisman, eds, *Colonial Discourse and Post-colonial Theory: A Reader*, 222–37 (London: Harvester Wheatsheaf).

— (1996a) 'When Was the Post-Colonial? Thinking at the Limit', in Iain Chambers and Linda Curti, eds, *The Post-colonial Question*, 242–60 (London: Routledge).

— (1996b) 'Introduction: Who Needs "Identity?"', in Hall and Du Gay, eds, *Questions of Cultural Identity*, 1–17.

— (1997) 'Aspiration and Attitude: Reflections on Black Britain in the Nineties', *New Formations*, vol. 33 (Frontlines and Backyards).

— (2002) 'Calypso Kings', *Guardian*, 28 June.

— (2004) 'Divided City: The Crisis of London', openDemocracy.net, 27 October, accessed at https://www.opendemocracy.net/en/article_2191jsp on 1 July 2019.

— (2011) 'The Neoliberal Revolution', *Soundings*, vol. 48, 9–27.

— and Paul Du Gay, eds (1996) *Questions of Cultural Identity* (London: Sage).

— and Tony Jefferson, eds (1991) *Resistance Through Rituals: Youth Subcultures in Postwar Britain*, 8th edition (London: Routledge).

— et al., eds (1978) *Policing the Crisis: Mugging the State and Law and Order* (Basingstoke: Macmillan).

Hancox, Dan (2018) *Inner City Pressure: The Story of Grime* (London: William Collins).

Bibliography

Harris, Roxy and Sarah White (1999) *Changing Britannia: Life Experience with Britain* (London: New Beacon Books).

Haslam, Dave (1999) *Manchester, England: The Story of the Pop Cult City* (London: Fourth Estate).

— (2015) *Life After Dark: A History of British Nightclubs and Music Venues* (London: Simon Schuster).

— (2018) 'How Ecstasy and the Haçienda Nightclub Changed Music Forever', *Guardian*, 8 February.

Hebdige, Dick (1974) *Reggae Rastas and Rudies: Style and the Subversion of Form*, Stencilled Occasional Papers 24, Centre for Contemporary Cultural Studies, University of Birmingham.

— (1979) *Subculture: The Meaning of Style* (London: Methuen).

— (1987) *Cut'n'Mix: Culture, Identity, and Caribbean Music* (London: Routledge).

Hebditch, Stephen (2015) *London's Pirate Pioneers: The Illegal Broadcasters Who Changed British* Radio (London: TX Publications).

Henriques, Julian (2011) *Sonic Bodies: Reggae Sound Systems, Performance Techniques, and Ways of Knowing* (London: Continuum).

Henry, William (Lez) (2006) *What the Deejay Said: A Critique from the Street!* (London: Nu-Beyond, Learning By Choice!),

Hesmondhalgh, David (1997) 'The Cultural Politics of Dance Music', *Soundings*, issue 5.

— (1998) 'Club Culture Goes Mental', *Popular Music*, vol. 17, no. 2, 247–53.

— (2000) 'International Times: Fusions, Exoticism and Anti-Racism in Electronic Dance Music', in Born and Hesmondhalgh, eds, *Western Music and Its Others*, 280–305.

— (2013) *The Cultural Industries*, 3rd edition (London: Sage).

— and Leslie Meier (2018) 'What the Digitalisation of Music Tells Us About Capitalism, Culture and the Power of the Information Technology Sector', *Information, Communication and Society*, vol. 21n no. 11, 1555–70.

— and Caspar Melville (2002) 'Urban Breakbeat Culture: Repercussions of Hip-Hop in the United Kingdom', in Mitchell, ed., *Global Noise*, 86–111.

Hesse, Barnor (1993) 'Black to Front and Black Again: Racialisation Through Contested Times and Spaces', in Pile and Keith, eds, *Geographies of Resistance*, 162–82.

— (2000) 'Diasporicity: Black Britain's Post-colonial Formations', in Barnor Hesse, ed., *Un/settled Multiculturalisms: Diasporas, Entanglements, Transruptions*, 96–121 (London: Zed Books).

Hinds, Donald (1980) 'The "Island" of Brixton', *Oral History: Journal of the Oral History Society*, vol. 8, no. 1, 49–51.

Hiro, Dilip (1991) *Black British White British* (London: Grafton Books).

hooks, bell (1984) *Feminist Theory: From Margin to Center* (Boston, MA: South End Press).

Hughes, Walter (1994) 'In the Empire of the Beat: Disco and Discipline', in Andrew Ross and Tricia Rose, eds, *Microphone Fiends: Youth Music and Youth Culture*, 147–57 (New York: Routledge).

Hutchinson, Kate (2018) 'A Sweaty Night Out in London's New Jazz Scene', *New York Times*, 19 October.

Bibliography

Hutnyk, John and Sanjay Sharma (2000) 'Music and Politics: An Introduction', *Theory Culture and Society*, vol. 17, no. 3, 55–63.

Huttman, Elizabeth, Wim Blauw and Juliet Saltman, eds (1991) *Urban Housing Segregation of Minorities in Western Europe and the United States* (Durham, NC: Duke University Press).

Huxtable, Paul (2014) *Sound System Culture: Celebrating Huddersfield's Sound Systems* (London: One Love Books).

Iton, Richard (2008) *In Search of the Black Fantastic: Politics and Popular Culture in the Post-Civil Rights Era* (Oxford: Oxford University Press).

Jackson, Nicole (2015) 'A Nigger in the New England: "Sus", the Brixton Riot, and Citizenship', *African and Black Diaspora: An International Journal*, vol. 8, no. 2, 158–70.

James, Robin (2015) *Resilience and Melancholy: Pop Music, Feminism, Neoliberalism* (London: Zero Books).

— (2018) 'Poptimism and Popular Feminism', *Sounding Out*, 17 September, accessed at https://soundstudiesblog.com/2018/09/17/poptimism-and-popular-feminism on 17 September 2018.

James, Winston (1993) 'Migration, Racism and Identity Formation', in James and Harris, eds, *Inside Babylon*, 231–89.

James, Winston and Clive Harris, eds (1993) *Inside Babylon: The Caribbean Diaspora in Britain* (London: Verso).

Johnson, Philip (1996) *Straight Outa Bristol: Massive Attack, Portishead, Tricky and the Roots of Trip Hop* (London: Hodder & Stoughton).

Jones, Simon (1988) *Black Culture, White Youth: Reggae Tradition from Jamaica to UK* (London: Macmillan).

— and Paul Pinnock (2017) *Scientists of Sound: Portraits of a UK Reggae Sound System* (Birmingham: Bassline Books).

Joppke, Christian (1996) 'Multiculturalism and Immigration: A Comparison of the United States, Germany and Great Britain', *Theory and Society*, vol. 25, no. 4, 449–500.

Kamugisha, Aaron (2016) 'The Black Experience of New World Coloniality', *Small Axe*, vol. 20, no. 1, 129–45.

Katz, David (2014) 'Zion in a Vision: Jamaica's ' 90s Rasta Renaissance', *Red Bull Music Academy Daily*, 22 April, accessed at http://daily.redbullmusicacademy.com/2014/04/rasta-renaissance-feature on 20 June 2018.

Keith, Michael (1993) *Race, Riots and Policing: Lore and Disorder in a Multi-racist Society* (London: UCL Press).

Kelly, Karen and Evelyn McDonnell, eds (1999) *Stars Don't Stand Still in the Sky: Music and Myth* (New York: New York University Press).

Keyes, Cheryl (2013) '"She Was Too Black for Rock and Too Hard for Soul": (Re)discovering the Musical Career of Betty Mabry Davis', *American Studies*, vol. 52, no. 4, 35–55.

Kushnik, Louis (1993) '"We're Here Because You Were There": Britain's Black Population', *Trotter Review*, vol. 7, no. 2, article 7.

Lawrence, Tim (2003) *Love Saves the Day: A History of American Dance Music Culture, 1970–1979* (Durham, NC: Duke University Press).

— (2011) 'Disco and the Queering of the Dance Floor', *Cultural Studies*, vol. 25, no. 2, 230–43.

Bibliography

— (2016) 'Life and Death on the Pulse Dance Floor: Transglocal Politics and Erasure of the Latinx in the History of Queer Dance', *Dancecult: Journal of Electronic Dance Music Culture*, vol. 8, no. 1, 1–25.

Lefebvre, Henri (1994) *The Production of Space*, translated by Donald Nicholson-Smith (Oxford: Blackwell).

Lentin, Alana and Gavan Titley (2011) 'The Crises of Multiculturalism', openDemocracy.net, 18 July, accessed at https://www.opendemocracy.net/ourkingdom/alana-lentin-gavan-titley/crises-of-multiculturalism on 18 September 2018.

Lipsitz, George (1994a) *Dangerous Crossroads: Popular Music, Post Modernism and the Poetics of Place* (London: Verso).

— (1994b) 'We Know What time It Is', in Ross and Rose, eds, *Microphone Fiends*, 17–27.

— (2007) 'The Racialization of Space and the Spacialization of Race', *Landscape Journal*, vol. 26, no. 1, 10–23.

Lynsky, Dorian (2011) 'Frankie Knuckles Invents House Music', *Guardian*, 15 June.

— (2014) 'Tony Colston-Hayter – The Acid House Fraudster', *Guardian*, 15 January.

Malbon, Ben (1999) *Clubbing: Culture and Experience* (London: Routledge).

Malik, Kenan (2002) 'Against Multiculturalism', *New Humanist*, accessed at https://newhumanist.org.uk/articles/523/against-multiculturalism on 3 March 2018.

— (2007) 'Against Multiculturalism', openDemocracy.net, 31 May, accessed at https://newhumanist.org.uk/articles/523/against-multiculturalism on 4 June 2007.

— (2014) *Multiculturalism and Its Discontents: Rethinking Diversity After 9/11* (London: Seagull Books).

Mandler, Peter (1999) 'New Towns for Old: The Fate of the Town Centre', in Becky Conekin, ed., *Moments of Modernity: Reconstructing Britain, 1945–1964*, 208–27 (London: Rivers Oram Press).

Marcus, Greil (1989) *Lipstick Traces: A Secret History of the Twentieth Century* (Cambridge, MA: Belknap/Harvard University Press).

Marks, Andrew (1990) 'Young Gifted and Black: Afro-American and Afro-Caribbean Music in Britain 1963–88', in Oliver, ed., *Black Music in Britain*, 12–26.

Martin, S. I. (1996) *Incomparable World* (London: Quartet Books).

Massey, Doreen (1992) 'Politics and Space/Time', *New Left Review*, vol. 1, no. 196, 65–84.

— (1994) *Space, Place and Gender* (Minneapolis, MN: University of Minnesota).

— (1996) 'Space/Power, Identity/Difference, Tensions in the City', in Merrifield and Swyngedouw, eds, *The Urbanisation of Injustice*, 100–17.

Matera, Marc (2016) *Black London: The Imperial Metropolis and Decolonization in the Twentieth Century* (Berkeley, CA: University of California Press).

May, Rueben and Pat Goldsmith (2018) 'Dress Codes and Racial Discrimination in Urban Nightclubs', *Sociology of Race and Ethnicity*, vol. 4, no. 4, 555–66.

McCann, Ian (1995) *The Complete Guide to the Music of Bob Marley* (London: Omnibus Press and Schirmer Trade Books).

McKitterick, Katherine (2006) *Demonic Grounds: Black Women and the Cartographies of Struggle* (Minneapolis, MN: Minnesota University Press).

— and Alexander Weheliye (2017) '808s and Heartbreak', trueleappress.com, 12 October, accessed at https://trueleappress.com/2017/10/12/808s-heartbreak on 3 May 2018.

Bibliography

McQuaid, Ian (n.d.) 'Gone to a Rave #51: Paul Ibiza Gets Real', Ransom Note website, accessed at https://www.theransomnote.com/music/gone-rave/gone-to-a-rave-51-paul-ibiza-gets-real on 7 January 2017.

McRobbie, Angela (1998) *British Fashion Design: Rag Trade or Image Industry?* (London: Routledge).

— (1999) 'Come Alive London: A Dialogue with Dance Music', in Angela McRobbie, ed., *The Culture Society: Art Fashion and Popular Music*, 144–57 (London: Routledge).

— and Jenny Garber (1991) 'Girls and Subcultures', in Hall and Jefferson, eds, *Resistance Through Rituals*, 182–93.

— Paul Gilroy and Lawrence Grossberg, eds (2000) *Without Guarantees: In Honour of Stuart Hall* (London: Verso).

Melville, Caspar (1995) 'Sound Business, Carnival Guide London', *Touch* [magazine]/ *Time Out*, 24 August.

— (1997) 'Size Matters', *Touch* [magazine], 7 July.

— (1998) 'The Dreem Team', *Touch* [magazine], No. 79, April.

— (2001) 'Jennifer Lopez: My Part in Her Downfall', openDemocracy.net, 13 June, accessed at https://www.opendemocracy.net/node/429 on 14 June 2001.

Merrifield, Andrew and Eric Swyngedouw, eds (1996) *The Urbanisation of Injustice* (London: Lawrence and Wishart).

Middleton, Richard (2000) 'Musical Belongings: Western Music and Its Low Other', in Born and Hesmondhalgh, eds, *Western Music and Its Others*, 59–86.

Minton, Anna (2017) *Big Capital: Who Is London For?* (London: Penguin Books).

Mitchell, Tony, ed. (2001) *Global Noise: Rap and Hip Hop Outside the USA* (Middletown, CT: Wesleyan University Press).

Monrose, Kenny (2016) 'Struggling, Juggling and Street Corner Hustling: The Street Economy of Newham's Black Community', in Georgios Antonopoulos, ed., *Illegal Entrepreneurship, Organized Crime and Social Control: Essays in Honor of Professor Dick Hobbs*, 73–84 (London: Springer).

Moretti, Franco (1998) *Atlas of the European Novel 1800–1900* (London: Verso).

Morley, David and Kuan-Hsing Chen (1998) *Stuart Hall: Critical Dialogues* (London: Routledge).

Mosco, Vincent (2004) *The Digital Sublime: Myth, Power and Cyberspace* (Cambridge, MA: MIT Press).

Mudede, Charles (2013) 'Hip Hop Rupture', n.d., accessed at https://journals.uvic.ca/ index.php/ctheory/article/viewFile/14734/5745 on 11 March 2015.

Munson, Ingrid (1994) 'Doubleness and Jazz Improvisation: Irony, Parody, and Ethnomusicology', *Critical Inquiry*, vol. 20, no. 2, 283–313.

Nava, Mica (1999) 'Wider Horizons and Modern Desire: The Contradictions of America and Racial Difference in London 1935–45', *New Formations*, vol. 37, 71–91.

Nayak, Anoop (2003) *Race, Place and Globalization: Youth Cultures in a Changing World* (London: Berg).

Neal, Mark Anthony (1998) *What the Music Said: Black Popular Music and Black Public Culture* (New York: Routledge).

Needham, Jack (2017) 'The Beautiful Black Gay History of Chicago House's Birth', Dazed Digital, 11 May, accessed at http://www.dazeddigital.com/music/ article/35892/1/chicago-house-lgbtq-history-documentary on 8 January 2018.

Bibliography

Neely, Brooke and Michelle Samura (2011) 'Social Geographies of Race: Connecting Race and Space', *Ethnic and Racial Studies*, vol. 34, no. 11, 1933–52.

Nelson, Trevor (1994) 'Clubbed to Death', *Touch* [magazine], 7 June.

North, Adrian and David Hargreaves (1999) 'Music and Adolescent Identity', *Music Education Research*, vol. 1, no. 1, 75–92.

Nott, James (2015) *Going to the Palais: A Social and Cultural History of Dancing and Dance Halls in Britain, 1918–1960* (Oxford: Oxford University Press).

Noys, Benjamin (1995) 'Into the "Jungle"', *Popular Music*, vol. 14, no. 3, 321–32.

Nurse, Seymour (2010) 'Interview with Bülent "Boo" Mehmet', The Bottom End, accessed at http://www.thebottomend.co.uk/Bulent_Boo_Mehmet.php on 16 January 2017

O'Hagan, S. (2002) 'Norman Jay: Minister of Sound. Profile and Interview', *Observer* (Music Monthly), 23 June.

Oliver, Paul, ed. (1990) *Black Music in Britain: Essays on the Afro-Asian Contribution to Popular Music* (Oxford: Oxford University Press).

Olusoga, David (2016) *Black and British: A Forgotten History* (London: Macmillan).

Paccoud, Antoine (2016) 'Buy-to-Let Gentrification: Extending Social Change Through Tenure Shifts', *Environment and Planning A*, vol. 49, no. 4, 839–56.

Pannell, Norman and Fenner Brockway (1965) *Immigration: What Is the Answer?* (London: Routledge & Kegan Paul).

Patterson, Orlando (1994) 'Global Culture and the American Cosmos', Andy Warhol Foundation, 24 May, accessed at https://warholfoundation.org/grant/paper2/paper.html on 7 January 2016.

Peach, Ceri (1996) 'Good Segregation, Bad Segregation', *Planning Perspectives*, vol. 11, no. 4, 379–98.

— (1998) 'Trends in Levels of Caribbean Segregation, Great Britain, 1961–91', in Chamberlain, ed., *Caribbean Migration*, 203–17.

Perkins, William Eric (1996) *Droppin' Science: Critical Essays on Rap Music and Hip Hop Culture* (Philadelphia, PA: Temple University Press).

Petrides, Alex (2014) 'Frankie Knuckles: Godfather of House Music, Priest of the Dancefloor', *Guardian*, 1 April.

— (2016) 'Interview. Andrew Weatherall: "Anyone can make music. What a double edged sword"', *Guardian*, 25 February, accessed at https://www.theguardian.com/music/2016/feb/25/andrew-weatherall-interview-dj-disco-maverick on 15 July 2019.

Phillips, Mike (2001) *London Crossing: A Biography of Black Britain* (London: Continuum).

— and Trevor Phillips (1998) *Windrush: The Irresistible Rise of Multi-racial Britain* (London: HarperCollins).

Pile, Steve and Michael Keith, eds (1997) *Geographies of Resistance* (London: Routledge).

Pilkington, Edward (1988) *Beyond the Mother Country: West Indians and the Notting Hill White Riots* (London: I. B. Taurus).

Pini, Maria (1997) 'Cyborgs, Nomads and the Raving Feminine', in Thomas, ed., *Dance in the City*, 111–30.

Porter, Roy (1994) *London: A Social History* (London: Hamish Hamilton).

Potter, Russell (1998) 'Not the Same: Race, Repetition, and Difference in Hip-Hop and

Bibliography

Dance Music', in Thomas Swiss, John Sloop and Andrew Herman, eds, *Mapping the Beat: Popular Music and Contemporary Theory*, 31–47 (Oxford: Blackwell).

Putnam, Lara (2013) *Radical Moves: Caribbean Migrants and the Politics of Race in the Jazz Age* (Chapel Hill, NC: University of North Carolina Press).

Redhead, Steve, ed. (1993) *Rave Off: Politics and Deviance in Contemporary Youth Culture* (Farnham: Ashgate).

Reeve, Keisa (2009) 'The UK Squatters Movement 1968–1980', in Leendert Van Hoogenhuijze, ed., *Kritiek 2009: Jaarboek voor Socialistische Discussie en Analyse*, 137–59 (Amsterdam: Amsterdam University Press).

Reiner, Robert (2000) 'Crime and Control in Britain', *Sociology*, vol. 34, no. 1, 71–94.

Reynolds, Simon (1992) 'The Wire 300: Simon Reynolds on the Hardcore Continuum #1: Hardcore Rave (1992)', February 2013 (originally published as 'Technical Ecstasy', in *The Wire*, issue 105, November 1992), accessed at https://www.thewire.co.uk/in-writing/essays/the-wire-300_simon-reynolds-on-the-hardcore-continuum_1_hardcore-rave_1992 on 5 March 2017.

— (1994) 'Above the Treeline' (feature on ambient jungle, including interview with Rob Haigh), *The Wire*, issue 127.

— (1998) *Energy Flash: A Journey Through Rave Music and Dance Culture* (London: Picador).

— (1999) *Generation Ecstasy: Into the World of Techno and Rave Culture* (New York: Routledge [US edition of *Energy Flash*]).

— (2006) *Rip It Up and Start Again: Postpunk 1978–1984* (London: Faber & Faber).

— (2009) 'The Hardcore Continuum, or (a)Theory and Its Discontents', text of a talk delivered at FACT, Liverpool, 11 February, accessed at http://energyflashbysimonreynolds.blogspot.co.uk/2009/02/hardcore-continuum-or-theory-and-its.html on 5 March 2017.

— (2010) *Retromania: Pop Culture's Addiction To Its Own Past* (London: Faber & Faber).

Rietveld, Hildegonda (1998) *This Is Our House: House Music, Cultural Spaces and Technologies* (Abingdon: Ashgate).

— (2014) 'Voodoo Rage: Blacktronica from the North', in Stratton and Zuberi, eds, *Black Popular Music in Britain Since 1945*, 153–68.

Ritz, David (1970) 'Soul Music in the Ghetto', *Salmagundi*, issue 12, 43–53.

Roach, Joseph (1996) *Cities of the Dead: Circum-Atlantic Performance* (New York: Columbia University Press).

Robins, Kevin (2003) 'Beyond Imagined Communities: Transnational Media and Turkish Migrants in Europe', in Stig Hjarvard, ed., *Media in a Globalised Society* (Copenhagen: Museum Tusculanum Press).

Rose, Tricia (1994) *Black Noise: Rap Music and Black Culture in Contemporary America* (Hanover, NH: Wesleyan University Press).

Ross, Andrew and Tricia Rose, eds (1994) *Microphone Fiends: Youth Music and Youth Culture* (New York: Routledge).

Runnymede Trust and the Radical Statistics Group (1980) *Britain's Black Population* (London: Heinemann Educational Books).

Saha, Anamik (2017) *Race and the Cultural Industries* (Cambridge: Polity).

Sassen, Saskia (2001) *The Global City: New York. London, Tokyo*, 2nd edition (Princeton, NJ: Princeton University Press).

Bibliography

Savage, Jon (1991) *England's Dreaming: Sex Pistols and Punk Rock* (London: Faber & Faber).

Schwarz, Bill (1996) 'The Only White Man in There': The Re-Racialisation of England, 1956–1968', *Race and Class*, vol. 38, no. 1, 65–78.

— (2007) 'Living With Difference: Stuart Hall in Conversation with Bill Schwarz', *Soundings*, issue 37, 'Tales of the City'.

Segal, Ronald (1995) *The Black Diaspora* (London: Faber & Faber).

Sexton, Jared (2015) 'Don't Call It a Comeback: Racial Slavery Is Not Yet Abolished', openDemocracy.net, 17 June, accessed at https://www.opendemocracy.net/beyondslavery/jared-sexton/don%E2%80%99t-call-it-comeback-racial-slavery-is-not-yet-abolished on 6 October 2017.

Sharma, Ash, John Hytnyk and Sanjay Sharma, eds (1996) *Dis-orienting Rhythms: The Politics of the New Asian Dance Music* (London: Zed Books).

Sharpe, Christina (2016) *In the Wake: On Blackness and Being* (Durham, NC: Duke University Press).

Smith, Chris (1998) *Creative Britain* (London: Faber and Faber).

Smith, David and Jeremy Gray (1983) *Police and People in London, Vol. IV: The Police in Action* (London: Policy Studies Institute).

Smith, Susan (1993) 'Residential Segregation and the Politics of Racialisation', in Cross and Keith, eds, *Racism, the City and the State*, 128–43.

— (1997) 'Beyond Geography's Visible World: A Cultural Politics of Music', *Progress in Human Geography*, vol. 21, no. 4, 502–29.

Snead, James (1984) 'Repetition as a Figure in Black Culture', in Henry Louis Gates, ed., *Black Literature and Literary Theory*, 59–80 (New York: Routledge).

Solomos, John (1988) 'Institutionalised Racism: Policies of Marginalisation in Education and Training', in Cohen and Bains, eds, *Multi-Racist Britain*, 156–94.

— and Les Back (1996) *Racism and Society* (London: Macmillan).

Spillers, Hortense (2006) 'The Idea of Black Culture', *CR: The New Centennial Review*, vol. 6, no. 3, 7–28.

Stearns, Marshall and Jean Stearns (1994) *Jazz Dance: The Story of American Vernacular Dance* (New York: Da Capo Press).

Stennett, Enrico (2007) 'Racism in Britain and the Paramount Dance Hall', itzcaribbean.com, 13 July, accessed at http://www.itzcaribbean.com/uk/history/racism-britain-paramount-dance-hall on 23 April 2018.

Stewart, Alexander (2000) 'Funky Drummer: New Orleans. James Brown and the Rhythmic Transformation of American Popular Music', *Popular Music*, vol. 19, no. 3, 293–318.

Stillman, Josh (2013) 'Maceo Parker Talks 98% Funky Stuff: My Life in Music Q&A', *Entertainment Weekly*, 1 February, accessed at https://ew.com/article/2013/02/01/maceo-parker-talks-98-funky-stuff-my-life-in-music-qa on 3 March 2018.

Stratton, Jon and Nabeel Zuberi (2014) *Black Popular Music in Britain Since 1945* (Farnham: Ashgate).

Styles, James (1991) 'Rhythms of the Jungle', Independent, 5 October.

Sumsuch, Will (2016) 'Exclusive Interview with Jay Strongman', Barely Breaking Even Records, 13 July, accessed at https://www.bbemusic.com/feature/exclusive-interview-jay-strongman on 26 May 2017.

Swindells, Steve (2014) 'All Human Beings Welcome', Steve Swindells blog, 10 March,

Bibliography

accessed at https://steveswindells.wordpress.com/tag/steve-swindells/ on 12 February 2018.

Szwed, John (1997) *Space Is the Place: The Life and Times of Sun Ra* (Edinburgh: Payback Press).

Tackley, Catherine (2014) 'Race, Identity and the Meaning of Jazz in 1940s Britain', in Stratton and Zuberi, eds, *Black Popular Music in Britain Since 1945*, 11–26.

Tate, Greg (1996) 'Jungle Boogie', *Pulse* [magazine], issue 50.

Thapar, Ciaran (2018a) 'The Moral Panic Against UK Drill Is Deeply Misguided', Pitchfork, 12 September, accessed at https://pitchfork.com/thepitch/the-moral-panic-against-uk-drill-is-deeply-misguided on 12 December 2018.

— (2018b) 'The Future of UK Drill', *Red Bull Music Academy Daily*, 11 December, accessed at https://www.redbull.com/gb-en/future-of-uk-drill on 12 December 2018.

Thomas, Helen, ed. (1997) *Dance in the City* (London: Macmillan).

Thompson, Nigel [Jumping Jack Frost] with Andrew Woods (2017) *Big, Bad and Heavy* (London: Music Mondays & Straight Six Publishing).

Thornton, Sarah (1995) *Club Cultures: Music, Media and Subcultural Capital* (Cambridge: Polity).

Titmus, Steve (2013a) 'Nightclubbing: Crackers', *Red Bull Music Academy Daily*, 11 March, accessed at http://daily.redbullmusicacademy.com/2013/03/nightclubbing-crackers on 13 April 2017.

— (2013b) 'Nightclubbing: Dingwalls', *Red Bull Music Academy Daily*, 13 May, accessed at http://daily.redbullmusicacademy.com/2013/05/nightclubbing-dingwalls on 17 June 2017.

Toynbee, Jason (2010) 'Reggae Open Source: How the Absence of Copyright Enabled the Emergence of Popular Music in Jamaica', in Lionel Bently, J. Davis and J. Ginsburg, eds, *Copyright and Piracy: An Interdisciplinary Critique*, 357–73 (Cambridge: Cambridge University Press).

Tuckey, Bill (1991) 'Radio Column', *Touch* [magazine], July.

Turner, Graeme (2012) *What's Become of Cultural Studies?* (London: Sage).

Turner, Patrick (2017) *Hip Hop Versus Rap: The Politics of Droppin' Knowledge* (London: Routledge).

Vincent, Rickey (1995) *Funk: The Music, the People, and the Rhythm of the One* (London: St Martin's Press).

VJ, Dave, and Lindsay Wesker (2012) *Masters of the Airwaves: The Rise and Rise of Underground Radio* (London: Every Generation Media).

Walcott, Rinaldo (2005) 'Post-Civil Rights Music or Why Hip Hop Is Dominant', *Action, Criticism and Theory for Music Education*, vol. 4, no. 3, accessed at http://act.maydaygroup.org/articles/Walcott4_3.pdf on 3 May 2018.

Wall, Tim (2006) 'Out on the Floor: The Politics of Dancing on the Northern Soul Scene', *Popular Music*, vol. 25, no. 3, special issue on dance, 431–45.

Wallace, John and Jerald Bachman (1991) 'Explaining Racial/Ethnic Differences in Adolescent Drug Use: The Impact of Background and Lifestyle', *Social Problems*, vol. 38, no. 3, 333–57.

Walvin, James (1982) *Slavery and British Society: Problems in Focus* (London: Palgrave Macmillan).

Wates, Nick and Christian Wolmer, eds (1980) *Squatting: The Real Story* (London: Bay Leaf Books).

Bibliography

Whitehurst, Andrew (2015) 'Exclusive: General Levy's "Incredible" Journey', *DJ* [magazine], 19 January, accessed at https://djmag.com/content/exclusive-general-levys-incredible-journey on 29 May 2018.

Williams, Alex (2009) 'Invention or Discovery – or, When Is a Genre Not a Genre?', Splintering Bone Ashes, 30 April, accessed at http://splinteringboneashes.blogspot.com/2009/04/invention-or-discovery-or-when-is-genre.html on 17 March 2018.

Williamson, John and Martin Cloonan (2016) *Players' Work Time: A History of the British Musicians' Union, 1893–2013* (Manchester: Manchester University Press).

Wilson, Greg (2003) 'Electro-Funk – What Did It All Mean?', *ElectroFunkRoots*, November, accessed at http://www.electrofunkroots.co.uk/articles/what.html on 26 May 2017.

— (2009) 'How the Talking Stopped: The UK's Microphone to Mix Metamorphosis', *ElectroFunkRoots*, n.d., accessed at http://www.electrofunkroots.co.uk/articles/how_the_talking_stopped.html on 26 May 2017.

— (2013) 'Cutting Shapes – How House Music Really Hit the UK', Greg Wilson Blog, 18 July, accessed at http://blog.gregwilson.co.uk/2013/07/cutting-shapes-how-house-music-really-hit-the-uk/2018 on 3 March 2017.

Wilson, Olly (1983) 'Black Music as Art Form', *Black Music Research Journal*, vol. 3, 1–22.

Wolton, Alexis (2008) 'Teknival and the Emancipatory Potential of Technology', text based on a talk given at the One-Shot Art Festival, Berlin, October 2007, *Datacide Magazine*, October 2008, accessed at https://datacide-magazine.com/teknival-and-the-emancipatory-potential-of-technology on 17 August 2018.

— (2010) 'Tortugan Tower Blocks? Pirate Signals from the Margins', *Datacide Magazine*, n.d., accessed at https://datacide-magazine.com/tortugan-tower-blocks-pirate-signals-from-the-margins on 16 November 2017.

Woods, Clyde and Katherine McKitterick, eds (2007) *Black Geographies and the Politics of Place* (Boston, MA: South End Press).

Wright, Ian (2016) *A Life in Football: My Autobiography* (London: Constable).

Zephaniah, Benjamin. (2018) *The Life and Rhymes of Benjamin Zephaniah: The Autobiography* (London: Scribner).

Zlatopolsky, Ashley (2014) 'The Roots of Techno: Detroit's Club Scene 1973–1985', 31 July, *Red Bull Academy Daily*, accessed at http://daily.redbullmusicacademy.com/2014/07/roots-of-techno-feature on 14 July 2016.

Zuberi, Nabeel (2001) *Sounds English: Transnational Popular Music* (Urbana, IL: University of Illinois Press).

— (2014) '"New Throat fe Chat": The Voices and Media of MC Culture', in Stratton and Zuberi, eds, *Black Popular Music in Britain Since 1945*, 185–202.

Index

Note: 'n.' after a page reference indicates the number of a note on that page. Page numbers in *italic* refer to photographs.

Index

Index

Electric Ballroom, Camden 100–2, 107, 148, 181
Elms, Robert 72, 166
Eshun, Kodwo 164, 201, 226–7
Euro-techno 181, 191, 198, 202, 215

Fabio (Fitzroy Heslop) *VI*, 40, 149, 169–70, 175, 178–9, 187n.32, 187n.34
Family Affair parties 110, *110*
Family Funktion *110*, 111–13, 142, 150
Farley 'Jackmaster' Funk 170–1
Farley, Terry 13, 75, 76, 97–8, 149, 151, 187n.34
Fats Domino 55, 68
Faver, Colin 169–71, 173, 175, 178, 179, 204
Femi Fem *see* Williams, Femi
Fields, Barbara 85
Fields, Karen 85
Fiorito, Alfredo 147, 148
Fisher, Mark 230, 234
Flintoff, Jean Paul 48
Florence Mills Social Parlour 17, 53, 58
Floyd, Samuel 22
Flux, MC (Carl Thomas) 185n.13, 216
Foncett, Frankie 138
football firms 181, 183, 185n.13, 199
Ford, Kevin (DJ Hype) 231n.4
Froggy, DJ *see* Howlett, Steven
Fryer, Peter 29
Fung, Trevor 147, 178, 179, 205
funk 119, 120–1, 124, 126, 127, 179
Funkadelic (band) 120, 122, 135n.43
Funkadelic sound system 116
funki dread 105, 134n.30, 144
Fusco, Coco 129

gabber 201, 231n.8
garage 2, 160, 165, 193, 216, 217, 218, 229, 230
Gargoyle Club 94, 95, *96*, 132n.12, 168
Garvey, Amy Ashwood 16, 17, 58
Gates, Henry Louis 157, 186n.22
gay culture 136n.46, 146, 158, 160, 161, 168, 169, 183
Gee, Bryan 7, 43, 175, 176, 197, 202, 209, 211

Gelston, Rene 117
gender issues 88–9, 98, 122–30, 132n.6
George, Nelson 157
Gilbert, Jeremy 186n.21, 208, 217, 230, 231n.2, 234
Gilroy, Paul 3, 8–9, 11, 20–1, 38, 87, 92, 159, 227–8, 233n.23
Goldberg, David Theo 4, 38–9, 165
Goldie (Clifford Price) 201–2, 205, 207, 214, 215, 219, 222, 225, 229
Goldmine club 68, 72, 82n.31, 92
Goodhart, David 10, 11
Good Times sound system ix, 104, 120
Goodwin, Andrew 226
Gordon, Simon 173
Gossips club 94–5, 170
Grandmaster Flash 118, 211
Grasso, Francis 134n.27, 160
Grenfell Tower fire 236–7, 242n.4
grime 2, 193, 213, 229–30, 232n.13, 238–40, 242n.11
Groove Connection 204
Grooverider (Raymond Bingham) *VI*, 170, 178, 179, 187n.34, 227
Gutzmore, Cecil 62
Guy Called Gerald, A 192, 212

Hacienda club, Manchester 155, 185n.14, 190
Haigh, Pete 223
Haigh, Rob 227
Hall, Aaron 200
Hall, Stuart 1, 9, 34, 85, 235
Hamilton, James 68, 82n.29
Hancox, Dan 206, 232n.13, 238
happy hardcore 201, 202, 213
hardcore 179, 193–5, 200–2, 205, 207, 211–13
Hardy, Ron 149, 162, 163, 170, 185n.12
Harrington, Steve (Steve Strange) 94
Haslam, Dave 190, 191
Heaven club 150, 159, 169, 178, 179
Hebdige, Dick 20, 49–50
Hedonism club 169, 173–4
Heslop, Fitzroy *see* Fabio
Hesse, Barnor 7
Hill, Chris 68–73, 77, 82n.27, 82n.31, 104

266

Index

Index

Index

Index

Index

EU authorised representative for GPSR:
Easy Access System Europe, Mustamäe tee 50,
10621 Tallinn, Estonia
gpsr.requests@easproject.com